3 week

MANAGEMENT SKILLS

Making the most of people

MANAGEMENT

SKILLS

MAKING THE MOST OF PEOPLE

Robin Evenden
and
Gordon Anderson

ADDISON-WESLEY PUBLISHING COMPANY
Wokingham, England • Reading, Massachusetts
Menlo Park, California • New York • Don Mills, Ontario
Amsterdam • Bonn • Sydney • Singapore • Tokyo • Madrid
San Juan • Milan • Paris • Mexico City • Seoul • Taipei

Transferred to digital print on demand 2002

Printed and bound in Great Britain by Antony Rowe Ltd, Eastbourne

First printed 1992

ISBN 0–201–54448–2

British Library Cataloguing in Publication Data
A catalogue record for this book is available from the British Library

Library of Congress Cataloging in Publication Data Available

Preface

Core people skills in the future

Managers will need to develop and use new practitioner skills to master the people side of their roles as the twenty-first century dawns. Already many are involved in selecting their own staff; all will need to be effective at building positive and performance based relationships with them; and an increasing number are developing their own people through appraisal, coaching and training. There is a need for knowledge and competency in all three areas.

'Making the most of people' is the theme of the book. It quite unusually combines the spectrum of skills from recruitment, through achieving positive relationships, to training and developing people.

The core people skills covered are:

- The manager as recruiter: getting the right people
- Managing people positively: personal and interpersonal skills
- The manager as developer: enhancing performance

Who will benefit

This book is written for those who will manage the future. It is to help individuals undertaking graduate or post graduate management programmes, such as an MBA, not only to develop their knowledge, but to translate it into practical management skills. Others whose route to management is via promotion, the professions or business ownership will find guidance in the coverage of the central aspects of managing people.

Robin Evenden and Gordon Anderson have long experience in working at graduate and post graduate levels. They have combined this with running hundreds of short management skills courses for practising managers during the last twenty five years, in the areas covered by the book. This background highlighted for them the urgent need to bridge the gap between the view of management as primarily based upon concepts and reflection, and the approach which is based entirely upon action. This gap is often more like a chasm. Those who fall in are either suffering from the 'analysis paralysis' of thinking without ever doing, or the 'action fraction' of doing without thinking. We hope that with the aid of this book the reader will integrate both thinking and doing, and leap the chasm with a single bound.

The manager: continuous developer of self and others

Many progressive organizations regard themselves as having adaptation and survival orientations. Training and development are considered the major means of achieving this. Learning is becoming a strong organizational value, expressed by the pursuit of the creation of a 'learning organization', where training and development are continuous and geared to the needs of individual and organization. Personal growth has as much importance as technical development in the future, with attitudes, values and personal skills assuming equal significance to the traditional functional areas of management.

A Code of Continuous Development has been produced by Britain's Institute of Personnel Management. It emphasizes the connection between learning and future performance. Training and development are strategic activities and managers should be able to be flexible and skilled enough to meet new needs as they appear. The Code suggests that the emphasis should be upon the needs, problems and opportunities found in the daily activity of the learner. Such a connection between the job and learning, seen as the main source of development by most professional practitioners, means that the line manager, at all levels, has to be intimately involved with the process.

One implication is that the development of personal and performance skills needs to be led by the manager as trainer and coach to the protégés as they practise their competencies directly through the work situation.

The adaptive organization pursuing success in future uncertainty, requires that managers have the growth of their people at the centre of their role. This should be a significant performance criterion by which they are judged, and *Management Skills: Making the Most of People* has been written to assist the development of the skills and knowledge needed to excel.

The origins of the book

This book has been written largely through long distance collaboration, with Robin Evenden living in Horsham in the south of England, and Gordon Anderson in central Scotland. It has been stimulated from time to time by face-to-face meetings, often over highly enjoyable late breakfasts at Fortnum and Masons in London.

Robin and Gordon first met in 1977 on the residential International Teachers Programme (ITP) – a kind of mini MBA for teachers of management – held that year at Jouy-en-Josas, near Paris, in France. They met again ten years later in the same place, making presentations at a two-day reunion of former ITP participants. The book emerged from their conviction that there is a need for a book in this field which combines theory and practice in a rigorous but readable way. It draws upon their complementary interests and their diversity of experience as managers, teachers, researchers, writers and consultants.

How to use this book

In 1980 Robin Evenden wrote the *Human Aspects of Management* with Derek Biddle (Second Edition 1989, IPM) to provide managers with an understanding of people at work and their own leadership role. It is widely used as an introductory text, for example on MBA and professional studies programmes, and should continue to be used for this purpose. *Management Skills: Making the Most of People* takes a broader look at the manager's job, to include both recruitment and development skills. It also focuses in depth upon the skills for developing positive performance relationships. The two books are complementary management development texts.

This book is designed to support either independent study or tutor-led course work. Typically a section of **text** will include authoritative references to concepts, research or methods, related to a description of needs and problems. These will be followed by an **activity** to help the reader analyse and learn in a practical fashion.

Activities take several forms, including:

- Individual reflection upon experience; observations and analysis; and experimentation.
- Group discussion and exercises, such as role plays and feedback which are often suggested for group learning.
- A continuous and integrated case study (Insupply) which is used throughout the book to provide illustrations and a basis for individual and group learning.

Please note that after an Activity the authors will often offer a commentary, framework or outline answer. If you wish to undertake an Activity, remember not to read on after the question until you have completed it!

The book invites the readers to develop their own training and presentation skills. Some areas of the book have been converted into ready-made training modules for use by managers or tutors (see Appendix B). All parts of *Making the Most of People* lend themselves to similar modularization. To help this process, *all Figures which appear in this book may be used copyright free on courses, provided acknowledgement is given.*

About the authors

Robin Evenden is a management development and training consultant. His career in management and training includes the Bank of England, Marks and Spencer and Shell. He has conducted research and consultancy in Europe, the USA and Africa. Robin works on recruitment training with the Commission for Racial Equality, management development with HM Customs and Excise, and appraisal skills with London and Edinburgh Insurance Group. His publications include the IPM's *Human Aspects of Management*. Robin is a graduate of the London School of Economics, and a Fellow of both the British Institute of Management and the Institute of Training and Development. He is External Human Resource Tutor on Strathclyde Business School's MBA programme.

Gordon Anderson is Chairman and Director of MBA programmes in the Strathclyde Graduate Business School, University of Strathclyde, Glasgow. After gaining industrial and commercial experience with Ford and a stockbroking company, he pursued a university career, focusing primarily on the human side of management. While he has published widely in this field, Gordon's central interest has been designing and implementing systems of performance appraisal and performance management. He has acted as consultant to many organizations in this area. He is presently writing a book on performance appraisal systems. Gordon has considerable international experience, and has set up centres for the Strathclyde MBA in Hong Kong, Malaysia, Poland and Singapore.

Acknowledgements

Writing this book has been made possible through the help and support of many people. One of us (Robin) did his own wordprocessing; the other (Gordon) would like to express his gratitude to Gillian Watson for her high-quality secretarial skills in typing his chapters and for her toleration and good humour in coping often with barely-legible drafts.

Christine Reid, Librarian in charge of the Business Information Centre of the Strathclyde Graduate Business School has been enormously helpful in responding to requests, usually at short notice, for source materials.

Our publisher has provided help and encouragement throughout. Sarah Mallen helped get the book underway; Maggie Pickering gave guidance during the main phase of writing; as did Jane Hogg and Susan Keany in the completion stages.

Devoting time to writing a book while continuing to undertake other work makes demands on families. We would like to thank ours – Marjory, Nigel and Christopher Anderson, for their patience and understanding, and Jean, Kate, Ben, Matthew and Tim Evenden for going through it all yet again.

Finally, we would like to express our thanks to all those who have influenced our thinking and thereby contributed to this book. In particular, Robin would like to acknowledge his debt to Dave Barker, Neil Clark and Geoff Ward for the knowledge and creative ideas so freely shared. Many individuals and organizations have encouraged the application and development of approaches described in this book, not least many friends and colleagues in the Commission for Racial Equality, HM Customs and Excise, London and Edinburgh Insurance and NEM Insurance. I should mention them all, but space limits me to Erik Shopland, Derek Hall, Chris Turnbull and David Dolton.

Robin Evenden
Gordon Anderson
September 1992

Contents

PART TWO
Personal growth and interpersonal relationships   83

PART THREE
The manager as developer: enhancing performance   213

PART ONE

The manager as recruiter: getting the right people

1

Why are you recruiting?

With the application of care and skill, effective recruitment can bring into your organization people who have the potential to perform well. If it is your intention, they could also be embarking on a career which is satisfying for them and productive for you. In general terms, that is the purpose of recruitment. However, the question still remains. Why are you recruiting?

Do you need to recruit: Is there a job?

When there is a need for things to be done and there is nobody designated to do them or the present incumbent is leaving, recruitment should not be the only option considered. It is always worth thinking about the need, spelling out your requirements and asking yourself how they can best be met. A job is one part of a network of people and roles. It is quite possible that the best answer lies in making changes within that network rather than deciding upon straight replacement recruitment. What are the choices?

Redeployment from within the organization is one possibility, especially if there are changes or contraction in some parts. If people are available for redeployment, there will still need to be a selection process to assess their suitability, and many of the approaches to be considered shortly for recruitment will apply to this, or any other internal selection procedure.

Internal selection such as transfer or promotion is a choice that the manager may make, prior or in addition to considering external recruitment. There may be procedures where this is implemented automatically, or the arrangements may be entirely informal, in which case you would need to take initiatives with your peers, hopefully avoiding inter-departmental conflict from poaching other people's staff or having their problem people dumped upon you.

Reorganization may meet your need rather than recruitment. Indeed, the departure of a member of staff may give you an ideal opportunity to reassess how your part of the organization operates. It could be that redesigning the jobs in the network will provide an effective basis for achieving your results without replacing the person leaving. You will need to take into account the skills and motivation of the remaining staff, improved technology and its cost, as well as the emerging demands that are being placed upon your department.

After you have considered the alternatives you may still decide that you will need to reinforce your team by external recruitment. The first step is to decide not who you want but what it is you want the new recruit to do.

Job description: What is the job?

You may have a written job description. Do not assume that it is valid or complete. Unfortunately many job descriptions are rightly mistrusted by line managers. Frequent criticisms are that they are outdated, incomplete, inconclusive or simply not describing the job that has to be done and the context in which it is performed. Equally, do not assume that you know the job. Your perception may be distorted, for example, by the people who have done the job rather than the job that has to be done. It always pays to check your understanding of the job and where it fits.

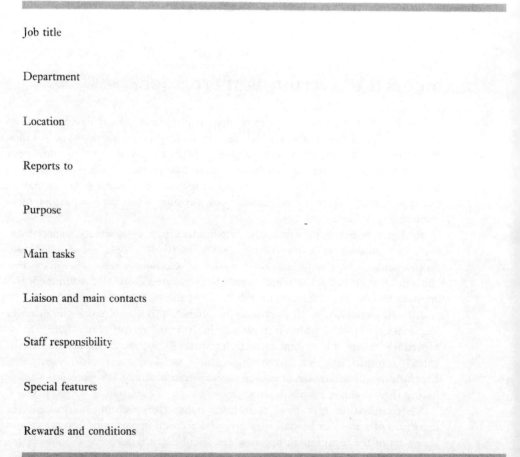

Job title

Department

Location

Reports to

Purpose

Main tasks

Liaison and main contacts

Staff responsibility

Special features

Rewards and conditions

Figure 1.1   Job description framework.

4

The elements of a job description should be determined by the use you intend for it. For recruitment you need to note the main purpose of the job and the main tasks to be performed; the social conditions of the job, such as reporting line, liaison role, internal and external contacts, and staff management; special aspects that are unusual or temporary; and the rewards and conditions attached to the job. Figure 1.1 suggests a framework to fill out.

Problems completing the job description

If you are unable to produce a valid, clear and comprehensive job description in terms of what has to be done, the clues and guidance about the kind of person you want will be weak or missing, so that the recruitment process will be compromised from the start.

Problems can inhibit the completion of the description.

Distortion can often result from the manager's angle of view on the job, which is different from others who have a stake in it. For example, you may emphasize the tasks performed directly for you as the boss; clients would emphasize what is done for them; the incumbent could give priority to thinking and judgemental aspects which are not observable by others; and staff may focus upon the job holder's relations with them.

Visualizing the whole job and identifying the most significant elements can be other difficulties. Faced with a framework to complete, some managers suffer a mental block or treat it superficially.

ACTIVITY 1.1

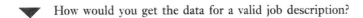 How would you get the data for a valid job description?

Getting ideas to complete the job description

▽ **Reflection and loose mapping** is a good way to start. Give yourself time to reflect and ruminate over the job. Many managers do not give themselves time to do this, but try to solve their problems by attempting to jump directly to the answers.

    (1) Let yourself wander around the job in your mind.
    (2) Think about it in all its phases.
    (3) What would you and others miss most if the job was not done?
    (4) Build a loose map of the job on paper. Doodle. Jot down key words and phrases as they occur. Circle and connect things.

    Don't try to be complete or detailed yet. Keep your mind walking the job.

Concrete comparison is another approach to getting the detail of a job, and equally important, identifying its priorities. It involves visualizing the job being done. Most people find that they get stuck thinking in abstract terms so this is a technique to think about real things in concrete terms.

(1) Identify three people who have done, or are doing, this job or similar ones. Let's call them A, B and C.
(2) Compare each person in turn with the two others, in terms of what they do in the job. See them doing it in your mind's eye.

The following uses the job description framework from Figure 1.1.

(1) What would be most missed if each did not do the job?
A –
B –
C –
Does this clarify the *purpose* of the job?

(2) Which *task* does each do better in comparison with the others?
A better than   B   –
A   C   –
B ....   A   –
B   C   –
C ....   A   –
C ....   B   –
Does this clarify the *main tasks?*

(3) Which *contacts* (up, down, side or outside) does each do better in comparison with the others?
A better than   B   –
A   C   –
B ....   A   –
B   C   –
C ....   A   –
C ....   B   –
Does this clarify the *contacts/liaison* part of the job?

(4) Which aspects of *staff management* does each do better in comparison with the others?
A better than   B   –
A   C   –
B ....   A   –
B   C   –
C ....   A   –
C ....   B   –
Does this clarify the *staff responsibilities* in the job?

6

(5) Are there any *special features* exclusive to A, B or C?

Talking around the job is a valuable aid to completing the job description. It will help you check for your own possible distortions and your ideas on detail and priorities. It involves identifying those with some stake in the job and getting their opinions about its main features, as well as developments affecting it.

Projecting the job. It is important to think about what changes may be imminent which could affect the job in the future. This will mean consulting those who are instrumental in bringing about change in your part of the organization. Your own manager will be a key figure here, as will others involved in strategic planning, system design and technology.

ACTIVITY 1.2

Prepare a job description using the approaches considered above either as an individual or group exercise.

If you are undertaking external recruitment as part of your management role, that would be an ideal subject for the practical activity.

A simulation would be helpful to give experimental and experiential meaning to the ideas. You could, for example, produce a job description of professor or lecturer.

Insupply case study: Job description

The Insupply case study recurs as an evolving situation throughout the book. It is intended as a means for the readers to apply and test ideas and to integrate and develop their learning in a practical way. We will not offer 'right answers' but will suggest ways of approaching the situations outlined. The exercises will encourage you to project your own imagined circumstances and personal characteristics onto the case scenarios. The case may be tackled either as an individual or group learning exercise.

An outline of the entire case will be found in Appendix A on page 347. The story unfolds chapter by chapter throughout the book as relevant topics are introduced.

Insupply supplies office equipment and stationery to a national market. It was formed three years ago with the merger of Buroquip, an equipment and furniture distributor, and Gloprint, a manufacturer of printing and paper products.

The integration was logical and was conducted without major organizational dislocation. The two units had dovetailed well and there were minimal job losses when some rationalization took place six months after the merger.

The headquarters was at Gloprint's site in Hometown and the distribution centre remained at Buroquip's Awayville warehouse, a 45-minute road journey apart.

There were now 300 employees and the company was growing quite rapidly as a result of good marketing, delivery and quality. Both sides of the business aimed at the quality end of the market and had landed some valuable contracts in the retail, financial and high tech sectors. A further boost was given when Insupply became the sole national agents for Kraft 2000, a leading overseas manufacturer of office equipment and furniture.

Colin Smith was the Company Secretary and Deputy Chief Executive. He had been Buroquip's Managing Director who had agreed the merger and had been largely responsible for conducting its legal, financial and organizational aspects. He had been heavily involved in setting up Insupply's administrative systems and he was responsible for its operation through three administrative officers.

Sally Bullen had run the typing pool for Colin Smith at Buroquip, and had been given the job of Administrative Officer: Staff and Buildings. The staff role was to arrange temporary clerical, secretarial staff as required throughout the company. Two assistants worked for her in this function.

Sally acquired responsibility for the buildings, including maintenance, security, health and safety. Most of these aspects were handled by external contractors, and another assistant helped her manage these.

Communications were described by Colin Smith as the lifeblood of Insupply. He had another administrative officer, Ekoku Inanga, to run the external and internal communications. Ekoku had a Masters degree in Communication and Media Studies, and he was recruited by Smith, just prior to the announcement of the merger, to handle the public relations aspects. Two years ago he was promoted to his current post to be responsible for mail, telecommunications, notice boards, the house magazine and quality circles in addition to PR. Ekoku had two assistants.

The third administrative officer was Peter Paine who, with an assistant, was responsible for the procurement of all materials and equipment needed by Insupply for its own use. Peter had had a similar role with Gloprint.

All three sections involved administering to the needs of all the departments of Insupply, including Production, Distribution, Finance and Accounts, Marketing and Sales, Personnel, and Information Systems. It also meant contact with Insupply's customers and suppliers.

Colin had enjoyed the access that his role gave him to all facets of the business, and he relished the challenge of making the wheels of administration run smoothly so that the other departments could get on with their tasks without unnecessary frustration. However, he and his fellow directors had agreed that he should divest himself of these particular responsibilities in order to cope with the increasing demands of growth and strategic management.

He would retain his legal responsibilities as Company Secretary, as well as those for organization development, but he would need to detach himself from direct supervision of the functions performed by the three sections. It was also planned that Insupply would move from its two sites in Hometown and Awayville to a purpose built facility in a new out-of-town complex midway between them, but he would not be able to give more than general oversight to the planning and implementation of this major corporate event.

CASE PROJECT 1.1

If you were Colin Smith, how would you tackle the organizational and resource aspects of the decision to change his role?

How Colin Smith tackled the organizational and resource aspects of the decision to change his role

Colin began by asking himself 'Is there a job?'

1. What would be left undone given his new role?
   (a) His administrative officers would be left unmanaged, in terms of objective setting, results management, task planning, monitoring, development, guidance and so on.
   (b) The relationships with major internal clients and the quality of the administrative provision would not be managed or coordinated.
   (c) The Executive's committee system would not be serviced.

2. What new or different things are emerging to be managed?
   (a) The move to the new site.
   (b) Sally has problems with the building side of her role.
   (c) Developing new systems and electronic technology on the new 'green field' site.

3. Can I reorganize?
   (a) No functions can be removed or easily integrated.
   (b) Another section could be set up for building.
   (c) Sally could take on the systems and technology.
   (d) Ekoku would do the Committee role well.

However there would still be many things not covered by such reorganization, especially the management and coordination aspects.

Colin decided that there was a job and considered his choices:

- Redeployment from elsewhere was not realistic.
- Reorganization was a possibility later, but not a full answer.
- Recruitment was necessary. He wanted an Administration Manager and would use Internal and External Recruitment.

CASE PROJECT 1.2

What is the job? Decide how Colin Smith should develop his ideas about the job of Administration Manager, and then, using the framework in Figure 1.1, produce the job description.

How Colin Smith developed his ideas about the job of Administration Manager

Reflection and loose mapping. Colin devoted an hour to letting his mind wander over the parts of his job that he would be delegating to the administration manager. He mapped out the people who were significant in his role network and jotted down the ideas that emerged about their needs and expectations of the new position. The exercise proved useful preparation for his subsequent consultation and analysis. (See Figure 1.2)

Concrete comparison. Colin concluded from his reflection that the roles of his three administrative officers would define many of the main task management responsibilities of the new manager. He was able, in addition, to identify the particular approach he found important for each of the three by comparing them in terms of their strengths and limitations. (See Figure 1.3)

Talking around and projecting the job. He had a clear idea whom he wanted to consult and what he needed to discuss with them.

(1) Hedi Lindstrom was the Chief Executive who had been brought in to run Insupply when the merger had been agreed. Her main requirements of the Administration Department were 'that it should enable us to have a silky smooth transition to the new location, and once we are there to be so good that we do not notice that they are there!' Colin Smith felt that this was enough to enable him to define the purpose of the job.

(2) The Co-Directors had three major requirements:
   (a) The move was a great chance to install new electronic systems and hardware. The new manager would need to manage the Administration and Information Systems Department interface.
   (b) They anticipated a changing employment pattern, with all departments having fewer permanent staff and the trend to consulting and contract staff needing to be handled by the Administration Department.
   (c) All the directors were certain that they wanted somebody with whom they could discuss their needs and problems and whom they could rely upon to deal with them effectively.
   Colin found this valuable in reminding him of the importance of relationships in the job, and it helped him to define some of the main tasks.

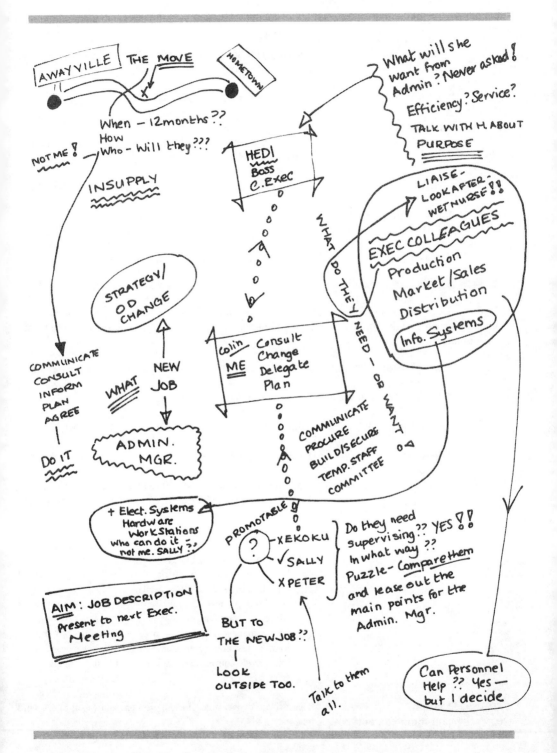

Figure 1.2 Colin Smith's loose map of the Administration Manager's job.

Sally's difference
>
> from Ekoku   guidance and advice on specific technical aspects of her job (building; security).

from Peter   more contacts to discuss her job.

Ekoku's difference
>
> from Sally   needs to keep me informed about his ideas; doesn't prioritize or use time well.

from Peter   frequent meetings with his important external contacts.

Peter's difference
>
> from Sally   resists change and appears frightened of new technology.

from Ekoku   passive during meetings; need to draw him out.

Figure 1.3 A sample from Colin Smith's concrete comparison of his administrative officers, identifying some of the special management attention that the current job holders require from their manager.

Job title   Administration Manager – Insupply

Department	Administration	**Location**	Hometown

Reports to   Deputy Chief Executive

Purpose   To provide smooth and efficient administrative support for the Executive and Departments to help Insupply achieve its corporate objectives.

Main tasks
(1) To manage the department's objectives, plans, control and coordination within budget.
(2) To liaise effectively with the Executive and client departments to meet their needs.
(3) To develop new administrative systems, with special reference to new technology.
(4) To manage the three sections handling communications, procurement, buildings management, Executive's committees, and temporary staff (internal and external).

Liaison and main contacts   Executive; department heads; junior staff; suppliers and clients.

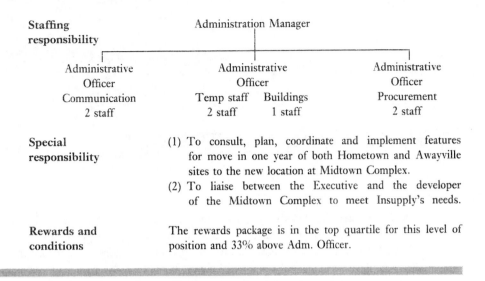

Staffing responsibility	Administration Manager	
Administrative Officer Communication 2 staff	Administrative Officer Temp staff Buildings 2 staff 1 staff	Administrative Officer Procurement 2 staff

Special responsibility

(1) To consult, plan, coordinate and implement features for move in one year of both Hometown and Awayville sites to the new location at Midtown Complex.

(2) To liaise between the Executive and the developer of the Midtown Complex to meet Insupply's needs.

Rewards and conditions

The rewards package is in the top quartile for this level of position and 33% above Adm. Officer.

Figure 1.4 Colin Smith's job description for the new position.

Colin Smith made notes in addition to the formal job description (see Figure 1.4), which would remind him of important things when he is deciding the kind of person he wants:

- Role of temps will grow at all levels;
- Increasing prevalence of electronics and innovation;
- Some senior people were 'difficult';
- Section Heads presented different managerial problems;
- Reorganization?

References for further reading

Boydell T.H. (1977). *A Guide to Job Analysis.* BACIE

Collinson D. (1987). Who Controls Selection? *Personnel Management Journal* May 1987

Herriot P. (1990). *Recruitment in the 90's.* IPM

Lewis C. (1985). *New Perspectives in Recruitment and Selection.* Hutchinson

Plumbley P. (1988). *Recruitment and Selection.* IPM

Torrington D. and Hall L. (1987). *Personnel Management.* Prentice-Hall

2

Who are you recruiting?

Once you have decided that you need to recruit and have established clearly what the job is, then you can use the job description to help you focus upon who you want. What you are now doing is producing a specification of the ideal person for the job. Not that you will necessarily expect to achieve that ideal, but it will guide you in the search for the best actual person. The person specification is an invaluable tool for all parts of the recruitment activity, including the matching process (see Figure 2.1).

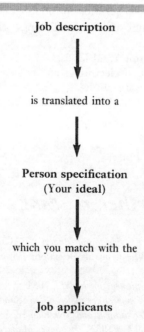

Job description

is translated into a

Person specification
(Your ideal)

which you match with the

Job applicants

and decide who is the best match with the ideal.

Figure 2.1 Recruitment as a matching process.

Uses of the person specification in recruitment

(1) **Describing who you are looking for.**
You need to be clear yourself at the outset. If it is a team effort, agree at the start what you are looking for and consensus will be easier when you need to make the selection decision.

(2) **Deciding where to look.**
Have you got one already? Is it worthwhile doing an internal search? Where to look externally? Do you need specialist help?

(3) **Identifying what and how to advertise.**
What to put in to attract applicants but to stop those with no chance from applying, by using cut off points identified in your specification. The latter applicants can often double your work.

(4) **Short listing.**
Systematic use of the specification is a good way of reducing the chances of the best fish escaping your net.

(5) **Deciding your recruitment method.**
Will the interview be sufficient, or will you need to supplement it with other methods, such as assessment centres or psychological tests with specialist help.

(6) **Preparing the interview.**
Sorting out what you know already, what you need to check and what you have to discover.

(7) **Handling and recording the interview.**
The specification can be used as a map to guide the interview and a framework for notes on the candidates.

(8) **Making the selection decision.**
Systematic comparison of candidates against the specification is an effective way of differentiating between them, and a good discipline when you are exercising your judgement. It assists not only in establishing the reasons for your choice, but also the reasons for not choosing. This can be important given legislation or codes of good practice regarding prejudicial employment, sex and racial discrimination.

Selection involves, as do all other aspects of management, the exercise of judgement upon information and evidence. Methods like job description and person specification do not dispense with the need for judgement, but they can certainly help to improve it. This will be true whether you use your specification as a document to guide you through each part of the recruitment process or as an initial preparatory exercise.

ACTIVITY 2.1

An organization is looking for a person to fill the post of Administration Manager. To help them in their search they specify that the successful candidate should have:

- good personality,
- extensive experience,
- suitable qualifications,
- smart appearance, and
- high motivation.

That seems fine, doesn't it? We would always like to have people like that in our organization, wouldn't we?

That list has the benefit of reminding us that those aspects are important, but as it stands it has very limited value.

What is wrong with the list as an aid to recruiting?

What should a person specification be like to help select the right person for the job?

What a person specification should be like to aid recruiting

It needs to relate to a particular job

There is always the temptation to recruit an 'all round good egg', or somebody who is like us, or our mothers or fathers! You need to specify things that relate to a particular job, not every job.

'Good personality' means everything and nothing. The kind of personality you want for the job needs spelling out. Some jobs need outgoing people, others need people who are more reserved. Other examples of describing differences are risk taker–careful, doer–planner. It may be sufficient to identify the characteristics that you feel are important, such as capacity to cope with the pressures in a job; the significance of membership and interpersonal skills; ability to influence and so on.

It needs to be specific

Stating that 'extensive experience' is needed says nothing about the quantity or quality of experience which is deemed important for this job. What is the person to have extensively experienced, and perhaps more significantly achieved, which will show suitability?

It needs to help us differentiate between people

It is useful if we can define standards so that we can decide what exactly we are looking for. 'Suitable qualifications' tells us nothing about the level that is desirable. It is often possible to devise a scale of educational and professional qualifications which serves both to help us be precise about what we want, at the same time as enabling us to differentiate between candidates.

You should be able to recognize it when you see it

How do you recognize a person of 'smart appearance'? My delivery man, bank manager, fast-food waitress, son's girlfriend and the local football team are all very smart. They are also very different. In this case the degree and nature of smartness needs to be spelled out in relation to the job and its social impact context.

You need to be able to assess whether a person meets it

All of the things you specify should be assessable and you need to be sure that you will be able to get evidence of some kind to help you do it. You would need to say what is meant in this job by 'high motivation' and then establish how you will find it out. For example, you could check on what motivational rewards the job offers and then assess from the person's career history whether they would both keep and stimulate the person in the job.

Person specification: Defining the categories

Our example person specification, as we have seen, was not related to a particular job, neither would it help us specify clearly what was wanted, recognize it when we saw it, assess it nor differentiate between people so that we can decide which one to choose. If these problems can be avoided the person specification will become an indispensable tool in getting the right person for the job.

What we are looking for is a comprehensive set of categories which are useful for specifying the personal characteristics which will predict success in a particular job.

A number of schemes have been developed. Those produced by Alec Rodger (1952) and John Munro Fraser (1978) have proved to have practical value as an aid to recruitment. Categories which feature in some form in many person specification schemes are:

- Physical,
- Qualifications,
- Work experience and achievements,
- Learning and change,
- Special skills,
- Interests,
- Personality,
- Personal circumstances.

Physical

(a) Impact on others – What are the standards of dress, speech and other factors that you feel are important in this job? The job description will remind you of the type of contact needed with people inside and outside the organization.

(b) Health and physical characteristics – are there any features in the job which lead you to specify any special needs regarding health, fitness, strength, hearing or eyesight? Does the job make any special demands such as colour vision, hazards, physical stress?

Qualifications

Are there any educational, training, technical, professional qualifications that are essential? What would be desirable? Bear in mind the possibility of over-qualification for the job.

Check the job and reflect on people you know who have done this or similar jobs to an acceptable level. Do they have what you specify? It is common to overspecify, thus excluding applicants who could do the job well.

Work experience and achievements

What type of experience and achievements would you want somebody to bring to this job which would predict success? You may wish to specify the minimum essential and add a desirable list. Do not expect to get everything. What could the person have which could compensate for a gap? Could the applicant overcome a deficiency with training, for example?

Remember to check not only what they have done, but how well they have done it.

Learning and change

How important is the capacity to learn in this job? What emphasis do you place on personal development, keeping up to date and seeking new ideas? Relearning and unlearning are related to introducing and reacting to change? The job description will give you clues about what you will want to specify and look for in the applicants. What do you want and what can they demonstrate?

Special skills

Are there any special skills desirable or essential? Check the job description; examples are numeracy, keyboard, DP, presentations, creativity.

Interests

(a) Personal interests – are there any personal hobbies or interests which might suggest a fit with the job?

Does the job indicate, for example, a social person, one who works well alone, or one who pays attention to detail? What a person does out of work may give interesting insights into their work. Be led by the job description, not your own interests.

(b) Work interests – motivation is a vital and often overlooked aspect of recruitment. This is one of the main ingredients of performance and keeping a person. People do not have a general motivation, but are switched on and off by different things at work.

What are the motivators that this job has, and does the applicant respond to this type of stimulus? A job which offers challenge may not appeal to a person who wants security and vice versa. Some to consider as possible motivators in a job are achievement, professional challenge, responsibility, recognition, advancement and development.

Personality

What personality is likely to fit the job? By this we mean personal attributes that vary from person to person. Again this may be a major determinant of fit with a role and success in it.

Examine the job to identify the things you think indicate which personal aspects are significant. Some examples are leader, team member, influencer, interpersonal style, stability, coping with the pressure of this job, self reliance, handling conflict, approach to subordinates, flexibility and risk taking.

Personal circumstances

Are there any special features of this job against which you wish to assess the applicant?

There may be some unusual requirements which may disqualify some people. Other aspects are so obvious that they are overlooked. For example, a car driver with a clean licence, unsocial hours, air travel (many people are phobic) and attitudes to clients who may present a value clash are others. It is important not to infringe legal or moral rights to equal opportunities in this or other categories.

Methods for constructing the person specification

Ways of specifying your 'ideal' person

- Descriptive: simply writing down what you are looking for. For example:
  - Numerate and literate: At Age 16 Top 40%;
  - Average examination passes: At Age 18;
  - Qualifications in business or related fields;
  - Membership of relevant professional body.

- Grading: identifying grades, say A to E and specifying the grades required, for example:

A	B	C	D	E
Higher degree	Degree	18 year Average	16 year Average Good literacy numeracy*	16 year Below average

A	B	C
Business	Business	Business
and	or	or
professional	professional	technical
qualification	qualification	qualification

B specified;   A or C acceptable if other conditions met.

* Specifications for lower grades apply to higher grades.

- Points: Allocating points to parts of a category and totalling them, for example

Points	General education level (one score only)
0	16 years below average attainment
1	16 years good literacy and numeracy
2	16 years average attainment
3	18 years average attainment
4	Degree or equivalent, e.g. professional exam
5	Higher degree

Points	Vocational (cumulative score)
1	Technical qualification
2	Business qualification, e.g. diploma
2	Membership of professional association

You may wish to specify a minimum score in each category of your person specification, for example:

Person specification category: Qualifications
Minimum score acceptable for this position is 4

The method you use is a matter of personal preference. Some people feel that grades or points makes the comparison between candidates easier. Either may save time, particularly at the short-listing stage, where you may have many people to assess and would welcome a simple way of quantifying and comparing.

There is a temptation, however, to invest greater credibility to grades and scores compared to a verbal assessment of people, because they have the appearance of being more objective or scientific. This is not valid, especially if the written specification is clear and precise in its wording.

It is important to remember that points and grades are only as good as the decisions behind them. Schemes are not substitutes for your judgement, but only ways of guiding and recording it. Always bear in mind the limits of the scheme you decide to use. In the example, for instance, the decision to give one point to technical qualifications could arguably have been two points. The minimum score acceptable was four, but this was a judgement based on assessment of the job description. Another person could have decided on three or five. In addition, how do you decide that a higher degree is worth five points, and does this really equate to five points say for personality or work experience? Be conscious of a method's limitations.

Many people find points or grades very helpful, but do avoid excessive complexity if a simple description will do the job.

Weighting

It is useful to give different weights to different parts of a specification according to their judged relative importance. The simplest way to do this is to describe some parts essential and others desirable. **Essential** defines the minimum acceptable, or lower cut-off point, below which you would not want to employ that person in that job. **Desirable** means good to have over and above the minimum, and the person you select would be the one who had the most desirable qualities. It is sometimes thought necessary to have an upper cut-off point. This would exclude those who would be over-qualified or over ambitious for the particular job and whom you would judge likely to be frustrated or just using it as a short term stepping stone. It is useful to spell out **contra-indicators** or things that would disqualify an applicant. If you have chosen to design a points scheme, you will be able to use your judgement to give different points quotas to different categories. If you feel that the 'Work experience and achievements' category is three times more important than 'Physical', then you give it three times the points.

As we have already seen, in a points scheme it is possible to give different weights to different aspects of a single category, for example Qualifications: Technical = 1 point; Business = 2 points.

Deciding what to put in each person specification category

It is necessary to decide what to include in specifications and the technique of concrete comparison can be very helpful. It involves simple and systematic comparison between people who hold or have held the job in question, or similar jobs (see page 6).

ACTIVITY 2.2

▼ Produce a person specification concrete comparison either for a job known to you or for the Insupply Case Study Administration Manager, based on your knowledge of administrators or people doing administrative tasks.

First think of up to four job holders, and compare them in pairs. Keep in mind a concrete mental image of them both in the job. At what parts of the job was one better than the other, and vice versa. At what different aspects were the next pair better or worse, and so on. Note these factors and see which categories they fit into. Include in this the ways in which the people you were comparing were better or worse than each other, for example:

Impact	ANNA	different from	PAT
	Conservative		Loud dress
	dress		and strident voice

This will help you identify what it is important to put in the specification and to define the standards you want.

Example of a concrete comparison: Person specification for the Administration Manager at Insupply

▽ The comparisons are between four Administration Managers (not applicants) known to Colin Smith of Insupply. Their names are John Ball, Charles Argent, Anna Friedmann and Pat Ryan. Some of their different approaches to the role suggested significant things for the person specification when Colin looked at them in the light of the job description for the new post of Administration Manager at Insupply.

After Colin had listed the differences, he added a column in the margin linking them to the different person specification categories:

PH	Physical
Q	Qualifications
WEA	Work experience and achievements
LC	Learning and change
S	Special skills
I	Interests (P–Personal; M–Motivation)
PE	Personality
PC	Personal circumstances

The categories are boxes of convenience. The issue should not be which is the correct place to put your specifications, but have you included all the important things somewhere.

Category

	John	different from	Charles
PE	Approachable		Aloof
PE	Diplomatic		Tactless
WEA/PE	People a priority		People a low priority

		different from	**Anna**
PE	Copes with pressure		Panics
PE	Flexible		Works 9–5 only
WEA/PE	Communicates with all levels comfortably		Awkward with senior people
WEA/PE	Has influence skills		Passive
I/M	Sets high standards for self		Sets easy standards

		different from	**Pat**
I/M	Proactive		Reactive
LC	Likes change		Avoids change
I/M	Tackles anything		Works to rule

	Charles	different from	**Anna**
Q	Professional member		Certificate in office skills
Q	Business diploma		16 years level

		different from	**Pat**
WEA	Knows product well		Low knowledge

		different from	**John**
WEA	Experience in Buildings & Security		Low experience
WEA	Delegates well		Tries to do all

	Anna	different from	**Pat**
PH	Conservative dress		Untidy; colourful
PH	Pleasant voice		Loud; strident
S	Advanced admin. equipment skills		No advanced equipment skills
LC	Recent study in software application		No study in any area for years

		different from	**John**
WEA	Good prioritizer and time manager		Low sense of the urgent/ important

		different from	**Charles**
PH	Healthy/energetic		Overweight/tired
PH	Absence through illness rare		Illness absence frequent
PH/I/P	Active fitness/ social interests		Inactive solo interests only

WEA	Planner and doer		Analysis paralysis
WEA	**Pat** Procurement tasks in previous job	different from	**John** No procurement experience
WEA	Ran communication systems		Little activity in communication systems
I/M	Relishes autonomy	different from	**Charles** Wants help often
PE/I/M S	Likes teamwork Likes all travel		Likes isolation Can't fly
WEA	15 years' experience in administration	different from	**Anna** 3 years only in administration

The need next would be to review the concrete comparison notes against the job description, and to select the parts that appear relevant to the new post of Administration Manager. It could be that there are additional personal characteristics or attributes that are not in the notes which needed to be added to it.

ACTIVITY 2.3

▼ Produce a person specification using the above notes or your own. Use description, grading or points, and weighting.

Recapitulation Summary

Job description   Insupply Administration Manager.

Objectives   Smooth support and collaboration with others.

Main tasks   Meet objectives within budget.
 Liaison.
 New administrative systems and technology.
 Management of people; communication;
  buildings and security;
  temporary staffing;
  Executive committees.

Special features	Major move and site development.
Person specification guide	Relate it to the job in question. Be as specific and factual as possible. Make sure your specification helps you differentiate between people. Check that it describes things that are recognizable and assessable.
Methods	Description or grades or points; weighting, such as essential/desirable; concrete comparison.

Insupply case study: Person specification for Administration Manager – illustrations and interpretations from the Insupply case

1. Physical: Combined maximum 20 points

1.1 Impact (Maximum 8 points)

Desirable (6)	*Contra-indicator*
Conservative dress; pleasant voice & manner; relaxed and attentive	Untidy; extravagant dress; loud or inaudible voice; tense mannerisms

Colin Smith knew that the job would call for extensive face-to-face contact with clients and others. He felt the AM's impact would need to be consonant with their expectations, so the contra-indications were important. However, he thought it would be unnecessary to specify essentials in this category. An individual could fall a little short of the specifications and still be acceptable for other compensatory reasons. (Mildly scruffy but with charisma and a proven track record in precisely the areas needed, for example!) The desirable specification would serve as a reminder that this aspect has significance. He felt that this part could be confidently assessed during the interview.

1.2 Health (Possible 4 points per item, maximum 12 points)

Desirable (10)	*Essential* (8)	*Contra-indicator*
Excellent health. rare medical consultation	Health sound. no severe problem	Poor health with continuing treatment for severe problem

| Very low absence | Low absence | Poor absence |
| Very fit & active | Fit & active | Low fitness & energy |

Colin felt that a high essential specification was important given the nature of the job and the range of tasks, travel and the spread out nature of the work locations, which often required a great deal of walking and climbing. It was also important to set high desirable and clear contra-indicators given the key part the AM would have to play, for example on the move to the Midpoint Complex. Even modest absence would cause severe problems and would possibly delay the move at considerable cost.

The health specification could be assessed by the application letter, interview exploration and with a medical examination prior to confirmation of offer.

2. Qualifications: Maximum 10 points

Desirable
Business and/or professional qualifications (5)
Graduate or postgraduate (5)

Colin decided that it was not necessary for this particular job to specify essentials or contra-indicators for qualifications. He felt that anybody who matched the other parts of the specification well could do the job, even if they had minimal qualifications.

He gave weight, however, to the desirable specification, feeling that they could reinforce evidence in other categories and support inferences, such as:

- The applicant with business or professional qualifications would have a range of tools and knowledge to draw on, and a good contextual background for doing the job in current and future situations.
- A graduate could be expected to have a sound capacity for analysis and conceptual thought, which would aid planning and policy.
- High qualifications could indicate a potential executive.

You may think that this is sufficiently important to classify these as essential, but as we have seen, person specifications are judgements, with no absolute right or wrong.

3. Work experience and achievements: Maximum 60 points

3.1 Administration (Maximum 36 points)

Aspect	Knowledge	Experience	Achievement
Major move	2	2	2
Administration technology and systems	2	2	2

Building administration	1	1	1
Security	1	1	1
Procurement	1	1	1
Temp/contract staffing	1	1	1
Senior Committee administration	1	1	1
Company communications	1	1	1
Product knowledge	1	1	1
Budget management	1	1	1

Maximum 36   Desirable 30   Essential 20

Colin judged that 20 would indicate a minimum breadth that could be built upon, if the individual had good management competence, vision and a track record of learning.

He chose this checklist and points approach because he felt it would be easy to score during assessment for the short list and conducting the interview, in a category with several important elements.

3.2 Management (Maximum 24 points)

Aspect	4	2	0
Communication with all levels	Yes	Adequate	No
Influence: Assertive not aggressive or passive	Yes	Adequate	No
Delegation: skill and will	Yes	Adequate	No
Plans and Does	Yes	Adequate	No
Prioritizes: Urgent/important	Yes	Adequate	No
Good balance between the people and technical aspects of role	Yes	Adequate	No

Maximum 24   Desirable 20   Essential 12

Colin saw these as vital for success in this job. It will require communication with widely different people and a need to get results, but without bullying. The wide responsibilities could only be exercised with good delegation. The central role in future developments requires planning skills and implementation of the plans to deadlines. The diverse demands call for time management and prioritizing skill and the will to practise it. People and technical aspects are important and a strong bias one way or the other would be undesirable.

Assessment will require careful question preparation and skilled interviewing to gain evidence.

4. Learning and change: 5 points per item, maximum 20 points

Desirable	Essential	Contra-indicator
Enjoys change and looks for it	Accepts change as necessary	Avoids and resists when possible
Handles change by involving others	Consults over changes	Directs people to change
Evidence of recent development and plans for future	Attended courses and willing to learn more	No recent courses and no real interest in own development
Self motivated to learn/experiment	Interested in learning/new ideas	Negative/neutral to new ideas

Maximum 20   Desirable 16   Essential 12

Colin Smith believes that Insupply is a dynamic, growing and innovative organization. The Administration Manager's role will be to facilitate this and help others contribute to it. He is looking for a person who supports change and who handles it with conviction and confidence. This is the essential part. It is desirable that the individual positively welcomes it and there will be some important cross references with the category which covers motivation. Closely linked to change is the desire to learn and the will to unlearn.

Track records and attitudes to change and personal development can be checked at all stages of evidence collection (application, interview, references).

5. Special skills: Maximum 10 points

Desirable
Operation of advanced administration methods and equipment.
Proficiency in languages

Neither of these special skills identified by Colin Smith is regarded by him as essential nor as a contra-indicator, but both are desirable given the nature of the job, in terms of technical change and innovation, and overseas clients/suppliers.

6. Interests: Maximum 20 points

6.1 Personal (0 points)

Community and group interests, with perhaps physically active pursuits, could reinforce other aspects, such as management, learning and change, personality and physical. Hobbies and their significance for the person could give some clues (for example, obsession!).

Colin felt it would be misleading to read too much into this aspect, and decided that he would give it a zero weighting.

6.2 Work interests: Motivation (maximum 20 points)

4	2	0
Sets and achieves high personal targets	Sets modest targets with some success	Sets easy targets or no clear goals
Enjoys taking initiative	Initiates within limits set by others	Reacts to others' prompts only
Welcomes variety in tasks and challenge	Accepts some variation to basic routine	Prefers fixed routine. Variation disliked
Wants autonomy	Prefers some independence	Wants direction
Thrives on responsibility	Accepts responsibility	Sees increases in responsibility as threatening

Maximum 20   Desirable 16   Essential 10

Colin thought about the nature of the job. The person in it would not be closely supervised and would need to respond to the opportunity for self motivation. To get results it would be necessary to be a high achiever and self starter. There would be a great deal of autonomy and extensive responsibility, which would increase as Insupply grew, as well as a wide variety of different tasks with an unpredictable pattern. He knew some people would find this threatening, others would be highly motivated by the challenge and it would be crucial to find out which was which during the selection process.

7. Personality: Maximum 20 points

	4	3	2	1	0	
Approachable	.	.	.	.	.	Aloof
Humour	.	.	.	.	.	Humourless
Diplomatic	.	.	.	.	.	Tactless
Stable	.	.	.	.	.	Anxious under pressure
Team person	.	.	.	.	.	Unsupportive or aggressive

Maximum 20   Desirable 15   Essential 10

Colin knew that the job would require a person who could get on with staff who were not the easiest people to manage. The senior members and clients of Insupply could all be difficult. He wanted an ally as diplomat and smoother of ruffled feathers. There was going to be much stress in the role with diverse demands and competing deadlines. A stable person who knew how to cope and relax was needed. There was a strong team dimension to the job. He knew these would not be easy to assess, but felt he could look for clues during the interview from the applicants' behaviour and evidence from their careers.

8. Personal circumstances

The job needed a person who could drive and fly and whose circumstances did not prevent frequent stays away from home. These were things to explore, but did not require points.

Comments on the person specification: Administration Manager

Colin had reviewed thoroughly his idea of the job description and found it helpful to compare people he had known in similar positions. This enabled him to identify the kind of person he was looking for.

He found that it was easier to be precise and factual in some categories than in others. Motivation and personality were difficult to describe, but the terms he used were clear to him. He thought he could make a good attempt to assess the characteristics he had identified by the way people behaved, and how they talked about their approach to work and people. He knew he would have to interpret this and that it would not be easy. These aspects were so important that he had to make the effort. He felt that others using the specification would also understand them, and so be guided to make useful judgements.

The 'essential', 'desirable' and contra-indicators and his points weighting would make assessment of suitability and the final decision easier. He had experimented with a number of ways of setting standards and defining differences.

ACTIVITY 2.4

▼ If you produced a person specification compare it to that created by Colin Smith. If the four people in his concrete comparison were applicants, experiment by comparing them to either or both specifications. Would you recruit one of them?

References for further reading

Anderson G.C. and Kelly J. (1986). *Personnel Selection and Recruitment*. HMSO
Boydell T.H. (1977). *A Guide to Job Analysis*. BACIE
Fraser J.M. (1978). *Employment Interviewing*. Macdonald and Evans
Plumbley P. (1988). *Recruitment and Selection*. IPM
Rodger A. (1952). *The Seven Point Plan*. National Institute of Industrial Psychology (NIIP), London

3

Setting up the search

Where to look?

Once it has been decided that there is a job and the person specification has been produced, the next step is to establish where to look.

Personal network

One option is to activate your personal network, either to identify potential recruits or simply to spread the word in the right quarters that the vacancy exists to members of staff, colleagues and appropriate professional and business connections. This would normally be to encourage promising candidates to apply and to supplement more conventional routes.

It has been shown that word of mouth can be as important as newspapers as a source of information about job availability, and it certainly costs less.

Internal

Most managers prefer to recruit from within their organization if possible. This supports morale in meeting advancement needs of employees, and can encourage others if they see that opportunities exist.

There is also greater knowledge of the person available to the recruiter, because the individual's performance and potential will have been assessed and probably reported upon. If this is an exclusive policy there would be problems should a particular set of skills be in short internal supply and could lead to an inward looking organization and few fresh approaches being imported. There are often procedures for internal advertising, and if a pool of sufficient quality is not forthcoming there is no choice but to look outside.

External

The external pool is vast and you may feel it is necessary to engage specialist help to fish it. Should you have a personnel department or choose external agencies, it is important that you are precise in your wants and expectations and it helps to have knowledge of the options so that you are in a position to manage the relationship. You may want to hand over most of the activity or merely some parts of it, but if you are the person who owns the job requirement, it will benefit you to define the job and the person at least, and to share in key decisions. Recruitment is a costly exercise and failed recruitment even more so.

Choices of media include radio and TV, but the most frequent is the press. Possibilities range from the specialist journals to national, overseas and local newspapers.

Professional and specialist journals have the real advantage of appealing directly to a pool which should be well stocked with the type for which you are fishing. A problem may be that you are competing with others angling for the same fish. It is probable that the circulation will be restricted in numbers, if not relevant quality. They are published at much less frequent intervals than newspapers which is a disadvantage if you are in a hurry. They are usually cheaper, often 10% of the cost of the quality national newspapers for equivalent space.

Newspapers are the most common medium for advertising vacancies. They have a massive circulation compared to journals and are usually proportionately more expensive, although it could be argued they could be cheaper in terms of the cost per viable applicant. One estimate is that a moderate size full display advertisement will cost rather more than one month's average European or United States salary. Newspapers have different readerships and different reputations with job seekers. They often appeal to different job clusters at different times, so modest research may well pay dividends in terms of reaching the right audience.

It is often worth approaching a recruitment agency which will handle the advertisement at no fee to you. They take a percentage of the fee paid by you to the paper and will advise on content, timing and placement and take care of design.

Do not discount the local press for even senior and specialist appointments. You may well find the person you want on the doorstep. Many people may be tired of commuting and could welcome a move closer to home. It could also be quicker and cheaper if no house move is involved. Although you are not likely to rely exclusively upon local newspapers for senior recruitment, at low additional cost it is often worth the investment.

Keeping a record of the results from the different placements in terms of cost per viable applicant is a good way of managing recruitment costs.

How to look

The advertisement

The purpose of the advertisement is to attract the promising applicants and deter the unpromising. It should be striking so that it is noticed and have information which interests those you wish to interest.

ACTIVITY 3.1

 What should be included in an advertisement?

CASE PROJECT 3.1

If you were Colin Smith of Insupply, what would be the information you would give the advertising agency to include in the advertisement for the Administration Manager?

Organization's name	Insupply	**Location**	Hometown
What it does	Fast growing supplier of high quality office equipment and paper products.		
Motif/eyecatcher	Go to the top with us in this new post.		
Job title	Administration Manager.		
Main purpose, tasks and responsibilities	To manage a department which provides the support needed to maintain Insupply's success and to lead our relocation to new premises at Midpoint Complex.		
Main features of specification	We hope the person appointed will have professional or business qualifications with foreign language proficiency, but more important will be self-starting energy and a desire for challenge, allied to good management skills, and a proven track record in areas such as contract staffing, company communication, procurement, building management and technical change.		
Reward package	Top quartile for this level.		

Figure 3.1 Information in Colin Smith's job advertisement.

It could be argued that Colin Smith has given too much away to potential applicants (see Figure 3.1), so that they have clues about the image to project in their application and in the subsequent interview. However, if the advertisement gives too little information and focuses only on the attractions of the post, there may be a flood of candidates who do not fit at all, and this can be a very time- and cost-consuming exercise. It is useful to include key factual elements in it, in order to enable some realistic preselection and self 'selecting out' to occur.

The middle course is to give a feel for the company self image and culture (motif/eyecatcher, for example). Most emphasis should then be placed on the factual elements of the job:

- qualifications,
- track record,

rather than on personality aspects:

- self starting energy,
- desire for challenge,

which probably do not lead to people selecting themselves out nor to people including themselves who otherwise would not have done so. There is evidence that people are honest with you and themselves about facts, but not about interpretations of ability and personality characteristics. Perhaps we all think we are energetic self starters who love challenges, or if we don't we are sure we have other qualities which will do just as well. These factors are important for you to have in your specification, but for you to make judgements upon rather than advertise.

Recruitment agencies and consultancies

There are a variety of agencies which can undertake the chores or major responsibility for recruitment. They appear extensively advertising vacancies in the media and are easy to contact. Like all service providers, there are sharks and charlatans alongside the professional and ethical businesses. It can be a very expensive exercise with no certainty of success at the end.

Recently a company of modest size decided that its future lay with bright and intelligent young people who could be trained to handle the market and technical turbulence anticipated in the future. This was interpreted by them to mean high level graduates. They had not recruited at this level before and they had nobody on their staff they felt could do this. The Chief Executive had recently attended a conference where he met the director of a training and consultancy organization, which was invited to undertake the recruitment

The consultants were not, in fact, experienced in the field of graduate recruitment. Nevertheless, they contracted to find eight graduate trainees for the company. The company agreed to a daily fee rate and the advertisement attracted 800 applications, of whom 100 were interviewed to produce a short list of 24. The others were contacted by the consultants and informed that they had been unsuccessful.

In the discussion with the consultants the client appeared to rate academic standards and 'drive with ambition' above everything else. The resulting specification and the weightings were not discussed in any detail with the clients, and they were used for the advertisement and short-listing.

The Executive of the company was confronted with a group of outstandingly qualified high achievers attracted by the consultant's advertisement and their own supporting literature, which substantially oversold the job, its rewards and prospects.

At the interviews, the company realized it was going to over-recruit in nearly all cases, and that there was little chance of a mutual fit. Eventually they appointed four of the original 800, two of whom left in the first three months. The cost to the company was the equivalent of the full annual salaries of those four recruits.

ACTIVITY 3.2

 The above case was a costly mistake for the company, and the consultants. How was the recruitment process mishandled by the clients and the consultants?

Check them out
    Ask them about their relevant track record.
    Who would work on the project?
    What experience do they have?
    Who have they recruited for in the past?
Test their professionalism
    Find out the methods they use.
    Assess them against your own knowledge.
    Ask them about difficulties and how they
      increase the chances of success.
    Discuss how they would involve you.
    Are they good listeners?
    Seek their views upon the case.
    Are they confident and assertive?
Do not surrender responsibility
    Insist upon being consulted at key stages and before major decisions.
    Demand feedback at key points, e.g. see the job description and person
      specification before they are acted upon; check out the advertisement.
Take care with the contract
    Treat it as you would any supply contract.
    Get more than one quote and modus operandi.

Figure 3.2 Working with recruitment consultants.

There were faults with both the consultants and the client in the recruitment case. The client became a victim of its own propaganda. The person specification fitted their own rosy image of themselves, rather than what they really needed. Their advertised reward package was less than truthful and oversold the job to nobody's gain. They failed to manage either the consultants or the project.

The consultants should have checked their understanding and tested their plans with the client. They made assumptions, for example, about the specification, which should have been tested. There were some basic errors, such as not confronting the client about overspecifying and releasing too early those not making the initial short list.

A knowledge of the methods and techniques of recruitment can help the professional manager reduce the risk of mistakes with agencies and consultants. Unless you know them well or have good reason to trust them, check out their professionalism by asking about their other clients, and finding out how thorough they are in the areas we have examined, such as job description and person specification. Ask what recruitment methods they propose and if they seem to be selling a particular line, such as the latest thing in computerized psychological tests, do seek evidence of validation that they actually do get the right person for the job.

Points to bear in mind when working with recruitment consultants are summarized in Figure 3.2.

Planning the recruitment project

To be efficient and successful, recruitment needs detailed planning and thorough administration. As with any other activity which involves contact with the world outside, it is an opportunity for image enhancement or tarnishing. There are many aspects to be included in the plan and preparation.

1 What is the recruitment time span?

- When do you need the person?
- Where are you advertising? when will it appear?
- When will the application deadline be?
- When will you short-list?
- How much notice will you give those short-listed?
- When will you interview/assess the short list?
- When will you make the offer?
- When will you inform the unsuccessful?
- When do you hope to see the person in post?

It usually takes longer than you think. You will benefit from making a detailed schedule and agreeing diary dates with others involved as early as possible.

Short-listing can take a considerable time.

Interviewing times should allow for preparation and reflection. The temptation to cram in too many interviews should be avoided. Five hours face-to-face in one day is a reasonable load. More than this and you will not do yourself nor the applicants justice.

2 Who is going to be involved in the project?

- Planning stage.
- Administration.
- Assessment and decision making.

Involve those who are on your recruitment team at the planning stage, including the person responsible for its administration. There is always a great deal of administration and clerical work associated with most recruitment and this can have a marked effect upon success and the PR aspects. The line boss of the person being recruited should always be part of the team. It is usually thought desirable that as few as possible should take part in interviewing as too many interviewers can put undesirable pressure on the applicants. Perhaps the future boss and one other important stakeholder is best, either separately or together, but certainly planned and coordinated.

3 What information will you give the potential applicants?

- Job description?
- Organization literature?
- Standard/non-standard letter?
- Application form/guide?

An application form restricts the choice of the applicant but gives the recruiter the chance to direct the information required. The open-ended letter may reveal things about the applicant that the standard form could miss, but key details could be omitted. Another choice is to send an application guide, identifying the basic details wanted but with some flexibility.

4 How will the short-listing be organized?

- Construction/agreement of the person specification?
- Who is doing the short-listing?
- How many on the short list? reserves?
- Date flexibility to accommodate applicants?
- Invitation letter and details: date, time, who will interview, map?

Short-listing is sometimes delegated. If this is the case, it is important that the senior parties involved in recruitment give a clear indication of their specification to the short-listers. Factual cut-off points, such as a candidate not having essential experience, are the means of eliminating applicants at this stage.

Some flexibility in your interview timetable to accommodate a candidate who is unable to meet your date or time may mean you do not lose your best candidate.

5 Methods of recruitment?

- Interview? who? solo? series? panel?
- Second interview?
- Other methods? tests? group selection?

The interview is still the most common method of recruitment, but other approaches are sometimes used to produce additional evidence to assist the decision process. These include tests of ability or personality and group assessment. These are usually sophisticated methods, and their proponents suggest that they need to be conducted and interpreted by specialists.

6 Decision process?

- Who decides? how? consensus? majority? you?

Comparing the applicants to the person specification and each other is the hub of the process. If there is more than one person involved in the decision the specification is usually a good way of focusing the discussion and sharing judgements. Decisions will be easier if the specification has been agreed and discussed prior to the interviews. If there is a panel then how it will be guided and organized, as well as how the selection decision will be made, should be considered at the planning phase.

7 How will you make the offer?

- Letter and/or telephone? negotiate? subject to satisfactory referees and medical?
- What will be the contract of employment?

Part of the project planning should be the contract and reward package to be offered or negotiated with the successful applicant. It is also necessary to identify the policy on references and medical examination at this stage.

8 What are your induction plans?

- What will the successful person need to learn?
- Will there be a guide and mentor?

Success or failure following recruitment often depends upon induction, which can often be considered appropriately at the planning phase.

Insupply case study recruitment plan

Colin Smith produced the following plan.

(1) Time span

Week 2 – Advertisement appears in local and regional press and two appropriate journals.

Week 5 – Application deadline and short-listing; rejections except short list and reserves.

Week 7 – Interviews, offer and rejections after satisfactory acceptance.

Week 16 – Target start date for the successful person.

(2) Who will be involved?

Personnel Administration would conduct the routine parts of the search and were involved in the planning.

Hedi Lindstrom, his Chief Executive, agreed to meet all six short-list candidates.

(3) What information would be given to potential applicants?

They would be sent the full job description and a copy of the advertisement, which would form part of the contract of the successful applicant. Copies of Insupply's promotional literature would also be included.

They would also have an application guide.

(4) Organizing the short list

Personnel would conduct the initial vetting of the applications in order to produce a 'long list', with notes indicating why they were recommending rejection.

The long list would then be reviewed by Colin Smith, using the person specification to produce a short list of six with two reserves. Personnel would administer the process, including the invitations.

(5) Methods of recruitment

The interview would be the main method of recruitment, but Colin planned to use a short test to assess management style. He was aware of the need to exercise caution in interpreting the test, but it was very easy to administer and he felt it could give insights. It would be interesting to see how the applicants responded to the request to take the test. He would interview each of the candidates for two hours, and the Chief Executive would then meet them for half an hour. Colin's plan was to hold two interviews on each of three consecutive days with a vacant slot in each day, and be prepared to offer alternatives. He would meet the Chief Executive late on Thursday to discuss the decision, and arrange with Personnel to make the offer and rejections.

(6) The decision process

Colin planned to delegate the long-listing to Personnel, working to his specification. He would select the short list himself and after the interviews discuss his conclusions with the Chief Executive and take account of her opinions, hopefully arriving at agreement. She had indicated that it would be Colin's decision, but he obviously planned to consider her views carefully.

(7) Making the offer

Once the decision had been made, and one or two reserves decided upon, Colin would write to the first choice offering the position. He would follow this with a phone call, and agree terms and conditions. The offer would be conditional upon adequate references and medical report. Personnel would send the formal offer and contract for written acceptance.

(8) Induction planning

Colin would discuss induction with the successful person. They would agree what the new Administration Manager needed to do to become familiar with Insupply and the role. External training and internal attachments would be organized. Colin intended to become the Administration Manager's guide and mentor during the induction period, progressively moving away from close contact as the new person became established.

CASE PROJECT 3.2

Evaluate Colin Smith's recruitment plan.

What would you include in your application guide if you were Colin, in order to get sufficient information to assist your short-listing judgement?

Colin Smith's application guide is shown in Figure 3.3.

You are requested to present your application for the position of Administration Manager in the following sequence. Your application should not cover more than three A4 sheets.

1 Name, address, telephone number, date of birth, marital status and dependants.
2 Educational and professional qualifications. Include schools, colleges and dates of awards.
3 Development during the last 10 years, including courses.
4 Career review, including organizations, positions held, dates, salaries and reasons for leaving.
5 Highlight your experience relevant to this position.
6 Outline the reasons for your application.
7 Summarize your health record.
8 What are your personal interests?
9 Give the names and addresses of two referees who are in a good position to comment upon your work.
10 What period of notice is required?
11 Any other information to support your application.

Figure 3.3   Illustration of the application guide sent to potential applicants by Colin Smith.

References for further reading

Anderson G.C. and Kelly J. (1986). *Personal Selection and Recruitment*. HMSO
Herriot P. (1990). *Recruitment in the 90's*. IPM
Plumbley P. (1988). *Recruitment and Selection*. IPM
Torrington D. and Hall L. (1987). *Personnel Management*. Prentice-Hall

4

Conducting the search

Long-listing and short-listing

Long-listing is the first step. This involves weeding out the obvious mismatches to arrive at a group of possible recruits. If the total number of applicants is high a quick means of elimination is helpful, but it is important not to sacrifice valid assessment on the altar of speed.

Some intriguing methods have been developed by some recruiters to save time. One rejects all who apply on coloured notepaper; another dismisses those who write long hand, as opposed to a third who will not see those who type. These approaches reflect the prejudices of the recruiter, rather than the qualities of the candidates, and are likely to substantially reduce the effectiveness of the recruitment.

Perhaps a more understandable criterion is differentiation in terms of neatness and clarity of presentation, but it could be a mistake to reject an applicant on these grounds unless untidy presentation is a clear contra-indicator for the job. It is best to use the person specification to identify a few essentials and contra-indicators for the post, which can readily be identified at a glance. Typically these could be minimum experience type or range; qualification cut-offs; and some would have age limits that they wish to apply.

Short-listing means careful matching of the applicants to your specification of the 'ideal' person. However, you may find it helpful to modify your detailed specification to accommodate the nature and limitations of the written evidence at your disposal when short-listing. An example of a modified person specification is shown in Figure 4.1.

Even though you may have steered the applicants to give you information needed as evidence for assessment in their written application, you will find that some categories are hard, perhaps impossible, to assess at this stage. Impact needs face-to-face contact; motivation and personality may or may not be inferable from the application, but the inferences may be unreliable and you may wish to reweight them for this stage, focusing on more concrete, factual aspects. You could then revert to your original full specification at the interview.

Category	Points Essential Maximum		Comments and Notes
1 Physical			
Impact	0	0	Only assessable at interview.
Health	8*	12	Record requested in application. Infer from interests. Check at interview. Medical needed.
2 Qualifications			
Business/prof		5	Not essential, but desirable and
Grad/postgrad		5	identifiable from application.
3 Work experience			Identifiable from application. Use the
Administration			main specification factors. Point weight
Knowledge	7*	12	less here. Achievement assessed at
Experience	7*	12	interview.
Management			
Experience	7*	12	Quality and approach not easily assessable from application. Weight less. Experience only.
4 Learning and change		5	Courses identifiable from application but not attitude to change.
5 Special skills		4	Identifiable from application but weight less to avoid imbalance with more relevant factors.
6 Work motivation		4	
			6 & 7 both important, but clues in application unreliable so weighting lower than main specification.
7 Personality		4	
8 Circumstances		0	Assessed but not weighted.
TOTAL		75	

* Four contra-indicators to use to arrive at the long list and identifiable from the written application.

Figure 4.1 Modified person specification for short-listing (from the Insupply case study).

The short list can be arrived at by identifying the closest fits to the person specification. This could be achieved by classifying each individual simply as 'See'/'Not see'. The marginals could be assessed by closer scrutiny of the desirable aspects of the more highly weighted categories.

The points system can be used to place people in order. The easiest method is to take the top group for your short list. It is safer to compare at least the borderline cases again as a double check.

You may think that an individual's points score 'feels' wrong. Examination of their application may reveal assets that are not accounted in the specification, in which case you probably should revise it. If somebody has a lower score than others, and you feel you want to see that person in preference, then do so. As was suggested in Chapter 2, you should not be a slave to your system but it should be a servant to you. It is a good idea to have one place on a short list for a 'wild card'. That is somebody whom you have a feeling about, but can't explain what it is that makes you believe they have possibilities.

Evidence for a category may be entirely absent in one application. You may wish to scale up the points score. For example, a person may give no clue about learning and change and, say, has in effect a score of 42/70. This is the equivalent of 45/75, and it may be better to use the latter score.

Insupply case study: Short-listing

Colin Smith began the implementation of his recruitment plan and used an agency to design and place the advertisements.

Three weeks after the advertisements for the Administration Manager (page 33) appeared in the press, Insupply had received 70 applications for the post. Personnel reduced this to a long list of 30, in consultation with Colin Smith, who then set about producing his short list of six, with two reserves.

The applications of two of the long-listed people are shown below. They both used the application guide (Figure 3.2) to structure their letters.

Colin Smith had to decide which of the two should have the sixth and final place on the short list and which should become a reserve.

CASE PROJECT 4.1

Examine the applications of Joseph Silva and Robert Armstrong. Using the modified person specification (Figure 4.1) or another which you devise yourself, assess them in each category and decide which of them would have the final short-list place.

Application from Joseph Silva

Mr Colin Smith
Deputy Chief Executive
Insupply

Dear Mr Smith

Vacancy: Administration Manager

When I saw your advertisement in the *North City Times* I was excited by the prospect of applying. It is exactly the opportunity I want at this stage of my career and I hope that you will feel that I am the person you require. Without, I trust, appearing immodest, I think I have the qualities and experience needed for what I am sure will be a demanding position in a growing company.

I enclose a brief career history which follows the format suggested in your application guide.

I would be very pleased to discuss my application in more detail and look forward to hearing from you.

Yours sincerely,

Joseph Silva

Career history: Joseph Silva

1 Personal Details

Joseph Silva, 24 Dukes Avenue, North City.
Phone 9432 8907.
Age 32 years. Married to Tina. We have one boy age 2.

2 Educational and Professional Qualifications

Studied at North City Central.
Age 16 Level Examination: Passes in English, Spanish, Mathematics, General Science, History.
Age 18 Level Examination: Passes in major subjects English and Economics.

Local Government Examination: Passes in Law, Public Accounts, Public Relations, Property Management, Administrative Management.

3 Courses

I studied for the Local Government Examinations which I passed fully at my first attempt seven years ago. Apart from an occasional conference or convention in Local Government Property Management, it has not been necessary to study or take other courses, as I have sufficient knowledge for my job.

4 Career Review

Jansen and Crabbe Accountants: Trainee Accountant
I joined them at 18 years of age and left after 2 years because I did not feel that I was suited to a career in accounting.

North City Local Authority, Solicitors Department:
Administrative Officer Grade 2
I provided support to the legal professional staff in Property, Debts, Finance and Planning from when I joined at 20 to my transfer and upgrading six years later.

North City Local Authority, Housing Department: Administrative Officer Grade 4

I was promoted from Grade 3 four years ago and I am currently in charge of two staff. I am responsible for the Authority's Property Management, which involves maintenance and new building work, security and liaison with architects and contractors.

5 Relevant Experience

I had experience of private business directly during my two years in accounting. My contacts with company clients were extensive and I spent much time working with accounting and administrative departments of companies like Insupply. My time in the North City legal department should prove helpful to the post of Administration Manager. Although I have no legal qualifications, I have a good knowledge of the law as it affects organizations.

In my current post I am responsible for contract building staff, arrange for the procurement of materials and manage the maintenance of the Authority property and new buildings. I believe I communicate well and have a working knowledge of Spanish. I have seen many changes in the last ten years so technical change would not be a problem. I am responsible for managing my department and the two staff and think that I have good management skills.

6 Reasons for my Application

I am applying for this post because after ten years I feel I want more of a challenge and regard myself as an enthusiastic self starter. I am ambitious and know I could achieve more with Insupply than with the Authority.

7 Health Record

My health is good. In the last year I have only visited the doctor three times with dietary-induced migraine and minor digestive problems. My absence record shows only eight days' absence in 12 months. I have had no major illness.

8 Personal Interests

I spend as much time as possible with my family. Apart from this, I enjoy reading, music and the theatre. My wife and I share an interest in genealogy.

9 Referees

My two referees are Mike Hanlan, head of the Housing Department and Jill Scott, head of the Legal Department.

10 Notice

My employers require three months' notice.

11 Other Information

I have found out about your products, and know that people speak most highly of them. Insupply has a very good reputation and I am sure I would be proud to work for such an organization. My career has centred around administration and management and this has been supported by my studies. I am sure that I could perform this job to a good level and have good experience in many aspects of it.

I look forward to an opportunity to discuss my application with you.

Application from Robert Armstrong

Mr Colin Smith
Deputy Chief Executive
Insupply

Administration Manager Vacancy

Dear Mr Smith

Thank you for sending me the details of the above position. I am pleased to submit my application and have provided the information below in the way suggested by you.

1   Robert (Bob) Armstrong
    274 Oak Drive,
    Hometown
    Phone 9420 34356

    I am 36 years old. Divorced. Ex-wife has custody of our two children. My new partner has a daughter and I hope to remarry shortly.

2   I attended Middleton County School and at 16 achieved pass grades in English, Maths, Physics, Craftwork and Geography. I passed my standard Banking Institute examinations at 26. After evening study I have recently been accepted as a Member of the Institute of Administration after successfully completing their examination.

3   Since the age of 18 I have attended many courses not only related to my positions at the time, but also to my future career. I have been fortunate in having mostly had employers who have supported me in this, and good managers to learn from. I have been involved in a great deal of changes in my roles and career and my development has had to match them.

4   At 16 I made the mistake of not continuing my education but went to work in the family store. I have to confess I soon found this boring and wanted to do more with my life, so at 18 I joined the police. After three years I was promoted to Sergeant and came to specialize in Crime Prevention, liaising with industry and commerce. I spent time, for example, advising banks and when my marriage got into difficulties over the demands of my police work I

was able to start a new career at 24 in banking. I enjoyed the responsibility for cash and meeting the public at all levels.

I was promoted to Assistant Manager: Small Businesses and enjoyed this work for two years. I was involved also in training the regional staff in personal computing and the implementation of new systems. Unfortunately my employers, Southfield Bank, merged with the Country Bank and promotion became blocked. At that time, one of my small business clients approached me to run their administration. This was JB Distribution, a company at the time employing 20 staff distributing local free newspapers and advertising material.

My title was Administrator and it involved doing everything that needed doing, from introducing basic hardware and software to increase our distribution efficiency to operating the equipment myself. We doubled in size in two years and had to move to larger premises on the edge of town. I was responsible for the planning of the move and persuading the staff that they would be better off. I think I was successful because nearly all stayed with us in spite of the increased journey time to work.

After four years with JB I felt the need for more professional development. The owner did not really understand this, and did not feel able to support me in my pursuit of further education. I was accepted on the Institute of Administration part time course at Hometown, where I moved three years ago, taking up a post as Assistant Administration Manager with Middleton Booksellers. My responsibilities cover many of those in your post, such as purchasing, which includes much of Insupply's product range! I am happy at Middleton, but your vacancy is too good an opportunity to miss trying for.

5 I think I have wide and varied experience of many of the duties in the position advertised and would feel able to tackle those aspects new to me.

6 I want to be responsible for a department of my own and to enjoy new aspects such as building management. I would like 'to go to the top with Insupply!'

7 I am very fit and have a good health record.

8 I have many interests. I run a rock climbing club and organize climbs once a month. House and car maintenance are both a necessity and a hobby. I am also involved in charity work.

9 My referees are Steve Jameson, Regional Manager, Southfield Country Bank, and my current Chief Executive, John Stein.

10 Two months' notice would be needed.

11 No further information, but I would welcome the chance to talk with you about the outline I have given in more detail, and to find out more about the new position.

Yours sincerely,

Bob Armstrong

Colin Smith's short-list assessment and decision

Joseph Silva	Category	Bob Armstrong
He suggests his health is good, but his record doesn't support this.	1.2 Health	Claims good but no evidence. Needs a check but reasonable to infer he is from other clues.
8		10

Cross references to information provided elsewhere to support inferences can be helpful. Colin refers to other clues, such as Bob Armstrong's frequent rock climbing expeditions and other active interests.

Colin is probably correct not to accept an applicant's evaluation of what is good, but to seek other evidence to test it. Candidates will tend to distort such evaluations in their own favour. Joseph Silva's assessment of his health record as good suggests also that he may be operating to different standards from those of a healthier person. What is good to Joseph may be below average to somebody else. His record of three visits to the doctor and eight days' absence in one year raises the issue of what a bad year would be. Colin has to be clear on the standard he wants. He is optimistic about Bob, who seems active and energetic, but cautious about Joseph whose life style seems more sedentary. The points are for short-listing and would be reassessed at interview stage.

Joseph Silva	Category	Bob Armstrong
Local Government exams in relevant subjects.	2. Qualifications	Bank exams equate to LG exams. He also has an Inst. Admin and passed Police exams.
3		6

Colin Smith equated the two initial professional examinations. He was impressed by the Institute membership, which along with the police exams he felt merited more than the 5 he had allocated in his scheme for this category. Therefore he borrowed a mark from the 5 available for graduate qualifications and gave Bob 6 points. This is perfectly sound. No scheme can catch all the qualities you will meet in candidates and flexibility to cater for this is important. The aim is to compare and assess people, not to stick slavishly to a scheme which will not fit every circumstance.

Colin was not weighting education at 18 and below.

Joseph Silva		Category		Bob Armstrong
		3. Work experience (Administration)		
Supporting experience (liaison architects etc.).	1	Location move	4	Ran JB's move. Knowledge + experience.
Some doubtful claims for Tech. Change.	1?	Admin. technology	4	With Bank & JB. K+E and change.

Good K+E.	2	Building	1? Probable. JB & Mid'ton.
K+E at North City.	2	Security	2 Police work.
K+E at North City.	2	Procurement	2 K+E at Middleton.
Contractors at NC?	1	Temp staffing	? No K or E shown.
Supporting experience.	1?	Committee	1? Support experience.
No evidence.	0	Communication	1? Surely at JB?
Research worth a point.	1	Know product	2 K+E at Middleton.
Some in Local Authority.	1?	Budget	2 Surely JB & Mid'ton?
Legal & Accounts useful.	2	Bonus (5 max.)	3 Law, banking and small business.

14   **22**

Colin Smith felt that his plan to have less than 14 as a cut-off point was wrong in the light of the relevant experience of some applicants, which he hadn't anticipated in his original scheme. He realized that he would have excluded some who were worth interviewing . He decided to keep his minimum of 14, but to add five bonus points for unspecified valuable experience. The maximum total for this part now became 29, and overall 80.

Colin also gave credit for experience which would be of relevance to a job description factor, even if the person had no direct experience of that factor. Joseph's good experience of working with architects and builders would be very relevant to managing the development of the new location prior to the move, even if he had no experience of managing a move as such.

The recruiter always hopes that the applicant will translate their experience in terms of the person specification and the job requirements. Applicants will often try to do this, in their own interests, but they are not mind readers and often will not spell out knowledge or experience they possess which would support their case. Colin Smith, in his efforts to arrive at the best short list, often had to make reasoned guesses about the applicants, sometimes giving them the benefit of the doubt.

The question marks on his notes (?) indicate where he has guessed at experience and knowledge which has not been stated. This is a good argument for giving applicants as full information as possible about the job tasks and responsibilities, so that they can provide you with the relevant facts about themselves.

Joseph Silva	Category	Bob Armstrong
	3. Work experience (Management)	
2	Communication	2
2	Assertion	2
1	Delegation	?
1/2?	Planner + Doer	2
1	Time Manager	1
1/2?	Technical/People	2
7		**9**

Colin found the management category difficult to assess from many of the letters. Some said very little directly about their responsibilities and fewer still described their approach to management. He knew what he was looking for but found little direct evidence in the applications to help him make assessments. Joseph and Bob were unfortunately typical in this respect. Colin felt the mistake was his, not theirs, and that he should have been explicit about the need to spell out their approach to management in his application guide.

He decided to assess quantity of experience as one criterion, and to attempt to infer qualities and approach from the tone and clues in the applications. He was aware that those who gave no clues would be penalized and he decided to treat low scores with caution.

Joseph had had some unspecified departmental management responsibilities for at least four years. There was probably a high people content. He had two staff reporting to him and high financial responsibility given the property element. He had been upgraded three times in ten years which meant he was not assessed negatively in North City Authority. His application was clear and confident. Given the amount of work Colin guessed would pass through his area, Joseph probably had to delegate to survive. Building and maintenance required a sense of priorities and time management skills, but Colin could find few clues about either planning/doing or technical/people balance.

Possibly because Bob had had a more diverse experience and partly due to his fuller narrative style in the application, Colin felt he had more clues about him as a manager. He talked about 'good managers to learn from', which suggested that he saw the people side of management as important. He was promoted by the bank to a position which required influence and good communication skills as assistant manager for small businesses, and his training role also supported this. Promotion to police sergeant after three years suggested leadership attributes. Bob's work with JB Distribution suggested planning, doing and influencing achievement in relationship to the move, and a good record with the staff. Colin wondered about Bob's delegation. It was possible that he was a person who liked to do it all. He had several years good managerial experience.

Joseph Silva	Category	Bob Armstrong
	4. Learning and change	
Seen many changes. Technical change 'no problem'.		Introduces change including technical. Welcomes personal change.
No recent courses – 'has sufficient knowledge'.		Enthusiastic to learn. Left JB to do it.
1		5

Colin was as unimpressed with Joseph's complacent attitude to learning and change as he was impressed by Bob's. He felt confident there was a real difference between them here.

Joseph Silva	Category	Bob Armstrong
	5. Special skills	
Spanish – working knowledge.		Operates advanced administrative equipment.
2		2

6. Work motivation

	Category	
Modest goals.	Goal setting	Sets high and achieves.
'Self starter' claim. Evidence?	Initiates	Enjoyed this at JB in creating systems/change.
Has not sought yet.	Variety/Challenge	Enthusiastic about it.
Would he value it?	Autonomy	Guess he enjoys it?
Has it. Wants it? I am not sure.	Responsibility	Says he wants more. I believe him.
1		4

As he continues his assessment, Colin finds himself warming to Bob and discounting Joseph. This is mainly based on the evidence in Bob's application and perhaps the lack of it in Joseph's. There is a risk that he is developing a predisposition to rate Bob high and Joseph low which should be avoided. However, it is valuable to try to develop a feel for the whole person, and not to treat recruitment simply as an analytical exercise. Bob's enthusiasms come through his writing and Colin's assessment seems sound on the evidence, but Joseph's style and confident unsupported assertions may work against him. He could be under-assessed on motivation.

Joseph Silva	*Category*	*Bob Armstrong*
	7. Personality	
Non-social interests. Family centred. Does he suffer from stress – migraine/ digestion? Letter impersonal. Few clues about the person. Is he complacent?	Approachable Humour Diplomatic Stable Team person	Social and organizing interests. Probably good with relationships (training/JB). Seems open – admits mistakes. Team person – needs to trust others rock climbing. Diplomatic in police & bank roles?
2		3

Once again Colin found this very difficult to assess. He searched for clues and made inferences which he recognized may be wrong. He felt, nevertheless, that it was worth attempting to make judgements but he avoided giving too much weight to personality at this stage. At least it would give him something to pursue at the interview. His task at the moment was to find the best candidates for the short list and it was these interpretative areas that he would have to guesstimate in order to differentiate between close contenders.

8. Personal circumstances

Colin felt it would be important to check that the candidates were drivers, comfortable travellers and content to work unsocial hours, often away from home.

Colin Smith's short list decision

Colin Smith rated Bob Armstrong ahead of Joseph Silva in all aspects of the person specification. He had question marks about Joseph's health and fitness in relation to the job demands, and further reservations on his attitude to learning and change. He was uncertain about his motivation, in terms of the motivators he felt would apply. Joseph's qualifications and work experience indicated that there was a possibility that he would fit this part of the specification, but not as closely as several others, including Bob Armstrong. He was a marginal reserve for interview and had 38/80 points, with no contra-indicators.

Bob was rated highly by Colin in most categories. Particularly well rated were his health, work experience, capacity to learn and attitude to change, all factors seen as important in the Administration Manager's role at Insupply. He had one of the highest points total, 61/80.

Colin Smith intended to use his analysis of the applications to identify things he wanted to check or explore in the interviews. He would revert to his original person specification, although he would review it in the light of the experience of short-listing. For example, he would consider more weighting for work experience, with space for 'other unpredicted factors'. The points scores for short-listing would not necessarily count for anything at the interviews. The final assessment would be based on all the evidence from all the available sources, including applications and interviews.

References for further reading

Anderson G.C. and Kelly J. (1986). *Personnel Selection and Recruitment*. HMSO
Fraser G.M. (1978). *Employment Interviewing*. Macdonald and Evans
Plumbley P. (1988). *Recruitment and Selection*. IPM

5

Selection: getting the evidence

There are a range of approaches which can provide evidence to assist the selection decision. They are not mutually exclusive. Indeed, if several are used together they will reinforce each other and increase the chances of the right choice being made.

The line manager without substantial professional support is most likely to gather information from the application, the interview and the reference report. Research suggests that these methods are often not used effectively, so that their value may be little more than picking a person for the post at random. As these remain the most popular ways of getting selection evidence, we will examine practical ways of maximizing their effectiveness.

There are other, probably more valid and reliable tools which are better predictors of an applicant's success in a particular job, which are usually seen as the province of the selection specialist. However, some can be used by line managers who are under-resourced and do not have access to personnel specialists. It will require a little ingenuity and creative use of your time to increase the probability of a good selection decision. These include assessment centres and work sampling. Psychological tests have greater effectiveness than most managers want to accept, but are usually best left to those with specialist training.

Selection methods and their effectiveness are shown in Figure 5.1.

Application information: biodata	Popular. Easy to get. Reasonable predictor.
The interview	Popular. Low skill means poor prediction.
Reference reports	Popular. Yields poor predictive results.
Psychological tests	Less popular but good prediction value.
Assessment centres	Increasing popularity. Costly. Useful predictor.
Work sampling and work tests	Infrequently used. One of the best predictors.
Computer recruitment networks	Useful resource when available.
Genetic screening	Rare and specialized to assess health hazards.
Astrology and graphology	Best left to the popular press and fairgrounds.

Figure 5.1 Selection methods.

Application information: biodata

Research indicates that this is one of the better ways to gain helpful evidence to assist selection decision making. (P. Makin *et al.*, 1986). People rarely lie when giving factual information. This may be because they are intrinsically honest. An additional factor is that they may feel it is checkable, perhaps through references. The recruiter needs to steer the applicant to provide the information required, otherwise important facts may be omitted by accident or design.

The current jargon for application information from the applicant is **biodata**. This can be structured by forms prepared for the applicant to complete, or a letter and career history with the sequence and content of the application influenced by an application guide.

Applications should provide key factual information, which can be used in conjunction with the person specification to produce the short list. It will also produce some evidence for the final assessment and selection, as well as identifying areas to explore and clarify during the recruitment process.

Care has to be taken that application forms do not offend equal opportunities legislation, for example regarding gender and race. Equal opportunity employers may use part of the form to seek ethnic origin information for equality monitoring.

The basic factual information required is shown in Figure 5.2.

Personal details: Full name; title; date of birth; address; telephone number.

Education, training and qualifications: Establishments attended; awarding bodies; details and dates.

Work experience: Employers; positions; dates; main tasks and responsibilities; salaries; reasons for leaving.

Personal interests.

Health: fitness; disability.

Work interests and career hopes/plans.

Why do you want this post?

Any additional information to support your application.

Ethnic origin to assist equal opportunities monitoring: African; Afro-Caribbean; Asian; White; Other.

Referees.

Figure 5.2   Applications: basic factual information.

The selection interview

The interview as a selection tool is fallible. It relies upon information exchanged and interpreted by people with personal interests and biases so that judgement is distorted and decisions open to error. As a predictive tool Makin's study suggested that it is marginally better than references and too close for comfort to being no better that selecting staff at random.

Common reasons for the weakness of the interview as a selection device are:

- Distorted and premature judgement.
- Inadequate preparation.
- Poor use of support tools like person specifications.
- Lack of rapport with applicants.
- Poor panel teamwork.
- Weak and unfocused questioning.
- Poor listening.
- Bad interviewing conditions.

As it remains the most frequent recruitment tool it is important that it is used to maximum effect. The ways to achieve this are the subject of Chapter 6.

References

References are a popular part of the selection tool kit. Surveys indicate that 82% of recruiters use them in the USA. The figure reaches 96% in one United Kingdom study reported by Paul Dobson (1989). Initial return rates can be as low as 35% although this improves with second shots and telephone requests.

These may be taken up prior to making a decision, or simply to check veracity before confirming an offer. Many applicants would not want their current employers to be approached until a job offer has been made, for fear of prejudicing their position.

The purpose of references is to verify essential facts about qualifications with academic or professional bodies, and experience and performance with previous employers. They are also potentially valuable second opinions from people who have had the opportunity to observe the applicant in circumstances relevant to the post for which application has been made. However, whatever use is made of them, if they are part of the selection process they need to have validity and reliability in order to assist prediction of success in the job.

References have a very significant indirect contribution to make to the process. If an applicant knows that references may be taken up, it is a strong inducement to tell the factual truth in the written application and during the interview stage.

Due caution should be exercised about the non-factual aspects of references, especially if the referee is not known to you. Their value is increased if you supply the referee with full details of the post and specify the aspect upon which you would welcome comments. Suggest to applicants that you would like referees who have seen them perform at work. If you have doubts, or want clarification, you could always speak with the referee. It is sometimes necessary to read between the lines or understand what is not being written in a reference. For example, a reference which said only that the person was an excellent timekeeper and never absent, but nothing about what they did and how they did it when at work, should raise question marks!

The question remains about their usefulness in selection. Makin suggests that their predictive value is usually very poor, barely better than tossing a coin. Research has shown that whilst references can be predictively valid, typically they are not.

References can be made more effective by using the following suggestions:

- Supply the referee with relevant job information, such as a copy of the advertisement, job description and person specification.
- Ask specific questions related to the post to be filled.
- Seek facts and concrete illustrations.
- If you want a personal characteristics assessment, define them clearly and seek illustrations.
- Ask the applicant to supply referees who have been able to observe their recent job performance.
- Seek yes/no answers rather than offering rating scales, which will often produce a leniency bias.
- Talking to the referee is probably better than relying on the written word. Try to do this if you feel you have good reason, perhaps if you have reservations or the post is critical.

Psychological tests

Test are a specialized form of evidence. They can measure:

- aptitude   – the potential to learn to do something;
- ability   – being able to do something now;
- attitudes   – what you think about something, and therefore how you might respond to it;
- personality – what you are like as a person.

Recruiters range in their attitude from total mistrust to complete reliance upon them. The tests for ability and aptitude can be amongst the best predictors of future job performance (Makin et al.,1986). For example, tests for computer ability and manual dexterity can be valuable in specific recruitment circumstances.

Personality tests are more controversial. They have been challenged on ethical grounds for intrusiveness and professional grounds for ineffectiveness. Makin found them to have the same predictive value as biodata and assessment centres. The reality is that psychological tests can be an aid to recruitment, as a supplement to other methods.

ACTIVITY 5.1

 Figure 5.3 gives an example of a non-validated test, the T–P questionnaire which measures an individual's approach to leading a team.

Complete the questionnaire.

Do you feel it could have value as a selection tool? What reservations do you have?

The T–P leadership questionnaire

Directions

How would you most likely behave if you were a team leader?
Circle whether you would behave as described:

A   Always
F   Frequently
O   Occasionally
S   Seldom
N   Never

A F O S N   1   I would usually speak for the team.

A F O S N   2   I would want the team to work longer hours.

A F O S N   3   Members could have complete freedom at work.

A F O S N   4   Standard work procedures would be expected.

A F O S N   5   Members could decide how to solve problems.

A F O S N   6   I would emphasize beating other teams.

A F O S N   7   I would be team representative.

A F O S N   8   I would provoke the team to try harder.

A F O S N   9   I would test my ideas on the team.

A F O S N   10   Members could do their work as they feel best.

A F O S N   11   I would be trying hard for promotion.

A F O S N   12   I would put up with delays and uncertainty.

A F O S N   13   Visitors to the team would be my responsibility.

A F O S N   14   I would expect a high level of work activity.

A F O S N   15   I would leave members to get on with the job.

A F O S N   16   I would resolve conflicts in the team.

A F O S N   17   Details would overwhelm me.

A F O S N   18   I would represent the team at meetings.

A F O S N   19   I would not give the team much autonomy.

A F O S N   20   I would decide priorities and work methods.

A F O S N   21   I would demand higher output.

A F O S N   22   I would delegate to some members.

A F O S N   23   My predictions would usually be right.

A F O S N   24   The team would be very independent of me.

A F O S N   25   I would allocate the team tasks.

A F O S N   26   Changes would be welcome.

A F O S N   27   Members would be asked to make more effort.

A F O S N   28   I would trust the members' judgement.

A F O S N   29   I would decide work schedules.

A F O S N   30   I would not explain my actions.

A F O S N   31   I would sell my ideas to members.

A F O S N   32   The group could work at its own speed.

A F O S N   33   I would want the group to beat its targets.

A F O S N   34   I would not consult the team.

A F O S N   35   I would expect rules to be obeyed.

Scoring
(1) Circle the numbers 8, 12, 17, 18, 19, 30, 34, 35.
(2) Write 1 in front of a circled number if you answered S or N.
(3) Write 1 before an uncircled number if you answered A or F.
(4) Circle the 1s you have written in front of 3, 5, 8, 10, 15, 18, 19, 22, 24, 26, 28, 30, 32, 34, 35.
(5) Count the circled 1s. This is your P score for concern for people in the job.
(6) Count the uncircled 1s. This is your T score for your concern for the technical aspects of the job.

Figure 5.3 The T–P leadership questionnaire.

Review of Activity 5.1

▽   A P score larger than a T score suggests that your devote more of your energies to the people aspect of leadership. Only about 10% achieve this. A T score higher than P indicates a higher concern for technical aspects. About 80% achieve this. The rest are evenly balanced.

     The questionnaire is freely adapted from one developed by J.W. Pfeiffer and J.E. Jones as a discussion device to promote awareness of these aspects of management, not as a selection test. It has not been fully validated, although on a self-reporting basis, 85% of respondents believe it to be accurate. However, validation would require more than this. For example, the variables of 'technical' and 'people' bias could be defined and differentiated in behavioural terms, and individuals observed and assessed independently after taking the test. It could be seen if test scores and behaviour correlated.

Colin Smith, recruiting a manager in the Insupply case study, used this 'test'. He would have been unwise to give it too much credence, but tentative use in conjunction with other evidence could be acceptable. Scientifically and statistically such tests require validation by testing, observing and assessing people already in organizations.

Psychological tests: some criteria for effectiveness

- They should be developed by reputable practitioners from well conducted research into measurable aspects of people.
- They should have been validated. They should measure what they say they measure and predict, with reasonable probability, success or failure in a particular type of job.
- Validation should have been conducted by a body independent of the purveyors of the tests.
- Administration should be fair, under controlled conditions.
- They should be interpreted with caution, and by those trained to do so.

Many of the personality tests used at the moment meet these criteria. Some recruiters have favourite tests that do not meet them all, but in their judgement they do measure important things and indicate probable success or failure, especially if there are 'extreme' scores indicated. Unless this is based upon careful assessment and follow-up, the opinions are somewhere between an act of faith and a statement of fact. Sufficient to use the results with caution as marginal supporting evidence, perhaps.

Assessment centres

This is the name often given to group selection methods for recruitment or internal promotion and development. Candidates take part in a series of activities designed to produce behaviour related to that required in a job, or perhaps family of jobs. The behaviour of individuals is observed and assessed against the person specification. It provides supplementary or alternative sources of evidence to interviews and tests.

Critics argue that the situation is artificial and favours those who are extraverted or experienced in these types of activities. It is also suggested that there are design problems associated with developing exercises that actually will produce the relevant behaviour. Assessment requires considerable skill and poor assessments are likely from unskilled observers. Interpretation of the results is also regarded as complex and open to considerable error.

59

Its supporters claim that it provides evidence about vital aspects of an individual that can't be gained any other way. For example, if you want to assess decision and problem-solving skills, or effective team membership behaviour, what better way than giving candidates tasks which require just these attributes? They would say that looking at an individual behaving is more reliable than talking to a person about these aspects in interview.

Assessment centres are time-consuming and costly. To increase effectiveness they should be designed by people with expertise and experience in this field and all observer assessors should be trained. This makes it unlikely that a centre would be used for one-off or small-scale recruitment. The military have used these methods for many years and many large organizations, such as the Bank of England and HM Customs and Excise, make use of them for selection to senior positions.

With large-scale and proportionate resources it is possible to invest in sophisticated centres. This should not stop the creative manager, with smaller needs and budgets, from producing a mini-centre as an adjunct to their interviews. An awareness of the pitfalls and limitations is step one. You then need creative ideas, allied to the methods of job description, person specification and assessment techniques covered earlier. A good dose of pragmatism will help the manager gain a useful additional source of information about candidates. Experts have a vested interest in selling their expertise and persuading you that things can't be done without them. They often can be.

ACTIVITY 5.2

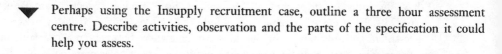

Perhaps using the Insupply recruitment case, outline a three hour assessment centre. Describe activities, observation and the parts of the specification it could help you assess.

The applicants would need to be informed that these activities are part of your recruitment process, just as it would be necessary if you were planning to administer tests. Some people have objections to these methods, so it is better that they have the opportunity to decline to take part at an early stage.

It is desirable to have more than one observer, and the observers should discuss at length what they are looking for and how they will recognize it when they see it.

Group exercises, similar to those often used in management training, are a good vehicle for observing the personality and motivational aspects of candidates relevant to many jobs. For example, a group discussion on, say, 'Rank the 10 most important characteristics of a good manager' will yield interesting information at the content level (what is said) and at the process level (what they do and how they relate).

Individual tasks, such as 'in-tray' exercises, can also be used to assess approaches to decision making, prioritizing and personal organization. Charles Woodruffe's book *Assessment Centres*, published by IPM, would help any manager contemplating this recruitment method.

It is worth considering their use. Makin rates them with biodata and personality tests as predictors in selection.

Work sampling and work tests

Work sampling and work tests were rated as the highest predictors of success in recruitment in the Makin study. They appear to be rarely used, but would probably repay the recruiter handsomely for the time and creativity needed to develop them.

They need to be specific to a job, and some lend themselves to sampling the work of applicants as part of the recruitment process. For instance, it doesn't require much ingenuity to ask a writer or photographer to produce a sample of work for assessment. In fact, anybody who produces work or a service which can be observed and documented as part of their job could be asked to provide a sample. Concrete evidence of individual performance is at a premium in recruitment.

Work tests require the applicants to show what they can do by getting them to perform tasks which form part of the position for which they are applying. This is superior to the assessment centre in the aspects it examines, because no simulation is involved. One example of work testing is from a British Rail Region, where potential bridge examiners were given the same task of examining a bridge under standard conditions. They each produced a report which was used as a significant element in the successful recruitment procedure.

The author, Robin Evenden, is currently working with HM Customs and Excise to select management trainers. There are a range of selection criteria against which the potential trainers are assessed. The evidence is gained by observing them experiencing, designing and running training activities identical to those they would run as trainers.

The process lasts five days and is costly but effective. The expense is small in comparison to the value placed by the Department upon the subsequent training activity of the successful candidates, who are themselves the subject of heavy development investment. The predictive value is high as judged by subsequent performance and the substantial majority of those who are 'unsuccessful' feel the method is fair and valid.

Computer recruitment networks

In the United Kingdom CV database have a computer based system to match employers and potential employees. The French have the Mintel network which helps potential candidates assess themselves against a vacancy specifications database. This self screening has proved effective in selecting out many who would have otherwise embarked upon a costly and fruitless recruitment exercise. It also provides an efficient means of bringing together supply and demand in the job market.

Genetic screening

This method is unlikely to be available to many recruiters. It has been developed in the USA to prevent those who can genetically be identified as high health risks if exposed to certain occupations. The motives are not altruistic so much as a desire to reduce liability and health claims.

The method may be considered as intrusive and unethical but it does illustrate the level of scientific sophistication that recruitment processes are now reaching.

Astrology and graphology

The previous method represents using the limits of science to assist recruitment. The following approaches illustrate the opposite, suggesting a return to magic for those with no faith in the judgement of mortals.

Even non-validated tests are better than using evidence based on astrology (birth signs and fate) and graphology (handwriting as an indicator of personality or character). These have been shown to have the same success rate as choosing people at random, yet some gullible recruiters still use them. Perhaps they have so little faith in their own judgement that they need to resort to the 'certainty' of magic and mumbo-jumbo.

References for further reading

Anderson G.C. and Kelly J. (1986). *Personnel Selection and Recruitment*. HMSO

Collinson D. (1987). Who Controls Selection? *Personnel Management Journal* May 1987

Dobson P. (1989). References. In *Assessment and Selection in Organisations* (Herriot P., ed). John Wiley & Sons

Forbes R. (1979). Improving the Reliability of the Selection Interview. *Personnel Management Journal* July 1979

Fraser G.M. (1978). *Employment Interviewing*. Macdonald and Evans

Goodworth C.T. (1983). *Effective Interviewing for Employment Selection*. Business Books

Makin P. *et al.* (1986) Selection. Where are the Best Prophets? *Personnel Management Journal* December 1986

Toplis J. *et al.* (1987) *Psychological Testing*. IPM

Woodruffe C. (1990). *Assessment Centres*. IPM

6

The interview: getting it right

The recruitment process is now reaching its final and critical phase. The analysis of the need for recruitment, careful definition of the job and identification of the 'ideal' person to perform it, led to the advertisement to attract a good group of potential high performers. A long list has systematically been reduced to a short list. The final stage is reached.

There are no certainties in horse racing and recruitment, but the professional attempts to reduce the odds on picking the winner. In both cases it is necessary to gather evidence to assess the form to try to ensure that your investment has the best chance of giving a good return. With horses it is possible to study previous performance and observe trials. With people too, their previous performance is the best predictor of the future, but the form has to be studied in a different way. This usually means talking to them about it, with the possible supplement of tests, trials and tips from referees.

The most popular method is still the interview. Its success rate is marginally better than the fortunes of chance. How can its predictive value be improved?

ACTIVITY 6.1

 How would you plan for the best results from an interview?

1	Plan the interview with the others involved.
2	What do you already know about the applicant?
3	What else do you need to find out?
4	Note the key questions you will ask.
5	How will you open the interview?
6	What is your preferred sequence of topics?
7	What approach will you adopt to the interviewee?
8	Prepare your interview guide.
9	What will the applicant want to know from you?
10	How will you conclude and refer to future action?
11	Check the time and location arrangements.

Figure 6.1 Checklist: planning the interview.

Planning the interview

▼ A checklist is given in Figure 6.1.

1 Plan the interview with the others involved

Whether you are involved with one other person or a large selection panel, it is vital for effective decisions to plan with them. You will need to discuss and ensure mutual clear understanding of the job description and the person specification, or you may find yourselves at unbecoming cross purposes. It is usually helpful to agree a structure, including topic sequence, division of labour and time allocation. This helps the interviewers and interviewee by providing cohesion and continuity, and if there is a series of solo interviews it will minimize repetition.

If you are chairing the process, discuss with the others how you plan to run it, the atmosphere you wish to create and how the decision will be reached.

2 What do you already know about the applicant?

You will have the applications, notes from the short-listing process and test results, if you have decided to use them. You may also have referees' comments, although these are often not taken up until an offer is made. People often want their application to remain confidential.

3 What else do you need to find out?

This involves careful comparison of the application to the person specification, with reference to any short-list notes and queries you may have made. You will have a lot of factual data that you probably will not want to repeat during the interview.

The emphasis is likely to be upon factual gaps or clarification, seeking evidence to support claims made by the applicant, and exploring categories of the person specification which are difficult to assess from a written application (impact and personality, for example).

4 Note the key questions you will ask

These will help you steer the interview, maintain the flow and give you the information you require. Some may be asked of all applicants (for example, 'Why did you apply for this job?') and some will be specific to an individual applicant. You will need to ask questions of a supplementary and spontaneous kind as well, but a core of prepared questions is always helpful.

5 *How will you open the interview?*

Think of some easy initial pleasantries, but also the first topic. Use the application as a guide to choose one about which you can both talk comfortably, as an ice-breaker.

6 *What is your preferred sequence of topics?*

You may decide to use the sequence followed in the application, although this is not always desirable if the first area is something like 'Health'. Be aware of the need to develop rapport and choose early topics which will help you do this.

If you anticipate tricky areas it is probably best to get on to these once a positive relationship has been established. Bear in mind the desirability of a logical flow and continuity

7 *What approach will you adopt to the interviewee*

Choices range from formal and structured to informal and unstructured, where the interviewer lets the applicant make all the running. Friendly neutrality, with a pattern set by the interviewer's questions and prompts but with scope for the interviewee to talk freely and initiate, is a sound and safe mid position approach.

8 *Prepare your interview guide*

A prepared guide can be a comfort and prompt to most interviewers. It could incorporate the person specification and some reminder facts about the individual. Photocopied as standard for all interviewees, it can be personalized for each interview, to include the specific questions for them, with space for notes and post-interview pen portrait and assessment.

9 *What will the applicant want to know from you?*

Although your aim will be to find out the things you need to know from the interviewee, and you will want to spend the bulk of the time listening, the applicant also needs to make a decision and will want the opportunity to ask you questions, in order to know whether to accept the job offer, should it be made. The job may also need selling, though certainly not overselling, and you will need to prepare for the public relations side of the interview.

It is as important to plan what you need to say, as it is to identify what you are going to ask. The tasks, responsibilities, organizational links, reporting and role relations will need to be thought through, in order to make a positive response and impression.

Applicants may be coy about asking questions about the reward package, but it pays to encourage them to do so. Misunderstandings here, as well as in the nature of the job, can lead to losing a good person, either because they turn you down or are disappointed after they join.

10 How will you conclude and refer to future action?

Prepare your final remarks with information about expenses, what happens next and when.

11 Check the time and location arrangements

The total time to be spent on each interview needs to be established and handover times agreed if there is to be more than one interview for each interviewee. Leave space between interviews for over-running, assessment and preparing for the next. It is worth producing a timetable for all involved.

Ensure that the reception for each person is friendly and efficient, and that attention is paid to their personal comfort. It will affect how they see your organization, and how they respond in the interview.

The interview room needs to be private and comfortable. The seating gives clear messages to the applicant about the interviewer and can help or hinder the process. What arrangement would you like if you were being interviewed? Interviews across a desk are seen as more formal, whereas seating at 120 degrees across a coffee table suggests a more relaxed approach. An offer of refreshments helps the climate. If the interviewee actually drinks the coffee, it will be feedback to you about your success in achieving rapport. Of course, arrange for no interruptions of any kind.

CASE PROJECT 6.1

Prepare for the Bob Armstrong interview, following the checklist in Figure 6.1.

Insupply case study: Illustrations from Colin Smith's preparation for the interview with Bob Armstrong

What does Colin Smith know and need to find out?

Physical

Colin needs to assess the impact Bob would have on the people he would meet in the job of Administration Manager by observing and conversing. He needs to check Bob's health and absence record by asking him and requiring a medical report if offered the job.

Qualifications

These are known but it might be worth finding out about the exam syllabuses and his motivation for study. (Cross refer to learning and change.)

Learning and change

Bob seems strong here from his written application but it needs checking carefully, as it will be important in the job. He could be asked about his attitude to exams and development.

Useful questions could be how he has developed in his current job and what direction his development would take if he joined Insupply?

Work experience: Administration

Bob has location move experience with JB. Colin could explore his role in this and assess whether he would be able to handle Insupply's move. A similar approach could be taken with administration systems and technology changes. A question might be, 'Some people feel that change in organizations is sometimes needed, but stability and certainty is the best basis for success. How do you feel about that?'

Colin should continue to check those areas which seem positive in the written application and explore knowledge or experience where Bob has possible gaps, such as building management, managing temporary and consulting staff, committee work, company communication and budget control.

Colin would ask direct questions on these areas to assess experience, followed by probing for evidence and examples of what he achieved and how he tackled these aspects. If lacking experience in some areas, how much of a handicap would this be and could the shortfall be made up?

Work experience: Management

Colin needs to assess Bob's management style, in terms of communication, influence and assertion skills, delegation, planning through to action, personal organization and time management, and finally how he balances the technical and people sides of the role. What is he like at delegation? Application clues are rare in these areas.

Information can be gained by asking the applicants to assess themselves and judge if they are being open. Colin could check Bob's self assessments by asking for illustrations and perhaps tossing a few cases to him to see if he has tackled anything like them, and if not, how would he want to handle them.

For example, 'How well organized are you? Can you tell me about a time when you were under pressure, with lot of demands and deadlines? Take me through your handling of it.'

Work motivation

Colin would probably get some helpful cross-reference clues from Bob's description of his experience of work and change. His application suggests that he responds well to the motivators anticipated in the Administration Manager's role, but it will be important to explore this for further evidence.

Illustrations of questions Colin could ask are, 'I'd like you to tell me what has motivated you in the past. What would you like to see in the job here that you would enjoy? I can't offer guarantees, but what kind of boss would you like me to be? Tell me about a time when you were demotivated.' The content of the answers and how he answers will give insights into Bob's motivation and link with personality.

Personality

This is difficult to judge and it will be important to reflect on this aspect during the interview.

It is possible to get a good impression about approachability, humour and so on from the way they get on in the interview. There is a risk of distortion here. Others could see him differently, so their opinions would be helpful. Perhaps the projection screen approach would give clues about his personality when Bob talks about other people. Examples are, 'Can you give me a pen picture of the best person you have worked with?' and 'Describe for me the worst manager you know.'

Colin Smith's interview plan

After settling in, a good lead topic would be Bob's rock climbing. It will give information about him as a social person and lead into the health aspect quite naturally.

His qualifications are sound and easy to explore, so they should make a comfortable second area, which should flow smoothly into Learning and Change. Picking up on the move and technical change could lead to Work Experience: Administration. At this stage rapport should have been established so some of the more difficult areas could be explored using self assessments, case responses and asking projection screen questions. This will lead to Management, Motivation and Personality.

Colin Smith's style and approach

His method is to assume he is going to recruit each interviewee so he tries to establish the relationship he would anticipate at work. For Colin this means a friendly and conversational style, but purposive and flexible. Colin planned a standard format for all the interviews, but tailored for each person. He prepared an interview guide with brief notes that will remind him of the salient points when he is making the assessment (see Figure 6.2).

What will the applicants want to know?

Colin clarified his thoughts on the job and how he saw it developing, as well as preparing to answer the kinds of thing he would want to ask if he was applying himself. This would include Insupply's future, the person's future, terms, conditions and the reward package. Some of this will be offered as a very short introduction, and he intended also to respond as appropriate to questions during the main body of the interview, as well as building in a period towards the end when questions would be invited. He planned to ask one of the senior staff to walk applicants around the site for ten minutes and to give them a five-minute break in the middle of the two-hour interview session.

Interview guide

Sample from Colin Smith's guide for his interview with Bob Armstrong.

Interview with
BOB ARMSTRONG: OAK DRIVE HOMETOWN

Time/Date
20 JUNE 0930

Qualifications/Education   MIDDLETON COUNTY : 16 OK (NO languages)
BANKING INST. EXAM
MIMA

Work
16/18 Family Store
19/24 Police: Sergeant : Crime Prevention ~ liaison with banks etc ·· (DOMESTIC)
24/29 A.Mgr: Southfield Bank - A.Mgr Small Businesses
　　　　　　　　　　　　 – Training in Personal Computing (MERGER /NO PROM)
29/33 Admin: JB Distribution – Papers:Advt   Administrator. Tech Innovation
　　　　　　　　　　　　 Grown 2x: Handled move.(DEV. NOT SUPPORTED)
33/36 A.Admin: Middleton Booksellers - Purchasing : + others

Personal
36.DIVORCED. REMARRY SOON ?
ROCK CLIMBING -organises monthly trips
HOUSE + CAR MAINTENANCE
CHARITY WORK
ELECTRONICS + COMPUTERS

Very Tall
Looks like
Jim R.
Non- Smoker

Person Spec	Questions	Answers/Comments	Assessment
	? ROCK CLIMBING ? →	Secretary of Club Weekend trips	WELL ROUNDED SOCIAL PERSON PULLS WEIGHT IN COMMUNITY
Pers. interests	? CHARITY →	Childrens Charity: Volunteer Helper	

Phys. impact — OBSERVE ↓ DRESS: VOICE: NON-VERBAL → Dark suit / Bearded / Pleasantly spoken / Relaxed — LIKED LOOK OF HIM. WOULD FIT IN Beard?? (8)

Health — ? FIT & HEALTHY FOR ROCKS?
? TELL ABOUT HEALTH RECORD
? - DOCTOR CONSULTED? • 3 yrs ago: broken toe.
? - ABSENCE? • None last year → HEALTHY ACTIVE ENERGETIC (10)

Qualifications
Police Exams - Content
• Relevant?
Bank + MIMA - Syllabus?
Motivation for Study?
Much training will be helpful in any role.
Covers all aspects of Admin. Role + Law/Banking/Acct.
• Likes learning new things
• Career prospects better
RELEVANT TO JOB (6)

Learn/Change ? What gained from MIMA ? - Prof. Discipline : Contacts : Ideas
? Recent Development? - Courses . Admin Tech:People Mgt
? Future ? → Interested in Strategy Planning / Personnel

Attitude → Describes change experienced as enjoyable → ENJOYS (4)

Handling → Consults and persuades. More involvement?? → CONSULTS (3)

Recent/Future → Has attended valuable course. Has ideas for more. Would seek guided experience in Building / P. Relations → LOOKING FOR DEVELOPMENT (5)

Drive → Self motivated from comments /track record → ACTIVE (5)

? " Organisations have to change, but } Bob disagreed positively
: stability/certainty needed for success?" } felt change and some risk taking very important

WE: Admin

Move — Your involvement? Negotiated the move: persuaded staff → (6)
Planned: implemented. Seemed thorough.

Tech change — An enthusiast. Knows a lot. Judicious evaluation? → (6)

Building admin — Not extensive experience. A practical person → (2)

Security — An expert ℓ → (3)

Procurement — Experienced purchaser → (2)

Temp/staffing — Limited experience: wants development in Personnel → (1)

Committee — Sec. to Executive at Middton Books. Seems competent → (5)

Co. communication — Internal fine: not PR / wants to train → (1)

Product — Uses our Products: would soon get to know range → (2)

Budget — Good experience: seems to have good control record → (3)

WE: Management

Communic. — I believe he would communicate well at all levels. His track record suggests this → (4)

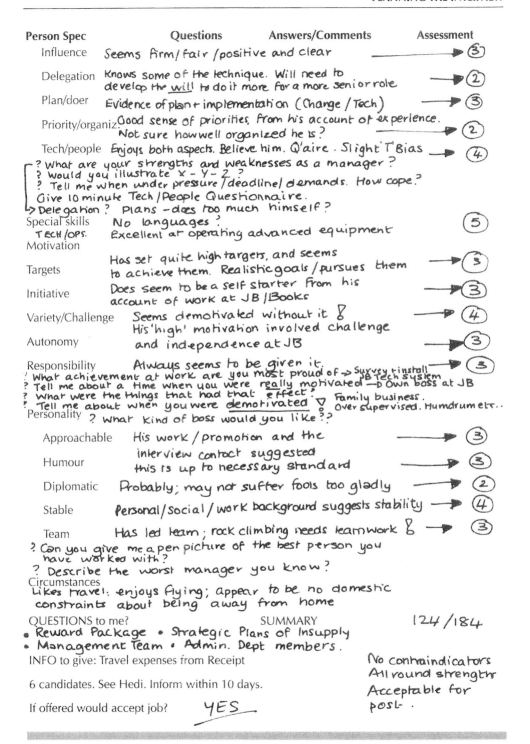

Person Spec	Questions	Answers/Comments	Assessment
Influence	Seems firm/fair/positive and clear		③
Delegation	Knows some of the technique. Will need to develop the _will_ to do it more for a more senior role		②
Plan/doer	Evidence of plan + implementation (Change/Tech)		③
Priority/organiz.	Good sense of priorities, from his account of experience. Not sure how well organized he is?		②
Tech/people	Enjoys both aspects. Believe him. Q'aire. Slight T'Bias		④

? What are your strengths and weaknesses as a manager?
? Would you illustrate X - Y - Z?
? Tell me when under pressure /deadline/ demands. How cope?
Give 10 minute Tech/People Questionnaire.
⤷ Delegation? Plans - does too much himself?

Special skills	No languages?		⑤
TECH/OPS.	Excellent at operating advanced equipment		
Motivation			
Targets	Has set quite high targets, and seems to achieve them. Realistic goals/pursues them		③
Initiative	Does seem to be a self starter from his account of work at JB/Books		③
Variety/Challenge	Seems demotivated without it 🗲 His 'high' motivation involved challenge		④
Autonomy	and independence at JB		③
Responsibility	Always seems to be given it.		③

? What achievement at work are you most proud of → Survey + install → JB Tech System
? Tell me about a time when you were really motivated → Own boss at JB
? What were the things that had that effect? ▽ Family business.
? Tell me about when you were demotivated ▽ Over supervised. Humdrum etc..

Personality	? What kind of boss would you like??		
Approachable	His work/promotion and the		③
Humour	interview contact suggested this is up to necessary standard		③
Diplomatic	Probably; may not suffer fools too gladly		②
Stable	Personal/social/work background suggests stability		④
Team	Has led team; rock climbing needs teamwork 🗲		③

? Can you give me a pen picture of the best person you have worked with?
? Describe the worst manager you know?

Circumstances
Likes travel; enjoys flying; appear to be no domestic constraints about being away from home

QUESTIONS to me?   SUMMARY   124/184
• Reward Package • Strategic Plans of Insupply
• Management Team • Admin. Dept members.
INFO to give: Travel expenses from Receipt   No contraindicators
                                                              All round strength
6 candidates. See Hedi. Inform within 10 days.   Acceptable for
                                                              post.
If offered would accept job?   YES

Figure 6.2 Interview guide – sample from Colin Smith's guide for his interview with Bob Armstrong.

The aims of the selection interviewer

- To get information to assess the interviewee's suitability for the position.
- To give information to the interviewees, so that they are in a position to decide whether to accept.
- To ensure that the applicants feel that the selection process has been conducted fairly.
- To give the applicants a favourable impression of the organization. They may become clients, suppliers or be in a position to affect your image positively or negatively.

Conducting the interview

Preparation

You have done your advance planning. The interview sequence starts shortly.

Check the reception arrangements for the candidates, making sure they will be welcomed and made comfortable. Of course, you will not keep them waiting, and you have double checked that you will not be interrupted.

Make a last check on the room and the seating.

Allow yourself five minutes to run through the interview guide. It will help you focus on the person about to come through the door and bring the salient features of your plan to the front of your mind.

Relax and prepare for a calm, confident and friendly reception.

Rapport

Exchanging information may be the reason for the interview, but unless good relations and rapport are established between you, the amount and quality will be doubtful. The selection interview is a high stress situation. It is likely that you will be feeling tense and this will communicate itself to the candidate, who is almost certainly feeling more anxious than you. If you have tricks to relax yourself, then use them. Smiling, handshakes and deep breathing are all good relaxers.

Rapport means being on the same wavelength and feeling comfortable with each other. It creates a climate in which the task of the interview can be conducted to good purpose and with goodwill.

ACTIVITY 6.2

 Visualize yourself in a selection interview. What kind of thing creates and maintains rapport?

Factors helping create and maintain rapport

(1) The tone of the written communication will be an influence on your relationship, even before you meet.

(2) Friendly reception by you and others will help.

(3) Be pleased to meet the other person and concerned to get on with them. This is not the same as being over the top, effusive and insincere.

(4) Non-verbal behaviour, or body language, is a major factor in rapport. Smiling with eyes and mouth, and shaking hands is significant and not accidental behaviour when meeting people. It has been shown by experience and research that this early contact affects the other person's initial impression and subsequent perception of the interviewer. Eye contact, facial expression, posture, gesture and voice tone all influence your rapport with the other person.

(5) Put the other person at ease. Relax yourself. Their physical comfort is important, but so are their feelings. Small talk is usually helpful at the start as long as it is not too prolonged, when it could actually reduce rapport.

(6) Choose initial topics that you think they will talk about easily. A person's own voice can be a great relaxer.

(7) Reassure and inform them about what is going to happen and how you would like the conversation to develop.

(8) Keep aware of the need to maintain rapport and reduce tension throughout.

Listening

It sounds obvious that listening is important in the selection interview. Ask yourself how well you listen. Experiment by listening to yourself listening! You will probably discover that you are far from perfect and stop yourself listening in a number of ways.

What are you listening to?

You want to hear the *words*, that is, what the other person is saying to you. This is the way they communicate to you their information regarding facts, ideas and opinions. However, if we are really tuned in to the other person, we should be detecting the *music* as well. We should notice how they are feeling and whether they are saying one thing and meaning or feeling another.

ACTIVITY 6.3

▼ Remind yourself how you listen to another person's music.

▽ We listen to their music by being aware of not only what they may say about their feelings, but also how they express them. This is usually through body language. Eyes, gesture, facial expression and other things you will recall when you reflect, give us clues about what feeling process is going on inside the other person. In selection this can be important for two reasons. First, it gives you clues about tension and rapport, and second, about whether they mean it or are truthful. In many interviews we may lose our sensitivity to the music.

How do we distract ourselves?

We have many ways that we switch ourselves off from the other person's communication of words and music.

We can listen to external distractors, like 'noises off', such as the people in the next room or the sound of birdsong on a summer's day. Even more potent are the internal distractors, or the ways we interrupt our own listening.

We can be distracted by our feelings, of boredom or anger, for example. They will often not be related to the events that are happening at the time, but things that happened earlier, such as an argument or enjoyable occasion. Anticipation of things to come can also remove us from close attention to the present.

We spend a surprising amount of time talking to ourselves. Think about how often we do this. Not usually out loud, but in our heads there is an almost constant internal dialogue. If we are listening to ourselves, our attention to the other person is reduced, and we may miss a lot of significance. We switch ourselves back for the last few sentences and move on from there, but have missed a lot in between. This internal dialogue could be thinking about our next question, puzzling over an earlier remark, making a judgement, or jotting notes. It affects our concentration and the attention we are giving the other person is much reduced.

Another distraction is talking too much. Remember your main task is to facilitate the interviewee's contributions, so that you get the evidence needed to make a selection decision. It is a major weakness of interviewers that they do not monitor the amount of their own talking.

A interviewer:interviewee ratio of 25:75 is a reasonable distribution. Most would settle for this 3:1 return, but nearly half of selection interviewers only achieve a 50:50 split, and a sizeable proportion actually talk substantially more than the person they are interviewing. Most are not aware that they do this.

How we do not listen

(1) We fail to hear the music.
(2) We miss the body language clues to tension and truth.
(3) We focus on external distractors.
(4) We allow internal distractors to take us from the present.
(5) We do not concentrate.
(6) We talk too much ourselves.

Active listening

Active listening is much more than concentrating on the other person. It is a skill which enables you to influence, indeed to orchestrate the contributions of the other person. As so many things do, it involves awareness and skills. The awareness is of your own behaviour and its impact, and the skills relate to doing the right things well.

Your need is to encourage the interviewee to speak comfortably and at suitable length about things relevant to the selection. Active listening, together with skilful questioning, is the means of achieving this. This involves displaying attentive behaviour and avoiding non-attentive behaviour.

ACTIVITY 6.4

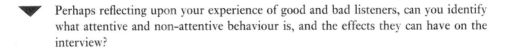

Perhaps reflecting upon your experience of good and bad listeners, can you identify what attentive and non-attentive behaviour is, and the effects they can have on the interview?

Attentive behaviour is simply showing the other person that you are listening with interest to what they are saying:

- Paralanguage. Speaking without words. The 'uh huh's and 'mm mmm's, which supplement your 'I see's and 'go on's are vital influences on the other person. It invites them to carry on talking, or to let you speak. Of course, inflection plays an important part in this. 'Yes' means 'stop' or 'go on', depending how it is said.

- Body language is used in conversation in a similar way to paralanguage. Smiles, nods and frowns are used to show we are listening and to encourage the other person to continue or to stop to let you say something.

- Reflecting back to the person a summary of their views or feelings is good listening and influencing behaviour. It shows that you are interested and listening, and gives a chance to get your understanding clarified.

We can all be attentive. The professional is self disciplined to make attentive behaviour a significant tool in their interactive or interviewing toolkit. To use these behaviours in a way that is not intrusive or insincere, but a real attempt to listen, is a powerful influence.

It is a great help to the nervous or shy person, because it reassures that you are genuinely interested in them. It is equally effective in orchestrating the talkative person, stopping or steering them in the direction you wish. It is a means of support and control which is unobtrusive and enhances rapport between you and the interviewee.

Non-attentive behaviour is a major threat to rapport. Doodling, yawning, looking at your watch, gazing out of the window and many other things are examples. They may not mean you are not interested, but that is how they will be interpreted.

Structure of the interview

The preparation of an interview guide, as we have seen, will provide a structure to the interview. It is helpful to have a plan but necessary to be flexible enough to depart from it. For example, it would serve no purpose to prevent an interviewee from giving you valuable information at the start of an interview, if your schedule had it earmarked for later! Applicants can be put off by either rigidity or an haphazard approach.

It is important to devote the first part of the interview to letting the applicants know what you plan to do, how you will set about it and what you expect from them. If you plan a 75:25 time split, tell them. Should you prefer to give them time at the end for questions, let them know. If you have a timetable, share it with them. It is part of the rapport process and they will find it helpful to know how to fit in with your plans.

You may find it useful to seek or give short periodic summaries as a means of charting your course through the interview. A rest or respite period is very desirable every two hours, if your applicant is going to be exposed to a long selection process, otherwise you may discover whether they can cope with chat marathons but precious little else.

Plan your conclusion to make it sharp, warm and businesslike.

Getting the information you need

Rapport and good listening are very important, as we have seen. To have an effective selection interview, however, you need also to get the information you require as evidence upon which to base your judgement about the candidate. This means developing and using your questioning skills.

You will already have decided the areas you want to explore at the interview. It is necessary to work out the basic questions you want to ask to harvest the information. There are several different types of question, and choosing the appropriate types can make the difference between a smooth-flowing, focused and relevant conversation and a stilted, disjointed exchange which is little help to either party. The types of question and their effectiveness are summarized in Figure 6.3.

Direct or Closed

These have the effect of yielding short answers like 'yes', 'no' or 'sometimes'.
'How did you travel?'

They are useful for the purpose of getting facts, but too much use leads to a staccato interview, and a short one if the applicant is nervous.

'How old are you?'
'Do you like sport?'

Leading

These lead the interviewee to give the answer that the interviewer expects or wants to hear.
'We are always in flux. You do like change, don't you?'

There is no value in this type of question, unless the interviewers have self deception in mind. Most interviewees would follow the lead.

Topic changing

Moving the interview on to a new topic.
'Thanks for the information on your qualifications. Would you tell me how you chose your career route?'

Necessary to control the move through your plan and your timing. Helpful in creating a smooth flow in the interview.

Probing and developing

These enquire more fully into an area, or encourage building upon an answer already given.
'Why did you say you prefer jobs which involve travel?'

Very important to seek evidence and test the interviewee's knowledge, experience, feelings and attitudes.

Open ended

These encourage full answers.
'Would you tell me about how you spend your leisure time?'
'Why did you apply for this particular job?'

The interviewee is given opportunity to answer at length, and to choose what to select to talk about. Very useful to get the person talking and involved in the interview. Good for shy people if allied to gentle persistence.

Reflecting back

Reflecting back to the person what they have said by restating their reply.
'Promotion is very important to you then?'
'Are you saying you are frightened of computers?'

These are important to make sure that your understanding is clear and accurate. It also shows that you are listening and interested in what the interviewee is saying.

Figure 6.3 Types of interview question.

It is always difficult to assess the reliability and validity of the information given by interviewees. Evidence suggests that they are likely to be honest on questions of fact, but to show themselves in a favourable light in qualitative areas. This is perhaps unsurprising, but it means that it would be unwise to accept claims and assertions of the quality of skills, experience and knowledge made by candidates without checking them out.

Information seeking guidelines

(1) Avoid simplistic questions like,'Can you cope with pressure?' or 'Are you good at...?' The answers to these kinds of questions are likely to be more positive and affirmative than reality would justify.

(2) Ask indirect questions to get closer to the truth in the aspects which interest you. 'Did you like your last boss?' may not yield such useful information as 'What type of boss do you like to work for?'

(3) Test the candidates' claims and assertions. Ask for evidence and seek examples. If the claim is that they handle change very well, test them by seeking an illustration from their experience. Get the candidates to talk about what they did rather than how well they believe they did it. Try to be in a position to make your own judgement rather than rely on that of the interviewee, who may well have a bias!

(4) Do not take the surface or initial response as valid. Be prepared to probe the candidate to get fuller information upon which to make the assessment.

(5) Use the 'projection screen' question, where the applicants can project themselves upon the 'screen' of another person or situation. `Which public figure do you admire most?' 'What motivates most managers to work well?'

(6) As a general rule do not ask leading questions, use direct questions sparingly and select the other types as appropriate.

(7) Avoid aimless conversation. All you say and ask should have some purpose relative to the interview objective. Work all topics around to the point where you will be able to assess some aspect of the person specification.

Note taking

Most people find it necessary to make notes during an interview of any length, rather than rely on their memory when they compile their post-interview summary. It does cause some concern, because of the possibility of interrupting the flow of conversation, hindering rapport and adding stress to the interviewee.

It is suggested that you explain at the outset that you plan to take brief notes upon your interview guide as an aid to your memory. Try to limit them to one key word or phrase which will act as a recall prompt after the interview.

Panel interviewing

In the private sector the one-to-one interview tends to be favoured, especially among smaller companies. By contrast, the great majority of public sector organizations use panel interviews. The principal argument in favour of the one-to-one interview is that it provides a better opportunity than in a panel interview for the candidate to relax and present an accurate picture of his background abilities and future aspirations. In the one-to-one situation it should be easier for rapport to be quickly established between interviewer and candidate, and for effective two-way communication to take place. The most obvious drawback of the panel approach is that the size of the panel and the formality of the situation may inhibit candidates. As a result, they may be unable to project themselves accurately to the interviewers.

Two broad arguments may be advanced, however, in support of panel interviewing:

(1) There is the proposition that the interests of the organization are better served by involving several organizational representatives in the selection interviewing process.
(2) It allows different expertise to be brought to bear on the selection process.

What criteria should be used in determining the size and composition of the selection panel? According to Palmer (1983), the composition of the panel should ideally be restricted to:

- the line manager responsible for the job (essential);
- the line manager's boss (possibly);
- a manager with direct interest in the successful performance of the job – for example, production director might participate in the panel interview for the position of head of work study;
- a manager who holds direct responsibility for ensuring a continuous supply of high calibre applicants – probably from the personnel department;
- for top management posts in the public service – a small number of elected representatives of the public.

Palmer's recommendations on the composition of the panel membership can be interpreted as emphasizing the importance of restricting representation on the panel to:

- those who will be part of the job network of the successful application – that is, those with whom the successful applicant will have direct vertical or lateral communications after taking up the vacant position;
- those who have the responsibility for assessing the policy implications of the selection decision – for example, elected representatives in the case of top management positions in a local authority context.

Practical and psychological considerations suggest that whenever panel interviews are used for selection purposes, every effort should be made to limit the size of the panel, to prevent the creation of too daunting an experience for candidates. Where the panel approach is used in the private sector, it is common to find the size of panel being limited as a matter of corporate policy to no more than two or three, thus trying to balance the two conflicting forces:

79

- for smallness to create better rapport and easier communication; but
- for a larger panel to ensure all appropriate organizational interests are represented.

According to the research studies of Forbes (1979) panel interviews are more reliable than one-to-one interviews. The two principal propositions put forward are that:

- interviewers in panel situations, conscious of the fact that they are being critically observed by fellow panel-members, formulate questions that are crisper and more to the point; and
- because there is multiple assessment of each attribute of the candidate, the element of bias is reduced, leading to objective decision making.

The panel approach to selection interviewing assumes that a number of underlying problems have been satisfactorily resolved. These are summarized in Figure 6.4 and cover three main areas.

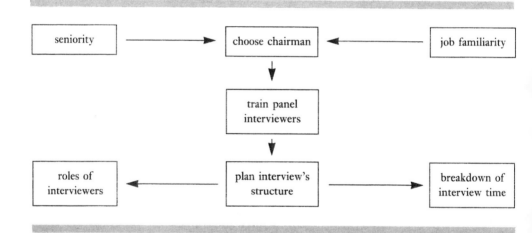

Figure 6.4   Problems to be resolved in setting up a panel interview.

(1) The chairman can have a major impact on the effectiveness of a panel interview. A difficult question to resolve in practice is whether the principal criterion in the selection of chairman should be seniority (that is, with the most senior member of the panel being expected to take the chair) or whether the criterion should be that of familiarity and knowledge of the job in question (pointing towards the immediate superior assuming the role of panel chairman).

(2) Panel interviewing is a more complex process than one-to-one interviews because of the multiple interactions involved. Those directly involved, namely the chairman and the panel members, should receive training to permit them to discharge their roles effectively. Without training the risks of disjointed interviews and inconsistent selection decisions become much greater.

(3) The larger the panel, the more important it is that prior discussion takes place to ensure that all panelists are aware of the roles they are expected to play, and

how the interview time is broken down into a number of elements to bring out an orderly, balanced interview. Without pre-planning, a panel interview could emerge as a very disjointed process, with detrimental effects upon both the candidates and the organization.

Making the choice

(1) Assess each applicant systematically against your person specification, highlighting strengths, doubts and weaknesses. Note your scores, grades and 'essentials', 'desirables' and contra-indicators, as well as the evidence for your assessment.

(2) Listen to others. Seek views on the applicants not only from those formally involved but from those who may have had contact in less formal circumstances. Valuable insights can be gained from reception staff, or those who may have given the candidates a tour of the site, for example.

(3) Compare assessments for each applicant from all formally involved. Move through each category of the specification. Often it is helpful to note the areas of agreement first before going back to examine where there is disagreement. Try not to get too entrenched in your assessment position by competing with your assessor colleagues. Remind them and yourself that this should be a collaborative exercise. Check the facts and the evidence and then discuss your different interpretations. Consensus may take a little time, but it is worth it. You all have to live with the results of your deliberations.

(4) Identify those who are not suitable. Even if you all agree, make a note of the reasons. This could be important in all cases where a job offer will not be made. Equal opportunities and unfair discrimination legislation and codes make this sensible practice. Candidates will sometimes contact the recruiter to learn the reasons why they were unsuccessful and you may feel that you would like to tell them.

(5) Compare the survivors. You will probably have reduced the list to two or three. Compare them against each other, category by category. Do they have all the essentials and no contra-indicators? If they do, begin the task of identifying who has the most desirables in terms of the specification. This process is often over quickly when there is a person who is clearly a better fit than the others.

(6) Judging a photo finish. Inevitably there will be times when it is difficult to decide between applicants. If there is an impasse, is a further interview feasible? It may be time to focus upon your feelings and intuition.
   (a) Call each of them to mind. Think of the whole person.
   (b) Visualize them against individuals you know in the job.
   (c) Picture them doing the job in difficult circumstances.
   (d) Who will develop the most?
   (e) Who would you enjoy working with the most?

Make your judgement and live with your decision.

The final stages

Having made your decision, the successful candidate also has a decision to make. Many recruiters at this stage prefer to telephone them to make the offer and conduct preliminary negotiations about the appointment, prior to writing with the formal offer and the basis of the employment contract. You hope that the candidate will now write an acceptance letter, which you should require fairly promptly as there are others awaiting news of your decision.

Your offer will not always be taken up. This means that you should consider carefully the suitability of the second and third applicants and decide whether you offer it to either of them or to go to the well again. If they would fit, it is better not to write to them until you have a firm acceptance or refusal from the recipient of your first offer.

Your task does not finish with the acceptance. Indeed it is only just beginning. Even the best person is unlikely to fit the job in all respects and you will need to draw up plans for their induction and development. What do they need to find out? Who can help them? Will they have a guide or mentor to help them get off to a good start and ease the frustrations and difficulties that so often beset new people in new jobs? Having applied so much skill and resource getting the right person, you will want not only to keep but also to make the most of them.

References for further reading

Anderson G.C. and Kelly J. (1986) *Personnel Selection and Recruitment*. HMSO

Forbes R. (1979) Improving the Reliability of the Selection Interview. *Personnel Management Journal* July 1979

Fraser G.M. (1978) *Employment Interviewing*. Macdonald and Evans

Goodworth C.T. (1983) *Effective Interviewing for Employment Selection*. Business Books

Palmer R. (1983) A Sharper Focus for the Panel Interview. *Personnel Management Journal* May 1983

Plumbley P. (1988) *Recruitment and Selection*. IPM

PART TWO

Personal growth and interpersonal relationships

7

Understanding the communications process

Once you have managed to recruit the right people, you become responsible for what happens to them, and for the impact they have now and in the future. This responsibility is massively important, because it bears upon the success and satisfaction not only for them, but for yourself and all others within their ambit. It is not absolute and exclusive responsibility. Others share it, not least the individuals themselves, but it is important to you, because you are accountable for its outcome in terms of performance and results.

In horticultural terms, you have selected the plant to fit into a planned design. It has within it its own potential and limits, but its survival and growth will be influenced greatly by the skill, knowledge and attention you give it.

Development is the process of bringing about growth. People can grow, and you can help them with their development. Part Three explores the links between the individual's development of job skills and knowledge, and your own direct involvement, for example, in their appraisal and training. Part Two will focus upon the equally important connections between your own development and the growth of the people you work with. It requires positive application and in many ways is a precondition for helping others develop their performance skills.

Good communications lie at the heart of personal growth, interpersonal relations and team development. Very frequently, interpersonal difficulties are attributed to communication blockages and communication breakdown.

A useful starting point is a framework or model to assist the analysis of communications, to identify the precise nature of communication problems that emerge, and therefore to permit appropriate corrective action to be undertaken. One model which provides a sound theoretical base and can readily be used to analyse practical communication problems is shown in Figure 7.1. This model can be used for the analysis of interpersonal communications, group communication problems and complex organizational communication issues.

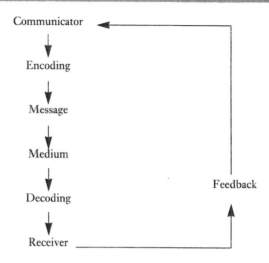

Figure 7.1 Model for analysis of the communications process.

The elements of the model will be examined.

Elements of the communications process model

Communicator, encoding, message and medium

The **communicator** is the individual or group with an intention to communicate, who will initiate some form of communication.

Encoding refers to the process of formulating a message. In the case of oral communication, encoding will consist partly of the choice of words used; it will consist also of the non-verbal elements of body language, including gestures, movement, eye contact and facial expression.

The **message** is the result of the encoding process; it represents what the sender wishes to communicate.

The **medium** is the carrier of the message. The precise form the message takes will depend to a large extent on the medium selected. In many situations managers make decisions about the choice of medium on the basis of custom and habit, almost at the subconscious level, without careful consideration of the issues involved. There is often a wider range of media choices available to the manager than may initially be apparent. In a typical organization, options will include:

- memorandum,
- circular,
- facsimile,
- electronic mail,
- telephone,
- telex,
- face-to-face meeting,

or some combination of these. Face-to-face meetings can be subdivided into:

- one-to-one meetings,
- one-to-small group meetings, and
- one-to-large group meetings.

Broadly, however, one of the important choices concerns the use of oral or written communication, or both. To ensure correct decisions about communications media are made, managers require a sound appreciation of the positive and negative aspects of oral and written communication. All too often, decisions about what media to use in communicating with others are made, without much conscious thought, relying largely on custom and habit.

ACTIVITY 7.1

 Note what in your view are:

(a) the main strengths
(b) the main limitations

of using oral methods of communication.

Repeat the activity, noting what in your view are:

(a) the main strengths
(b) the main limitations

of written communications.

Review of Activity 7.1

Assess to what extent your responses match those shown below.

Oral Communication

Strengths	Limitations
• Often perceived as highly acceptable.	• Speech depends on human memory.
• Feedback automatically present.	• Memory storage highly selective.

- Opportunity to use visual aids.

- Recall becomes less reliable over time.
- No record.

Written Communication

Strengths

Limitations

- More flexibility in encoding phase (for example, a writer, unlike a speaker, is less likely to use a wrongly-chosen word which may negate or distort the message, and can give more deliberation to precise encoding).
- More flexibility in decoding phase (for example, receiver can re-read the message, and/or seek help or advice from a third party in interpreting the message).
- Uniformity of coverage – everyone receives the same message.
- Preservation of a record.

- Feedback slow or non-existent (for example, if someone does not respond to a letter).
- Time-consuming to prepare.
- May be perceived as excessively formal and/or defensive.

The points shown illustrate some of the key considerations in helping managers decide whether to use oral or written communication. They do not provide an exhaustive analysis, and it is quite possible that you may have identified one or two relevant points not included above.

Decoding

Decoding involves the interpretation of the message by the receiver. Contrary to popular wisdom which thinks of decoding as a passive phase with receivers passively absorbing messages, research evidence (see, for example Biddle and Evenden, 1989) indicates that the interpretation of messages is a very active phase of the communications process. The hopes, fears, anxieties, values and experiences of the receiver all come into play, and impact on the way messages are decoded. As a result, the potential for messages to be interpreted in ways other than those intended by the communicator is substantial. While communication barriers and blockages can arise at any stage in the communications process, the propensity for distortion is particularly high in the decoding phase.

While the human brain possesses many truly outstanding qualities, it is often strangely limited in perceiving messages.

ACTIVITY 7.2

  (1)   FINISHED FILES ARE THE RESULT
       OF YEARS OF SCIENTIFIC STUDY
       COMBINED WITH THE EXPERIENCE
       OF MANY YEARS

Read the above sentence. How many letter Fs are there? Write your answer below.

(2)   Look at the picture in Figure 7.2. What do you see?

Figure 7.2

(3)   Study the diagrams in Figure 7.3. Your comments?

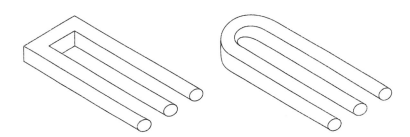

Figure 7.3

Review of Activity 7.2

Each of the elements of the activity draws attention to problems that can readily arise which can inhibit the accurate decoding of messages.

Detailed Responses

(1) Was your answer 3 Fs? If so, that is the commonest response – but incorrect!

89

The correct answer is 6 Fs – it is easy to overlook the word 'of' which occurs three times.

(2) The picture in Figure 7.2 contains two superimposed images. If you see initially the profile of a young woman, wearing a crown, you are in company with the majority. On the other hand a minority of people focus first on the old, witch-like face, with a large pointed chin. Most people find it difficult to hold the two images simultaneously – they tend to alternate in terms of what can be seen. Some people become so locked in on one image, that they find it difficult or even impossible to see the other.

Research evidence suggests there is a memory effect which influences perception, particularly in this type of situation. If someone looks first at a picture of a young woman and then transfers their gaze to this picture, then they are more likely to see the young woman's face. If, on the other hand, they look first at a picture of an old woman, they are more likely to perceive the old witch-like image. This illustrates the problem of selective perception, when we focus on part, and not the whole message.

(3) Did you find it difficult to look at the diagrams in Figure 7.3 for any length of time? If so (and many people find it uncomfortable to look at this kind of picture) it may well be because the diagrams shown do not appear logical, and do not match our experience of what is realistic and what is not. This tends to suggest that many of us have problems in interpreting messages that do not match up with our experiences.

Receiver and feedback

The **receiver** is the individual or group at whom the message is targeted.

The possibility for distortion and blockage at different points in the communication process emphasises the importance of **feedback**.

Feedback mechanisms are required to establish:

(1) Did the message get through to the receiver?
(2) If so, was it interpreted by the receiver in the way intended by the communicator?

Other factors affecting the communication process

Another relevant concept in examining the communication process is that of noise. It does not appear on Figure 7.1, but could be written across the whole diagram, because **noise** is defined as any factor that inhibits or distorts the communication process.

Examples of noise would include a telephone call interrupting an interview, or someone entering a meeting late.

The organizational **environment** has a major impact on how the communications process takes place, especially the culture of the organization and the levels of trust that exist among employees.

Observations from the literature

Drucker (1974) draws attention to four fundamentals of communications.

(1) Communication is perception.
(2) Communication is expectation.
(3) Communication makes demands.
(4) Communication and information are different.

Drucker draws attention to the obvious but often ignored fact that there is no sound unless someone can hear it. Drucker argues that it is really the receiver who communicates. The communicator only issues a message.

Expectation is closely linked to perception. The communicator requires some idea of what the receiver will expect, based on experience. Communication also, according to Drucker, makes considerable demands on the memory of the receiver, often leading to selective perception, broadly along the lines demonstrated in some aspects of Activity 7.2, with parts of messages being absorbed and other parts not received.

Information, in contrast to communication, is logical and is impersonal rather than interpersonal. All through history, Drucker argues, one of the challenges has been how to glean a little information out of communication, that is, out of relationships between people, based on perception. Cowling *et al.* (1988) stress that we give and receive non-verbal communication without conscious effort, and yet it can have a powerful effect on communication, and, in particular, on the decoding phase. When judging what others feel we trust facial expression first, tone of voice next and words last! When interviewing, negotiating and counselling we need to be alert to the various clues provided by non-verbal communication which may help in understanding the message of the other party – posture, gesture, tone of voice, rapid or hesitant speech, direction and duration of gaze.

ACTIVITY 7.3

▼ When watching a television interview, turn down the sound volume and focus on the non-verbal aspects of communication.

How far can you understand the nature of the dialogue by studying the non-verbal aspects?

Observe how people choose clothes, furniture and vocabulary to convey an image.

Handy (1990) suggests that we all make many assumptions based on a limited number of images. Covey (1989) explains that we all have two types of maps in our heads – maps of the way things are or realities, and maps of how things should be, or values – and that we interpret everything we experience through these mental maps.

Stanton (1982) concludes that communication is a selfless process in which, to stand any chance of success, we have to fight constantly our natural instinct to be self-centred. We have to guard against our natural instinct to concentrate on ourselves, on what we want to say, and try instead to think of the other party, the receiver, on what we need to do and say, to help them understand what we mean.

Covey (1989) stresses that one of the most important skills in dealing effectively with people is to recognize that people see things differently, each looking through the unique lens of experience – and to accept that others are not necessarily wrong, but that we see the world, not as it is, but as we are – or, as we are conditioned to see it.

The model shown in Figure 7.1 provides an excellent basis for self-assessment questions to assist in developing communication skills.

(1) Am I the right person to handle the communication (or should responsibility be delegated up or down the organization)?
(2) How well have I encoded the message I want to convey?
(3) Have I selected the right medium, or media, in communicating the message?
(4) Have I defined the receiver, or receivers of the message?
(5) Do I recognize they may decode the message in a variety of ways?
(6) Have I established feedback mechanisms, to establish the message is received as intended?

References for further reading

Biddle D. and Evenden R. (1989). *Human Aspects of Management*, Revised Edn. IPM
Covey S. R. (1989). *The Habits of Highly Effective People*. Simon and Schuster
Cowling A. G. *et al.* (1988). *Behavioural Science for Managers*. Edward Arnold
Drucker P. F. (1974). *Management: Tasks, Responsibilities, Practices*. Heinemann
Handy C. (1990). *Inside Organisations*. BBC Books
Stanton N. (1982). *What Do You Mean, Communication?* Pan

8

What are face-to-face skills?

Face-to-face skills are doing the right thing well, at the right time. If we succeed we may get the response we want and the results we are seeking. We get the satisfaction that comes from a smile or supportive agreement. If we fail, we may be faced with a scowl, indifference or hostility, and probably a reduced chance of getting what we want.

Behaviour is doing something, for example painting. A skill is behaviour which is controlled so that it achieves an objective. The skilled artist paints a picture commensurate with their skill level. Developing skill leads to higher possible standards of achievement. The artist paints better pictures.

Interpersonal or face-to-face behaviour is doing something that makes an impact on another person. They may barely notice it, or the effect on them may be profound, but either way, an impact is made. The effect may be primarily on the mind or it may be on the feelings, or both may be affected. Robert Bales (1950) distinguished between task and social emotional behaviour. **Task behaviour** is the 'words' we offer to the other person, which have a low or neutral emotive content, and give or seek facts or opinions.

In terms of work behaviour, the task is the stuff of information exchange, problem solving and decision making. If we were electronic beings, interpersonal skills would be confined to range and choice of language, structuring our ideas and presenting them clearly, so that logical and rational things could be done. Behaviour would be purely cognitive and our impact would be only on the other person's mental processes.

Social emotional behaviour comes from the heart, not the head, and is usually targeted at the same place in the recipient. Its impact is upon the relationship ('social') and the feelings ('emotional').

Task and social behaviours are summarized in Figure 8.1.

Task behaviour	Giving or Receiving words, facts, opinions, ideas
Social emotional behaviour	Affecting climate, relationships, feelings

Figure 8.1 Task and social emotional behaviour.

Bales suggests that the vital face-to-face skill is recognizing the difference between social emotional negative and social emotional positive behaviours, and being aware of both the need to be positive and the impact that you have upon others. In essence, a positive behaviour makes the other person feel good and a negative will make them feel bad. Examples of positive and negative behaviours are given in Figure 8.2.

In management's eyes, the task is the name of the game. This is the bottom-line behaviour which solves problems and gets the decisions made so that the right things are done to achieve the results. However, it is the social emotional behaviour which affects the climate in which the task is conducted. Indeed, if there are too many negatives the task may not be done at all.

Positive climate management is as important as good task contributions when we are face to face with others. There is a dynamic relationship between task, negative and positive behaviour in face-to-face contact. Research by Robin Evenden into meetings suggests that in order to achieve a 70% proportion of task contributions, positives need to outweigh negatives by two to one. A higher proportion of negatives may lead to their escalation at the expense of task contributions. Bales indicates that there is always a degree of tension in any human interaction, so social emotional behaviours are significant skills to develop. Most people not only prefer that kind of climate, but it is also more bottom-line effective.

Social emotional positive Producing good feelings	Showing warmth,	e.g. smiling, giving support, praise
	Reducing tension,	e.g. humour, helping relax
Social emotional negative Producing bad feelings	Unfriendliness,	e.g. hostility, putting others down, aggression
	Raising tension,	e.g. looking ill at ease, jokes at others' expense

Figure 8.2 Social emotional positive and negative behaviour examples.

Insupply case study: How important are face-to face skills?

In Part One we saw how Colin Smith, the Deputy Chief Executive of Insupply, was recruiting for the new position of Administration Manager. (For a summary see Appendix A). In general, Colin felt that he got on well with the staff, and that he showed interest and concern for people in his approach to management. He was satisfied with his relationship with his three administration officers, who would shortly be reporting to the Administration Manager instead of himself.

The Administration Officer: Communication was Ekoku Inanga, who had been with Insupply since it started three years ago. He was 27 years old, had a Masters degree and had a public relations background. He had been promoted two years ago. Ekoku was ambitious, confident and had proved very capable in his role.

He was a black African who had spent the last eight years living in a predominantly white community, and although he was on good terms with his immediate colleagues at work he was sensitive to colour prejudice which he experienced quite often in his daily life.

CASE PROJECT 8.1

Ekoku heard about the Administration Manager's job on the grapevine and phoned Colin to ask to talk about his interest in the post. Colin thought the position was unsuitable for Ekoku.

What should Colin do?

Colin considered two options

(1) Suggest that Ekoku should wait until the post is advertised, but tell him that he could not discuss it with him because it would be unfair to other applicants.

(2) See him and honestly tell him that the post was not suitable for him, giving the reasons.

He felt that the first would be the easier option. Ekoku would hopefully see that there were other more experienced and qualified applicants. He could be added to the short list for his pride's sake, before being turned down, with the reasons being explained in a counselling session. Ekoku would also see that this was a decision not just from Colin, but shared by the Chief Executive.

Colin chose the second option. He felt that it was more honest and would not raise false hopes that would be dashed and probably heighten any sense of grievance. Better to deal with the problem quickly, Colin felt. He would listen sympathetically and then explain rationally why Ekoku would not get the post.

He invited Ekoku to come to his office straight away so that they could talk about the situation and why the position of Administration Manager was needed.

The opening phase of the interview between Colin and Ekoku

Ekoku came into Colin's office at 4.30 p.m. He seemed agitated and upset, not responding to the suggestion that they should sit down at the coffee table, but walking to the window and glaring out. Colin offered him a coffee but again Ekoku ignored him, although it seemed more like he wasn't listening.

Without waiting for Colin to say anything, he burst out. 'I think you have treated me disgracefully. Why should I be the last to know that the Admin job is going to be advertised externally? I have just heard about it when I told Jean that I was coming to talk to you. It's terrible. To think that one of my own staff should tell me about it. It is a lousy thing when your own boss can't discuss something as important as this. I suppose you think that there is nobody good enough in Insupply to do the job. I really feel let down. I suppose an African is not good enough for you...'

CASE PROJECT 8.2

Thinking about task and social emotional positive and negative behaviour, can you visualize some of the face-to-face scenarios that could occur? How would you suggest Colin handles the situation? If you are studying in a group, a role play could provide good illustrations for discussion.

Can this type of problem be solved by good interactive skills?

Scenario One: Putting it on the line

Colin (standing and speaking loudly, glaring at Ekoku):

'That's enough. Just who do you think you are, talking to me like that. Now you sit down and listen to me. If you can't behave like a responsible adult then I have no wish to talk to you. You weren't in line for the job anyway and your behaviour proves how right I was.'

Clearly Ekoku was wound up by the way he heard about the situation, but given his role and other things we know about him, this outburst was untypical and was probably a response to a number of frustrations, not necessarily related to the external advertisement. His behaviour to Colin is obviously social emotional negative. It is aggressive, threatening, impolite and putting Colin down.

Negatives frequently beget negative responses in return, and they certainly did in the illustration above, when Colin returned the anger with bonus. Both men were expressing their bad feelings and their relationship is likely to deteriorate as a result of the episode. Even if Ekoku did sit down and shut up, severe damage would have been done. It is highly probable that he would leave, after three years' valuable contributions. There is little chance of negatives working long term and they usually make a difficult situation worse.

Scenario Two: Pouring oil on troubled waters

Colin (walking over to Ekoku and putting a hand on his shoulder with a concerned expression on his face):

'Come on. We've known each other too long to go to war. Let's sit down and talk about it. You seem to have a justifiable grievance and I want to find out more about it. First tell me exactly what happened, then we can talk about the person specification for the new job, and if you feel like it we can look at your own future.'

I don't think there are many people who would prefer Scenario One to Two, unless their major pleasure is taken in bloody battles. It is possible, however, that the first case is the more likely response, because negatives attract negatives. Given the aim is to retrieve the situation and retain a previously motivated member of staff, the second scenario shows a more controlled and skilled response from Colin Smith. It is a blend of supportive behaviour, offering recognition and conciliation, and task behaviour, seeking facts and problem solving. The skill is not just in the behaviours themselves, important as they are, but in showing control and awareness to behave in that fashion, when the temptation may well be to do the opposite.

Colin retrieved the situation by his skill, but behaviour was not the only cause and so can't be the only solution.

The advantages and limitations of face-to-face skills

As we observed in the case, lack of skill and negative contributions can make a bad situation much worse. It can also enable us to snatch defeat from the jaws of victory. It follows that the application of face-to-face skills helps to avoid this.

Good skill, balancing inevitable negatives with a higher proportion of positives, increases our capacity to handle the task in an appropriate collaborative climate. It can defuse tense situations and strengthen relationships. These are all highly desirable advantages, but there are limits. Face-to-face skills do not solve all interactive problems, but they usually assist in the solution.

Different interests and needs may not always be reconcilable. Ekoku would probably not be fully reconciled to not being considered for the post in the Insupply case.

We often have predispositions to respond to some people in a particular way. Individuals filter what happens in face-to-face contact according to their positive or negative prejudices, sometimes called the horns or halo effect. What a person sees as positive and negative will depend in part upon their attitude to the person with whom they are communicating.

Similarly, we will react partly to what a person does according to our experience and existing relationships with them. This would give Colin a good chance to rescue the interview with Ekoku, because of their previously good relationship.

The quality of a particular face-to-face contact will also partly depend upon its communication context. That is to say, it will be affected by the events that have occurred already.

In the case of Colin Smith and Ekoku Inanga, it is also about the events that should have happened. For example, if they had discussed departmental plans at an earlier date the specific outburst would not have taken place. Similarly, if they had discussed Ekoku's career aspirations during appraisal or some other time, the expectations and aspirations regarding the new job may have been different.

Face-to-face skills are by no means the only important tool in the manager's toolkit, but they should not be discounted. They are very significant in developing and maintaining relationships and enabling us to influence the learning and growth of others. They also have a marked effect upon the climate in which task objectives are achieved.

References for further reading

Bales R.F. (1950). *Interaction Process Analysis*. Addison-Wesley
Biddle D. and Evenden R. (1989). *Human Aspects of Management*, 2nd edn. IPM
Bolton R. (1979). *People Skills*. Prentice-Hall
Honey P. (1988). *Improve Your Skills With People*. IPM
Kakabadse A. *et al.* (1988). *Working in Organisations*. Penguin
Schein E. (1987). *Process Consultation* Vol. 2. Addison-Wesley

9

Developing our face-to-face skills

We cultivate face-to-face skills from birth, learning to choose and adapt our behaviour to others in order to get the response we want. If we can discover how we develop these skills, perhaps we can consciously learn more, and learn more effectively. We all have interpersonal blind spots. Nobody gets it right all the time. Developing these skills can improve our strike rate in getting positive responses from others.

If we can consciously learn interpersonal skills, do we have an unfair advantage over those less skilled? Will we want to pursue this advantage by manipulating others for our own ends?

There are wide differences between people in interpersonal effectiveness and influence, but there is no law that we must remain as we are, or change only by chance. Is it manipulation if we are better able to avoid defeats and meet needs as a result of improved skills? Ethical issues are raised if we exploit others by using power at their expense. This is true of all skills and knowledge and is a poor reason for us to remain ignorant or not develop ourselves. The ethical issue is how we choose to use the interpersonal power which is increased by learning, not the acquisition of knowledge itself.

ACTIVITY 9.1

▼ How do we learn our face-to-face skills?

Learning face-to-face skills

▽ When we are learning how to develop the skills which enable us to grow in terms of our interpersonal competence we need to consider two aspects. First there is the process by which we learn and second there are the development areas in which we learn.

The learning process

There are four stages in the interactive learning process (see Figure 9.1), developed from David Kolb's Learning Cycle (Kolb *et al*, 1974). We **experience** our contact with others, and those things in it which have a high impact, such as powerful feedback to us, lead to **reflection**. This reflection stage involves reviewing the episode, what we did, the response and how we felt about it. This is followed by the **ideas** stage, when we review our behavioural repertoire and re-evaluate what works for us in particular circumstances.

The fourth stage is **experimentation** or 'checking out' to test our ideas, to see if they work, or need modifying, or are hopelessly wrong. This may be at a low level of consciousness or a clear, rational test. We are then back full circle to the experience stage. If you experience it working you will be reinforced in your choice, if not you will reflect, modify, give up or try again.

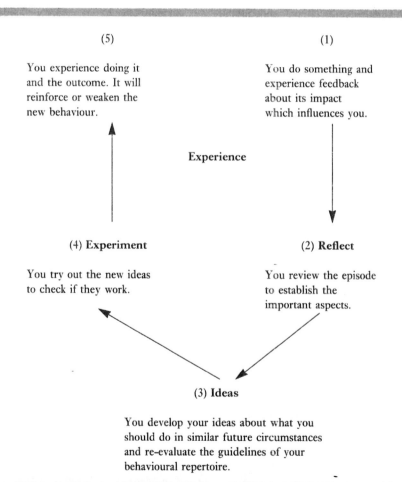

(5)

You experience doing it and the outcome. It will reinforce or weaken the new behaviour.

(1)

You do something and experience feedback about its impact which influences you.

Experience

(4) Experiment

You try out the new ideas to check if they work.

(2) Reflect

You review the episode to establish the important aspects.

(3) Ideas

You develop your ideas about what you should do in similar future circumstances and re-evaluate the guidelines of your behavioural repertoire.

Figure 9.1   Face-to-face skills: the learning process.

Development areas: the focus for face-to-face skills learning

There are four important areas to focus upon when developing face-to-face skills. They are **awareness** of our impact upon other people and what may be going on inside them; **self confidence** in our dealings with people; **influencing** others as a result of how we handle ourselves with them; and **behavioural skills**. Development in any one of the areas will increase our face-to-face skills, but they are all closely related and affect each other. The development areas are summarized in Figure 9.2.

(1) **Awareness**	Of ourselves and others
(2) **Self confidence**	How you feel about yourself in relation to others will influence what you do
(3) **Influencing**	Meeting your own needs positively, without negating the needs of others
(4) **Behavioural skills**	Developing positive behaviours and reducing negative

Figure 9.2   Face-to-face skills: development areas.

CASE PROJECT 9.1

Refer to the two face-to-face scenarios, between Colin Smith and Ekoku Inanga (pages 96 and 97).

Illustrate for yourself the four development areas:

Awareness
Self confidence
Influencing
Behavioural skills

Contrast each of the development areas with reference to Colin Smith's behaviour in both situations.

Insupply case study: Colin Smith and Ekoku Inanga scenarios

Awareness

In the first confrontational scenario, Colin was clearly aware of Ekoku's anger, but he was not aware of its causes and why he was behaving out of character. Again he was aware that he was being attacked and knew that his angry response would probably have a strong effect, although the direction was unpredictable. It could have been a bubble-bursting silence or escalated anger. If he was aware of the longer term damage it would have on their relationship, he discounted it and did not let it modify his behaviour.

In the second scenario, Colin was aware from his observation of Ekoku's body language that he was angry, but he also chose to detect that he was upset and under great pressure. His choice of response was based on this, and his awareness of the need to maintain their future relationship.

Self confidence

Uncertainty about yourself and your position is more likely to produce the response that Colin showed in the first case than the second. Aggression often comes from defensive feelings. It demonstrates self confidence if you respond calmly under verbal attack, and makes it easier to choose the behaviour that is most likely to get positive outcomes for both parties.

Influence

In the first case, Colin wanted to influence Ekoku, but it was entirely negative influence, intended simply to shut him up and to defeat him in verbal battle. As has been suggested this may have been achieved or the situation may have become more fraught. The negative influence adopted would not meet the needs of Ekoku (support, recognition, clarification) nor those of Colin (altering climate to deal with the problem). In the second case there is an example of positive influence, when Colin tries to defuse the situation by calming down Ekoku by remaining calm himself, so that both their needs in that situation could be met. It is probable that Ekoku would have responded to Colin's supportive intervention in a fashion that would enable them both to set about maintaining their relationship in a win–win, rather than a win–lose or even lose–lose mode. If Ekoku had such a head of steam that he continued in the same angry way, then Colin should himself carry on in similar positive vein, until Ekoku has let off his steam.

Behaviour skills

Earlier we defined behaviour skills as doing things that 'improve our strike rate in getting a positive response from others' and 'doing the right thing well, at the right time'. In the second scenario, Colin met these definitions with his aware and confident influence of Ekoku by behaving in a social emotional positive and task focused way.

References for further reading

Biddle D. and Evenden R. (1989). *Human Aspects of Management*, 2nd edn. IPM
Bolton R. (1979). *People Skills*. Prentice-Hall
Kolb D.A. *et al.* (1974). *Organisational Psychology – an experiential approach*. Prentice-Hall International

10

Developing awareness

Awareness which affects our interactive skills operates at two levels. The first is our knowledge of ourselves, in terms of what we do, how we are seen by others and the impact we have upon them. The second is our awareness of other people, with reference to their feelings and needs at the time of our contact with them. This 'sense' of the other person is our cue to action regarding them.

Increased awareness is important for face-to-face skills. It is central both to our own self development and the way we can help others develop.

Open self Your self knowledge which you share freely with others	Blind self Others' knowledge of you which you do not know about
Hidden self Your self knowledge that you hide from others	Unknown self That part of you that nobody knows – not even you

Figure 10.1   Awareness of self: the Johari window.

The Johari window (see Figure 10.1) is a famous explanatory model in social psychology developed by J. Luft and interpreted in terms of face-to-face skills by Edgar Schein. It represents our self as known or unknown to ourselves and others.

The **open self** are the parts of ourselves that we and others know about. These are the things we are confident and comfortable about that fit our image of ourselves.

The **hidden self** are parts of you that you choose not to reveal to others, perhaps through shame or, importantly for relationships, because you feel it is risky to reveal them. For example, a colleague has bad body odour, and you feel embarrassed by, but also for, them. In another case, your boss has a habit when excited of interrupting others, causing shy people to become more reticent and others to get angry, although the perpetrator is quite unaware of these effects.

You keep the knowledge and your feelings to yourself in both cases. Feedback to the other person about their impact would be disclosing this part of the hidden you. You perceive that it would be difficult and risky to do this, but the cost of not doing so is that you and others continue to suffer, as do the subjects themselves. It is an example of being unaware of a part of their **blind self**, although others are clearly aware of it and its marked impact.

The **unknown self** is that part of us which neither we nor anybody else knows about. It is the realm of the unconscious, and need not concern us in this context.

Skills which increase awareness of ourselves and others

In the illustrations of the blind selves, the route to move them into the open self domain is through *feedback*, which is a powerful and risky device. Clues about the hidden selves of others can be gained by *observation* and *listening*. These are the keys to increasing the level of awareness of ourselves and others, and as such are important skills to develop. They are summarized in Figure 10.2.

Feedback skills	Giving and receiving information about one person's impact on another
Observation skills	Watching how the other person responds to you, particularly in terms of their body language
Listening skills	Actively listening to the words and the music

Figure 10.2   Skills which increase awareness of ourselves and others.

Feedback

Feedback is giving a person information about how they affect others, or receiving information about your own impact.

Feedback can help you:

- Become more aware of your impact, reducing the blind self;
- Learn about the consequences of your behaviour choices;
- Identify behaviour which is effective for you;
- Help others become aware of their impact.

ACTIVITY 10.1

 (1) Think of times when you held back an opinion or feeling in contact with another person, when:
   (a) it helped to keep it hidden;
   (b) it hindered, and disclosure and feedback would have been preferable.

(2) Consider either of the cases in the Johari window hidden self illustration, or perhaps a similar real situation.
How would you give the feedback? What would you say? How would you say it?

What would you think are the rules for effective feedback?

Ways to give feedback

- Give it close to the event.
- Be specific.
- Observe and listen actively to the receiver when giving it.
- Give it as information.
- Avoid sitting in judgement. If the receiver feels you are putting them down, they will probably discount it.
- Don't overdo the amount. Keep it clear and straightforward.
- Remember feedback can be positive, and negative feedback can be given in a positive and constructive way.
- Try to ensure that the person will be receptive and try to be invited to give it.
- Get yourself into a calm and confident frame of mind.
- Take a task approach in a social emotional positive climate.
- Do not insist that it is the absolute truth, nor that the other person has to accept it.

Feedback can be a risky business. It may be accepted as helpful and acted upon, but there are many other possibilities. Your feedback may be rejected and you may be attacked or blamed, whilst the recipient may feel hurt, angry and defensive.

Following the rules of feedback will reduce the chances of a negative outcome. A final test before embarking upon feedback is to assess your own motivation for giving it. If your motive is really to make you feel better or superior in some way, don't expect the other person to accept it or thank you.

Ways to take feedback

If you want to discover part of your blind self, you will need to invite or at least listen to feedback.

- Explore it and discriminate. You do not have to swallow it all.
- Avoid arguing. Treat it as information to reflect upon.
- Seek specific feedback and ask for clarity and illustrations.

Observation

We generate a great deal of information when we are communicating with others, and much of it is non-verbal, or unspoken (see Figure 10.3). Observing and taking notice of body language is a skill that can reveal things that are 'hidden' by another person, and sometimes things about ourselves that are 'blind' to us.

There is usually so much non-verbal behaviour occurring during our contact with others that we ignore it or take it in without registering it as significant. Only when the body language is strong or unexpected are we likely to notice it, and take it into account in our interaction.

It can be helpful to develop our awareness of non-verbal behaviour in others, because of the clues it can give us about them. It can enrich the communication process and increase our understanding. One example of this is the mixed message, when a person says one thing but believes, or perhaps feels, something quite different.

'Oh yes, I'd be very pleased to ...', accompanied by avoidance of eye contact, hiding the mouth with a hand and fidgeting with a foot, would suggest that there is some feeling within the person, but you would probably be wrong to accept that it is pleasure.

We use non-verbal communication

- To control interaction
  e.g. hold up hand, palm out
  'Be quiet, I wish to speak.'
- To express feelings
  e.g. laughter; applauding.
- To conduct social rituals
  e.g. shaking hands.

The means of non-verbal communication are:

Appearance	Expressing who we are by dress and self display.
Movement	Whole body or parts ; hands, legs, head.
Posture	Slouch–straight; casual–alert; towards–away.
Voice	Tone quality; rate; intonation; loudness.
Position	Seating arrangement; distance apart; high–low.
Face and eyes	Expression; eye contact; mouth; eyebrows; cheeks.
Gesture	Hands; arms; fingers; shaking; pointing; touching.

Figure 10.3 Non-verbal communication: how we speak without words.

As we have seen, we often mask, or try to control the self shown to the other person, but usually tell tale signs can be seen or heard. These are referred to as **leaks**, in the sense of information leaking out rather than being offered (see Figure 10.4).

It is often not possible to be sure from the leak what the person's true feeling and thinking are, but you have a clue that all is not as it is presented. You may simply note that the person is not very pleased, in spite of their protestation. That could be helpful information to you both. You might have a hunch what is going on from the non-verbal behaviour, but you may be wrong.

Many different processes can give rise to the same body language. A frown as a colleague says, 'Yes, I see', may be interpreted several ways and your conclusion may in fact reflect your own state rather than that of the other person. If you are feeling defensive, you may see it as hidden disagreement. If you are confused, it may appear that the other person is puzzled. They may just be thinking about what you have said.

Although you need to be cautious about interpretation, body language can give you clues to think about, respond to or check out, by asking the other person about it or observing more closely.

Breathing	Catching breath; sighs; gasps; whistles; blowing; shallowness; irregularity; swallowing.
Eyebrows	Raising; beetling or lowering; frowning.
Feet	Twisting and angling; tapping.
Fingers	Tight fist; tapping; stroking and scratching; scrutinizing them; drumming.
Mouth	Tight lips; corner movement; pursing; sucking; hiding with hands; grimacing; smiling.
Eyes	Lowering; closing; avoiding eye contact; narrowing; moistening; glazing; rolling; focusing; 'looking through'.

It is not suggested that any single behaviour or pattern indicates a particular hidden feeling or thought. However, if some of the above aspects of body language are displayed, it is likely that something may be being held back.

Figure 10.4 Observation: where the hidden self leaks out.

Observation of others is a face-to-face skill which can help us understand them, and influence our responses to them. In a sense we can also observe ourselves for body language. The information we make available to ourselves can make us more aware of what we are doing and feeling, so that we can change.

One example of this is stress. In situations of some tension, there is usually a physical manifestation, and although we will probably be aware of feeling uncomfortable, and probably getting more uncomfortable by the minute, we are not likely to be observing our body 'message' too closely. Our stress, or unacceptable tension, almost certainly will be leaked to the other person, affecting the interaction process, usually in a negative way.

ACTIVITY 10.2

 You may find it helpful to check and test these ideas by reflecting upon your own experience and by practising your observation.

(1) How does stress manifest itself in body language?
(2) Does it affect interaction with others?
(3) How can it be modified if it is having undesirable effects?

Observation and body language: stress illustration

There are many body language indicators of stress noticeable in ourselves, some of which can be observed in others. These include sweating, clammy palms, clenched jaws, neck and shoulder tightness, white knuckles, shallow breathing, hugging yourself, legs twisted around each other and sitting uncomfortably, perhaps on the edge of the seat. It is surprising how we frequently fail to be conscious of these physical aspects of stress, which are symptoms of internal and external factors.

We will find that our interaction with others is likely to be as constrained and restricted as our bodies. We are unlikely to have too much control. It will be communicated to the other person and affect them. If they are dominating, they will become more dominating. If they are anxious they will become more anxious.

An external factor may reduce the stress and hence the non-verbal leakage. The cause may disappear, such as a threatening person leaving the room, another person entering, a good joke or the problem being solved. Or, having observed it in yourself, you take remedial action. You may choose to be different. Conscious relaxation of tight muscles, sitting 'four square', breathing deeply and regularly can lead to a change in you internal state and the external manifestation.

ACTIVITY 10.3

 You may wish to practise your observation skills.

 (1) Observing others
One safe method is to observe the non-verbal behaviour of people on television, the stage or films. Body language is exploited, if not exaggerated, by actors and observation with interpretation can be instructive and perhaps even entertaining. Switching off the sound can be a good exercise. If you are using video, the fast-search facility affords an excellent means of observing posture and gesture during interaction.

(2) Discovering hidden selves
If you are studying with others, one observation exercise is as follows:
Choose a topic to discuss with a colleague for 5–10 minutes, preferably one where one or both may wish to hide some opinions or feelings (for example 'My first impressions of you were...').

Afterwards share your observations about leaked hidden feelings and the body language that you felt showed it. Check any interpretations you may have with the other person.

Before exercises of this kind, agree to remain friends. Some experiments go wrong!

Listening

In considering ways to develop face-to-face skills, we have been looking at increasing our awareness of other people and also of our impact upon them. So far this has involved using feedback and observation. A third way of developing understanding is by listening.

In Part One, when the conduct of the recruitment interview was examined, it was suggested that we need to listen to the words (what people say) and the music (the way they express their feelings). Skilled **active listening** (see Figure 10.5) can steer us towards not only what the person is saying, but what is behind it.

Not only will active listening enable us to understand and recall what the other person is saying, but it permits us to influence the talker in a positive fashion by encouraging and steering them.

Listening and observing are parallel and related activities, providing checks and reinforcements of each other. If our eyes detect a mixed message from another person then we can use our ears for other evidence.

Active listening is important for maintaining relationships, developing trust and confidence, and helping our understanding.

Attentive behaviour	Smiles; nods; affirmation.
Avoiding non-attentive behaviour	Not yawning, clock watching, doodling or staring into space.
Influencing during their talking	Reflecting back their data to them; asking questions to steer them; seeking or giving illustrations; limiting or parcelling their data.
Reducing distractions	Internal: talking to ourselves; rehearsing what to say; anticipating them; letting our minds wander. External: noisy room; other people; interruptions.
Managing our receptivity	Physical support – appropriate comfort; self motivation to pay attention; mental organization.

Figure 10.5 How we listen actively.

References for further reading

Biddle D. and Evenden R. (1989). *Human Aspects of Management*, 2nd edn. IPM

Harris T.A. (1979). *I'm OK You're OK*. Pan

James M. and Jongward D. (1971). *Born to Win*. Addison-Wesley

Schein E. (1987). *Process Consultation* Vol. 2. Addison-Wesley

Schein E. (1988). *Process Consultation* Vol. 1. Addison-Wesley

11

Developing self confidence

Awareness of ourselves and other people, together with the associated skills of feedback, listening and observation, are important for our face-to-face contacts. However bringing ourselves to use behavioural skills and experiment with our repertoire depends partly upon *being* confident, and having an effect will depend upon *seeming* confident.

Self confidence is being sure of ourselves in situations which are uncertain, threatening or pressurized. It is confidence in ourselves stemming not from feeling better than the other person, but from an acceptance of our self and clarity about what we want. In an important sense, we can't give another person confidence but we can foster a positive self image by the way we treat them. Similarly, it is possible to undermine a person's confidence by what we do to them, but this will not happen to a person who doesn't give their confidence away.

ACTIVITY 11.1

▼ We influence our own self confidence to a substantial degree. The process of confidence boosting, in the vernacular, is 'psyching ourself up' for an encounter. Unfortunately, we can also 'psych ourself down'. Can you identify from your own experience some of these self-influencing processes?

Developing confidence: avoiding psyching yourself down

▽ There are many things that we do which undermine our confidence in ourselves generally, or in relation to a particular event which is important to us. Self confidence development requires that we recognize how we do this, catch ourselves doing it, perhaps with supportive help, and *stop doing it*!

Behaviour to avoid includes:

- Putting yourself down.
- Accepting the put-downs of others.
- Comparing yourself unfavourably with others.
- Going out of your way to invite negative judgements.
- Getting others to agree that you lack confidence.
- Having unrealistic personal standards doomed to failure.
- Reminding yourself of past failures.
- Believing that the worst possible things will happen.
- Rejecting compliments and praise.
- Not letting yourself feel pleasure from your successes.
- Being overcritical and not accepting yourself as worthwhile.

Developing confidence: psyching yourself up

Self confident people not only avoid frequent use of self put-down behaviour, but actively do things which boost their confidence.

Behaviour to adopt to enhance confidence:

- Remind yourself of the good feelings that confidence brings.
- Be convinced that your own needs and wants are important.
- Seek, accept and enjoy recognition and support from others.
- Accept that it is normal and human to make mistakes.
- Recall and review your successes and the good feelings that are associated with them.
- Visualize the best possible things that can happen and fix them in your mind.
- Set reasonable targets for yourself, and reward yourself when you achieve them.
- Support yourself before and during difficult events:
  - encourage yourself
  - give yourself rewards and compliments
  - physically support yourself by sitting or standing firmly and 'four square'; breath slowly and deeply.

Confidence in dealing with people you find difficult

We all have people and situations we find difficult. Practising the self confidence generating methods outlined above will give us the appropriate frame of mind to tackle them. In addition there are techniques to cultivate which will support confidence growth.

Handling the aggressive individual

The intention of a person behaving towards you in an aggressive way is that you should finish up being down and losing.

Aggression can be dealt with at a number of levels.

1. Dealing with unfinished business and the relationship

Neil Clark has pointed out that aggression may have more to do with unfinished business from previous encounters than with the immediate situation and conflict of interests. He suggests that in this case it is a good idea to offer the other person the chance to clear up these left over feelings.

In the confrontation Ekoku had with Colin in the Insupply case (page 96) some of the ways of defusing by tackling unfinished business are illustrated.

• Appealing to long-term relationship and expressing positive feelings	'Come on. We've known each other too long to go to war.'
• Inviting the other person to discuss the unfinished business	'Let's sit down and talk about it.'
• Accepting that the other person may have dissatisfaction	'You seem to have a justifiable grievance and I want to find out more about it.'
• Making sure that the task issues are on the table	'First tell me exactly what happened, then we can talk about the person specification for the new job, and if you feel like it we can look at your own future.'

Dealing with unfinished business may also involve offering to receive and to give feedback to the other person, so that things which may have been behind the difficulties can be identified and perhaps resolved.

It is important to create an opportunity to express your feelings about the previous contacts. Defusing the situation should not include surrendering your own needs.

2. Handling the immediate situation

There is often a conflict of interests, wants and goals. Aggression is a way that some people choose to handle such encounters, especially if they feel that they are in a win–lose situation.

If you can express what you want, invite the other person to say what he or she wants and then suggest that you find a way to achieve mutual satisfaction, it may remove the aggression from the meeting.

3. Coping with a constant aggressor

There are significant differences between the person who is showing aggression occasionally and the individual who is constantly aggressive. The former would probably respond to the rational and positive approaches just outlined. Unfortunately the latter may be immune to this, although it is always worth attempting as a first choice.

Constant aggressors find aggression normal, and it will have produced rewards in the past, such as triumph, winning and success. They will have resisted many approaches to deal with it by others, so long-term change is unlikely. The answer may well be either finding a way which works for you in switching off their aggression each time it erupts, or protecting yourself from it.

Tricky or risky approaches: can they work for you?

- Respond with your own aggression.
- Applaud the aggressive behaviour of the other person.
- Comment upon it ironically as it happens.
- Tell them how hurtful it is.
- Tell them how their behaviour appears to you.
- Laugh at them.
- Agree with them.
- Ignore them.
- Leave the room calmly.

Any of these may switch off constant aggressors for a short time and they may learn that it is better not to use verbal violence with you. Do assess the risk and your relative power position and experiment with what you regard are the safer methods.

Protecting yourself approaches

- Remind yourself constantly during the 'performance' that you are the one who is really in control.
- See the outburst as having nothing to do with you and everything to do with the other person. Enjoy it!
- Keep calm, rational and feeling good about yourself.

Practising this will help you develop protective immunity.

Getting on with people in authority

Many people have some difficulty in their dealings with individuals they recognize as having authority. This is often the power of a person's position, such as manager or supervisor, but it can also refer to those with high status or expertise such as doctors or lawyers, as well as those people with strong personalities.

These problems may manifest themselves by avoidance of the authority figures, shyness and anxiety in their presence or sometimes by rebelliousness or passive hostility. This response will obviously limit the person's ability to develop effective relationships and will affect how they are seen by the authority figure. The way they behave may actually produce the behaviour from the other person which in some sense they are afraid of facing, and the negative aspects are reinforced.

The rebellious approach to authority may stimulate an aggressive and negative response to the rebel, reinforcing their opinion and approach. (See the Insupply case, page 96). A shy approach often results in that individual being ignored, patronized, 'taken care of' or discounted in some other way which reinforces their attitude and behaviour to authority.

In most cases, it seems, the improvement in the 'getting on with' problem needs to stem from the person who has it.

Why do people have this problem?

Is it because they are:

- Trapped by their previous patterns of behaviour?
  (Compliance; hostility.)
- Governed by past difficult authority relations?
  (Parents; teachers.)
- Ruled by prescriptions they were made to swallow?
  (Respect your betters; all police are #@*s!)
- In the habit of undermining themselves?
  (I'll never be able to be as good as them.)

Ways of relating to authority figures

- Accept responsibility for the relationship.
- Decide to experiment with different ways of relating.
- Listen to your internal rules about how to behave and decide if they make sense.
- Visualize yourself in a position of power.
- Visualize the authority figure in a weak position.
- See them as they are rather than as you fear them to be.
- Relax yourself when you are with them, and practise being calm, positive and rational.
- Notice their weaknesses and your strengths.
- Discover ways that they need your help and support.
- Get them out of the habit of putting you down (if they do!).
- Get out of the habit of putting yourself down.

References for further reading

Back K. and K. (1982). *Assertiveness at Work*. McGraw-Hill
Berne E. (1977). *Games People Play*. Grove Press.
Bolton R. (1979). *People Skills*. Prentice-Hall
Clark N. *et al.* (1984). *Unfinished Business*. Gower Press
Harris T.A. (1979). *I'm OK You're OK*. Pan
James M. and Jongward D. (1971). *Born to Win*. Addison-Wesley
Schein E. (1988). *Process Consultation* Vol. 1. Addison-Wesley

12

Developing influencing skills

Making the most of people involves developing mutual awareness and confidence, conditions for the growth of both parties and their relationship. It is what many would describe as a mature relationship. It removes or prevents the stunting that can occur whenever threat, fear, uncertainty and bullying appear in a relationship.

This is not meant to imply that people should not make demands upon each other. This is a central part of interaction and living in groups within society. It is how those demands are made and responded to which is the measure of the relationship. It is to do with the skill we use in influencing each other.

ACTIVITY 12.1

 You may wish to think about the way you generally prefer to influence others. The questionnaire given in Figure 12.1 is designed to help you do that. Complete the questionnaire.

Directions

From each of the paired statements below, choose the one which best fits your views.

1.1 I am often wrong.

  2 It is essential to get what you want from life.

2.1 It is important to be in control.

  2 It is wrong to set out to 'get' somebody.

3.1 It is right to put the other person first.

  2 You have to be able to defend yourself in this world.

4.1 It is difficult to change.

  2 I do not mind saying what I feel.

5.1 I am often wrong.

  2 I am usually able to get what I want.

6.1 It is essential to get what you want from life.

  2 It is wrong to set out to 'get' somebody.

7.1 It is important to be in control.

2 It is right to put the other person first.

8.1 You have to be able to defend yourself in this world.

2 It is difficult to change.

9.1 I do not mind saying what I feel.

2 It is essential to get what you want from life.

10.1 It is wrong to set out to 'get' somebody.

2 I am often wrong.

11.1 I am usually able to get what I want.

2 It is right to put the other person first.

12.1 You have to be able to defend yourself in this world.

2 I do not mind saying what I feel.

13.1 It is difficult to change.

2 It is important to be in control.

14.1 You have to be able to defend yourself in this world.

2 It is wrong to set out to 'get' somebody.

15.1 I am often wrong.

2 I do not mind saying what I feel.

16.1 It is right to put the other person first.

2 It is essential to get what you want from life.

17.1 You have to be able to defend yourself in this life.

2 I am usually able to get what I want.

18.1 It is essential to get what you want from this life.

2 It is difficult to change.

19.1 It is important to be in control.

2 I do not mind saying what I feel.

20.1 You have to be able to defend yourself in this world.

2 I am often wrong.

21.1 It is important to be in control.

2 I am usually able to get what I want.

22.1 It is wrong to set out to 'get' somebody.

2 It is right to put the other person first.

23.1 I am usually able to get what I want.

2 It is difficult to change.

24.1 I am often wrong.

2 It is important to be in control.

25.1 It is essential to get what you want from life.

2 I am usually able to get what I want.

26.1 It is difficult to change.

  2 It is wrong to set out to 'get' somebody.

27.1 I do not mind saying what I feel.

  2 It is right to put the other person first.

Scoring

Put a circle around your choice for each pair, then add the circles in each column to give you your influence profile.

Statement pair	Passive style	Aggressive style	Assertive style
1	1	2	
2		1	2
3	1	2	
4	1		2
5	1		2
6		1	2
7	2	1	
8	2	1	
9		2	1
10	2		1
11	2		1
12		1	2
13	1	2	
14		1	2
15	1		2
16	1	2	
17		1	2
18	2	1	
19		1	2
20	2	1	
21		1	2
22	2		1
23	2		1
24	1	2	
25		1	2
26	1		2
27	2		1
Total circles			

Figure 12.1 Influencing style questionnaire.

Review of Activity 12.1

▽ The questionnaire consists of three sets of statements, each reflecting one of the three influencing styles: passive, aggressive and assertive.

Each statement of one style is paired in turn with each of the statements associated with the other two styles. If you chose the first statement of the first pair you would score one for 'passive style'. If you had chosen the second statement you would have scored one for 'aggressive'.

The most you can score for any style is 18 and the total score for all three styles is 27. A score of more than 9 would indicate that you have a preference for that approach to influencing. Similarly, a score of less than 9 suggests that it is less favoured by you.

This questionnaire does not pretend to be a scientific instrument or a personality test, although it is based on characteristics associated with the three styles of influencing. It is an heuristic device, intended to promote thought, discussion and learning.

Influencing styles

The aim of influencing skill is to meet our own needs and interests in an open and positive way, without negating the needs of others. Our aims may be to seek a change in them, to want something from them, or to modify their demands on us.

Dr Robert Bolton (1979) has suggested that when we are in circumstances where we have needs to meet, we can choose to behave passively, by being submissive, aggressively, by attempting to overpower others, or by being assertive. **Passive** behaviour involves a reluctance to make demands on our own behalf. We give in to others. **Aggressive** behaviour is trying to get what we want by dominance and with no concern for others. **Assertive** behaviour means being clear about what we want and pursuing it without 'defeating' the others.

These three influencing styles are illustrated in Figures 12.2, 12.3 and 12.4, respectively.

ACTIVITY 12.2

▼ Visualize yourself adopting each of the three influencing styles. Imagine the events as concretely as possible, and for each style note what you thought, felt, did (body language) and said.

Thoughts	I'm wrong and you are right.
	What's the point? I will not succeed.
	I have to take care not to hurt other people.
	I can't change in any way.
	Others are in control, not me.
Feelings	Depression
	Hopeless
	Worried
	Powerless
	Awkward
	Inadequate
Behaviour	Avoids eye contact
	Slouched
	Wrings hands
	Sighs
	Pleading or hesitant voice
	Wastes time
	Nervous mannerisms
Opening words	'Would it be at all possible ...?'
	'It is stupid of me, but I wonder ...'

Figure 12.2 Illustration of the passive influencing style.

Thoughts	I'm right and you are wrong.
	It is vital that I win.
	It doesn't matter if I hurt other people.
	Other people must change.
	I have to be in command.
Feelings	Anger
	Superiority
	Certainty
	Dominant
	Righteous
Behaviour	Glares and stares
	Physically looks down upon
	Clenched fist
	Snorts
	Loud voice or quietly with menace
	Demands instant action
	Points finger and hammers the table

| Opening words | 'You must ...'
'You have no choice in the matter.'
'Now just you listen to me.' |

Figure 12.3 Illustration of the aggressive influencing style.

Thoughts	We both have our views. We can both benefit. My feelings are important, and so are theirs. I have a right to seek specific changes from ... I am in control of myself.
Feelings	Calmness, anger, acceptance etc. as appropriate Confidence Contentment Powerful Fairness
Behaviour	Steady eye contact Upright posture Alert Four square and relaxed Clear voice Uses hands and voice for emphasis
Opening words	'I think ...' 'I feel ...' 'What I want is ...'

Figure 12.4 Illustration of the assertive influencing style.

Assertion and positive influencing

The aggressive approach to influencing implies coercion, and can bring about a win against those who are weaker and dependent. The win may be short-term or even illusory and the loser may strive hard to win next time and to minimize the victor's gains. It remains an influencing choice and is a style that many adopt, although not all admit to it or are necessarily aware that this is their approach.

The passive approach will only yield benefit to the person adopting that style if the other party is willing, supportive, kindly disposed and is able to get the passive individual actually to define what they want. The outcome is in the hands of the other person.

The assertive approach to influence is not at the expense of the other person. It involves controlling your own destiny and implies clarity of your own needs with firmness and persistence in their pursuit.

Influence through assertion is an orientation and set of skills that can be learned and developed with practice. It is not always easy, is not a panacea and will not always work, but it is a better bet than the other two in terms of meeting your own needs and maintaining positive relationships with other people.

It should be noted that aggressive people do not always notice the difference between assertion and passivity! This calls for confidence, persistence, interactive skills and patience. Similarly, passive people may take time to distinguish between assertion and aggression, in which case they may need encouraging out of their passivity to accept some ownership of the matters you wish to deal with.

The three steps in positive influencing

When you are deliberately setting out to influence using the assertive approach, there are three steps you need to take into the exchange.

(1) **Understanding**   Understand the other person's position, problem and needs. The first thing is to let them know that you do understand and that you are understanding. You make initial statements like 'I understand your difficulties...' and 'I can see what you are trying to achieve.'

(2) **Views**   State clearly and calmly your views and feelings on the matter, having clarified them fully beforehand in your own mind.
Be 'matter of fact' so that the other person does not become defensive.

(3) **Wants**   Having worked out in advance, if possible, what you want from the situation, make your statement based on your own needs briefly, clearly and calmly. Make and be prepared to repeat statements like 'I would like you to...' and 'No, I am unable to...'

Step three may require the **broken record** technique. This is where you put yourself in the groove of your 'wants' and repeat them as frequently as necessary until they are achieved. Do not be afraid to use the same phrases several times, although there is no reason why you should not prepare for the broken record beforehand by finding and rehearsing several ways to say the same thing.

123

Preparation for the influencing encounter

Rehearse	Visualize yourself going through the three steps. See both of you clearly in your mind's eye and yourself behaving effectively as planned so that the outcome is successful and you both are satisfied.
List the wants	Write down several different ways of expressing your wants. Prepare for the broken record.
Turn negative internal dialogue into positive	We talk to ourselves a great deal. This is called internal dialogue. It is negative when we put ourselves down and undermine our own self confidence. 'I could never do that!' 'I am certain to make a fool of myself.' 'Remember that disastrous time when...' It is likely that we do more to affect our own confidence level than a dozen enemies. We have first to cope with the enemy within. In preparing for the influence encounter, or indeed any circumstance when we need to be positive and confident, monitor closely your 'self-discounting'. Stop doing it! Turn all the negatives into positives. 'I can do that.' 'I am sure to be successful.' 'Remember that terrific time when...' Write it down. It helps to spell it out. Run through your successes and achievements. Find how you can trigger these good feelings associated with your successes so you can reproduce them during the influencing activity when the going gets tough. This is called 'anchoring'. Visualize and recall as vividly as possible the feelings associated with a triumph at the same time as, say, squeezing your wrist. Some people find they can later reproduce that feeling with a squeeze. A good trick! A positive influence checklist is given in Figure 12.5.

(1) What do you want from the other person?

(2) What are the three positive steps ?

	(a) **Understand**	Do you understand their position/viewpoint?
	(b) **Views**	What do you think and feel about it?
	(c) **Wants**	What do you want?

Broken	1.
record	2.
repeated	3.
in	4.
different	5.
ways	6.

(3) Are you having a negative internal dialogue? Turn the negatives into positives, in writing if it helps.

(4) Remind yourself of past successes and how you achieved them.

(5) Visualize and mentally rehearse. See yourself handling well the three steps and concluding with a 'win–win' outcome.

Figure 12.5   Positive influence checklist.

Insupply case study: Assertion and positive influencing

Three common circumstances when positive influencing techniques will be effective are:

(1) Giving negative criticism.

(2) Refusing to do something you do not want to do.

(3) Asking another person for something that you want.

Each of these three situations are dealt with below. Illustration of both the aggressive and the passive approach will be given and it is then suggested that you undertake an activity in the context of the Insupply case, when Ekoku Inanga confronted his boss Colin Smith about the recruitment of an Administration Manager. If you are studying in a group, the three situations lend themselves to role playing.

You will be asked to suggest an assertive positive influence approach to the three scenarios and will then be able to compare this to a set of illustrated guidelines.

The Insupply summary will be found in Appendix A and the three approaches will follow Ekoku's outburst on page 95 and Colin's positive initial response on page 96.

Positive influence: giving negative criticism

Aggressive approach	'That was a mindless thing to do.'
	'You are an idiot when you behave like that.'
	'In your position, you ought to know better than to behave in such an appalling fashion.'
Passive approach	'The Chief Executive probably wouldn't like it if she saw you doing that.'
	'It's up to you really, but I don't think it is possibly a very good idea.'
	'I am not sure that is the right way to tell me that you are not happy.'

CASE PROJECT 12.1

Assertive approach

How do you think Colin Smith should have given Ekoku Inanga feedback about his outburst? Are there any rules to follow? Suggest some appropriate sentences and phrases he could use.

Guidelines: giving negative criticism

(1) Careful choice of time and place. If the confrontation resulting from Ekoku's outburst had been stabilized and the discussion had become more positive and rational, Colin should have given his views on the outburst before they parted. It is always a good idea to give feedback close to the event, unless the feelings are so high that it would be counterproductive.

(2) Tell the other person how you felt and make sure they know the consequences for you. 'I was unhappy at the way you expressed yourself when you came into the room. It was embarrassing and you must see that it places me in difficulty when I am talked to like that.'

(3) Give specific information and illustrations. 'For example, you should not use phrases like "disgraceful" and it is unpleasant and unfair to describe me as racist.'

(4) Offer alternatives to the behaviour you did not like. 'It is much more constructive and helpful to tell me simply how you felt and why you felt like you did. Making personal comments will not help either of us to sort the problem out.'

Positive influence: saying no

Aggressive approach	'No chance!' 'To hell with that...' 'You are the last person I would suggest.' 'Get out of here!'
Passive approach	'Well... I'm not really sure you are the right person.' 'I will have to talk to the Chief about it. I do not think she will like it.' 'We will have to see. It is a bit early to make any decision on this issue.' 'I am doubtful about it, but you could try if you really want to.'

CASE PROJECT 12.2

Assertive approach

How should Colin say 'no' to Ekoku's wish to be the new Administration Manager? Are there any rules to follow? Suggest some appropriate sentences and phrases he could use.

Guidelines: giving a refusal

(1) It is your refusal. Own it. 'It is my clear opinion that the job is not appropriate for you.'

(2) Give your reasons not excuses. 'This is a position which requires wider experience than you have yet been able to acquire.'

(3) Give the other person the chance to draw the same conclusion as you. 'Here is the person specification. I'd like to hear how you see yourself measured against it.'

(4) Show you understand their feelings and that you are not rejecting them as a person, but just saying 'no' to this. 'It must be disappointing for you. You have done well in your current position and have a good career ahead of you. It is simply that, in this case, the job is not suitable for you.'

(5) You must be prepared to say 'no' as often as necessary. Don't be trapped into feeling guilty.

Positive influence: asking for something you want

Aggressive approach	'Give it me, or else...'
	'You have no choice. You must...'
	'You have got to...'
	'If you don't ...then...'
Passive approach	'Do you think you could see your way clear to...'
	'Would it put you out if ...?'
	'The Chief and I think it would be nice if you could...'
	'If only...I would be so grateful.'

CASE PROJECT 12.3

Assertive approach

How do you think Ekoku could have made his request to Colin Smith to be considered for the Administration Manager post, so that he would have increased his chances? Are there any rules to follow when asking for something? Suggest some appropriate sentences and phrases he could use.

Guidelines: asking for what you want

(1) It is your request. Own it. 'I would like you to consider me for the post.'
(2) Give your reasons and feelings. Show its importance to you. 'We have agreed that I have performed well since joining you. It is the next step for me. I feel that I need advancement and a fresh challenge that this job would give.'
(3) Be clear and specific. 'If I do not get this job there seems nowhere else for me to go with you.'
(4) Ask direct questions to get a clear answer. 'Am I in the reckoning for this job?'
(5) Be persistent. 'I have to repeat, I really want this job.'
(6) Bear in mind that at some point you may need to get the other to join you in the search for a solution and even a compromise. 'What other options are there for me here? I want to stay and I need a fresh challenge. I would like your ideas on this. Is there an answer?'

Insupply case study: attitudes and outcomes

If both Colin and Ekoku are both equally assertive, where will that lead them? There is a danger that one or both will slip into an aggressive mode with a clear win–lose orientation, when both may finish up losing.

Another possibility is that the person who is the most persistent or has the best case may persuade the other person. More likely is that if both stick with assertion and a collaborative approach, a mutually satisfactory outcome will be reached.

For example, Colin discovers that the real issues for Ekoku are his desire for advancement, and his belief that the Administration Manager post is the only option. He may already have ideas on Ekoku's future or he may rapidly develop some if he wishes to retain his services.

In the Insupply case, the outcome was a happy agreement based on collaboration. Ekoku found it easy to accept that the post was not right for him when Colin offered him a development and training programme, which if successful would lead to Ekoku moving into a new senior marketing post that Insupply would be needing in a year's time.

Positive influence: attitudes and outcomes

Giving criticism

Often we have attitudes or rationalize things in ways which make it difficult to give negative feedback, such as 'It is not the right time.', 'If I'm wrong I will look bad.', 'It will cause bad feeling.' Giving negative feedback can be viewed both as a sign of respect and trust in the other person, and if handled well, can improve a relationship.

Giving a refusal

We often fantasize about the bad things that will happen if we say 'No'. We think that people will become angry or cease to like us. We need to ask ourselves if it really is true that the way to be liked and respected is always to give in to the other person.

Asking for what you want

If another person turns down our request, we sometimes feel that they are actually rejecting us as a person. This is the reason many give for finding it difficult to ask for things they want. We need to be aware that we have a right to ask, but not to expect always to get what we want. Refusal is for something specific, not a total rejection of us.

References for further reading

Back K. and K. (1982). *Assertiveness at Work*. McGraw-Hill

Berne E. (1977). *Games People Play*. Grove Press

Biddle D. and Evenden R. (1989). *Human Aspects of Management*, 2nd edn. IPM

Bolton R. (1979). *People Skills*. Prentice-Hall

Clark N. *et al.* (1984). *Unfinished Business*. Gower Press

Cotler S. and Guerner J. (1979). *Assertion Training*. Champagne Illinois Research Press

Harris T.A. (1979). *I'm OK You're OK*. Pan

James M. and Jongward D. (1971). *Born to Win*. Addison-Wesley

Kelley C. (1979). *Assertion Training – A Facilitator's Guide*. University Associates

13

Developing negotiating skills

As well as developing influencing skills, the manager in dealing with interpersonal issues also requires an awareness of the principles and practice of negotiations, and the skills to negotiate effectively in a range of different situations.

Although at first sight negotiating skills may seem to represent a specialist area of expertise, used in industrial relations wage bargaining or commercial sales bargaining situations, in practice a typical manager will have opportunities to make use of negotiating skills in a range of relatively informal situations of varying degrees of importance. These could include:

- agreeing the timing of holidays with staff;
- discussing how best to use limited resources for competing projects;
- considering the salary and fringe benefits of a new employee;
- buying an item of equipment or an office service;
- the allocation of office space.

Negotiation involves the management of differences between two or more parties, with the implication that the parties involved will at some stage be willing to accept some movement from their original starting position, so that a solution acceptable to those involved can be reached.

Styles of negotiating

A range of different styles can be adopted in handling negotiations. Suppose your next door neighbour has the annoying habit (at least annoying to you) of getting up very early on a Sunday morning and cutting the lawn, upsetting your plans for sleeping late.

ACTIVITY 13.1

▼ How many approaches can you think of in dealing with the problem? List as many options as you can think of.

▽ You have a basic choice between 'harder' more contentious approaches, and 'softer' more conciliatory methods.

The model shown in Figure 13.1 suggests that in negotiating over differences your style will depend on:

- how assertive you and the other party are prepared to be;
- how cooperative you, and the other party are prepared to be.

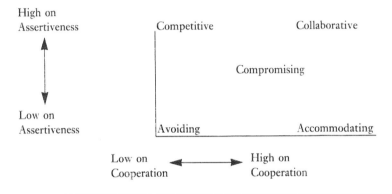

Figure 13.1   Negotiating styles.

Five distinct styles of handling negotiations emerge from this model.

(1) **Competitive** (high on assertiveness; low on cooperation)
This represents a battling, hard-nosed style, often typical of management and trade union negotiations and husband and wife arguments, with both parties striving hard to achieve their objectives, showing little cooperation towards each other. This style could be justified if, for example, unpopular courses of action such as cost-cutting have to be undertaken, or in emergencies when time does not permit other approaches.

(2) **Avoiding** (low on assertiveness; low on cooperation)
The kind of person who adopts this approach is likely to feel uncomfortable when facing negotiating situations, and prefers to avoid the problem of resolving differences through negotiation. In some situations this might be the right thing to do, if it is felt that the dangers of confronting the differences outweigh the benefits.

131

(3) **Accommodating** (low on assertiveness; high on cooperation)

This is very much the 'nice guy' or 'nice girl' approach in which the individual shows a high degree of cooperation towards the other party, but is often ready to yield on objectives, giving way to the other party. This approach could be justified if the issue over which negotiations are taking place is seen as trivial in importance. By yielding to the other party social credits may be generated, which can be used in subsequent negotiations on more important issues.

(4) **Compromising** (middle position on assertiveness; middle position on cooperation)

This represents a middle-of-the-road style in which the individual displays some assertiveness and some cooperation in negotiating with the other party. The person who adopts this style often enjoys the give and take of the tactics of bargaining in reaching compromised positions. It is often the case, however, that other factors may determine the use of the compromising style. The compromising style may be adopted if the issue under consideration does not justify the use of greater assertion associated with the competing and collaborative approaches. If both parties have roughly equal power and status but are pursuing opposite objectives, then the compromising approach to negotiation may be the only realistic option.

(5) **Collaborative** (high on assertion; high on cooperation)

This appears the most desirable style to adopt in negotiations, where alongside high assertiveness and determination to achieve objectives, high levels of cooperation are displayed in seeking a solution acceptable to all parties. This collaborative style is best illustrated in an ideal situation where two parties who are each pursuing their own, different objectives and advocating different courses of action A and B, talk through the issues in constructive, cooperative fashion and develop a new course of action C which permits both sets of objectives to be achieved.

While generally this is the preferred style for negotiating over major issues, there may be certain situations when, as previously noted, each of the other four styles can be justified.

ACTIVITY 13.2

▼ As a self-analysis and self-awareness activity to determine your preferred negotiating style, complete and score the questionnaire given in Figure 13.2.

Directions

Please read the following 30 pairs of statements marking with a tick your preferred option in each pair, in terms of which of each pair most closely fits your views and inclinations. Remember it is a forced choice exercise – to complete, you must select one of each of the 30 pairs.

1 A There are times when I let others take responsibility for solving the problem.
   B Rather than negotiate the things on which we disagree, I try to stress those things upon which we both agree.
2 A I try to find a compromise solution.
   B I attempt to deal with all of their and my concerns.
3 A I am usually firm in pursuing my goals.
   B I might try to soothe the other's feelings and preserve our relationship.
4 A I try to find a compromise solution.
   B I sometimes sacrifice my own wishes for the wishes of the other person.
5 A I consistently seek the other's help in working out a solution.
   B I try to do what is necessary to avoid useless tensions.
6 A I try to avoid creating unpleasantness for myself.
   B I try to win my position.
7 A I try to postpone the issue until I have had some time to think it over.
   B I give up some points in exchange for others.
8 A I am usually firm in pursuing my goals.
   B I attempt to get all concerns and issues immediately out in the open.
9 A I feel that differences are not always worth worrying about.
   B I make some effort to get my own way.
10 A I am firm in pursuing my goals.
   B I try to find a compromise solution.
11 A I attempt to get all concerns and issues immediately out in the open.
   B I might try to soothe the other's feelings and preserve our relationship.
12 A I sometimes avoid taking positions which would create controversy.
   B I will let them have some of their positions if they let me have some of mine.
13 A I propose a middle ground.
   B I press to get my points made.
14 A I tell him my ideas and ask for his.
   B I try to show him the logic and benefits of my positions.
15 A I might try to soothe the other's feelings and preserve our relationship.
   B I try to do what is necessary to avoid tensions.
16 A I try not to hurt the other's feelings.
   B I try to convince the other person of the merits of my position.
17 A I am usually firm in pursuing my goals.
   B I try to do what is necessary to avoid useless tensions.
18 A If it makes the other person happy, I might let him maintain his views.
   B I will let him have some of his positions if he lets me have some of mine.
19 A I attempt to get all concerns and issues immediately out in the open.
   B I try to postpone the issue until I have had some time to think it over.
20 A I attempt to immediately work through our differences.
   B I try to find a fair combination of gains and losses for both of us.
21 A In approaching negotiations, I try to be considerate of the other person's wishes.
   B I always lean toward a direct discussion of the problem.
22 A I try to find a position that is immediate between his and mine.
   B I assert my wishes.
23 A I am very often concerned with satisfying all our wishes.
   B There are times when I let others take responsibility for solving the problem.
24 A If the other's position seems very important to him, I would try to meet his wishes.
   B I try to get him to settle for a compromise.
25 A I try to show him the logic and benefits of my position.
   B In approaching negotiations, I try to be considerate of the other person's wishes.

26 A   I propose a middle ground.
    B   I am nearly always concerned with satisfying all our wishes.
27 A   I sometimes avoid taking positions that would create controversy.
    B   If it makes the others happy, I might let them maintain their views.
28 A   I am usually firm in pursuing my goals.
    B   I usually seek the other's help in working out a solution.
29 A   I propose a middle ground.
    B   I feel that differences are not always worth worrying about.
30 A   I try not to hurt the other's feelings.
    B   I always share the problem with the other person so that we can work it out.

Figure 13.2(a)   Negotiating style questionnaire.

Review of Activity 13.2

▽   Calculate the rank order of your results using Figure 13.2(b). Your highest score indicates your preferred negotiating style, your second highest score your preferred back-up style and so on. It is often of interest to take a careful look at your lower scores – indicating the style towards which you may have some feelings of aversion, and which you are probably likely to underuse.

Twelve is the highest score that you can obtain for any category, zero is the minimum, with six being the average. A second form of interpretation is to look at the spread amongst your five scores. If your highest score is a ten, eleven or twelve, and your lowest score a zero, one or two, this suggests that you have strongly held views and strong preferences regarding which styles you prefer to use or not to use. Alternatively if most of your scores are closely grouped in the five, six or seven area, this indicates relative indifference in selecting a style and a high degree of style flexibility, suggesting that you have few problems in shifting from one negotiating style to another.

It should be stressed that there are no right or wrong answers to this exercise. The activity is intended to encourage self-analysis and self-reflection. Do your results make sense in terms of the kind of work you do and the type of person you feel you are? Research evidence suggests, as previously noted, that there are situations where you could justify the use of each of the five styles identified. Two useful self-assessment questions therefore are:

(1) Do you tend to overuse the styles where you recorded a score in excess of six?

(2) Do you tend to underuse those styles where you recorded a score under six?

Principles of effective negotiation

Whatever the particular style adopted, there are a number of principles which, if followed are more likely to lead to effective negotiations.

Scoring

Circle the letters below which you circled on each item of the questionnaire.

	Competing (forcing)	Collaborating (problem solving)	Compromising (sharing)	Avoiding (withdrawal)	Accommodating (smoothing)
1.				A	B
2.		B	A		
3.	A				B
4.			A		B
5.		A		B	
6.	B			A	
7.			B	A	
8.	A	B			
9.	B			A	
10.	A		B		
11.		A			B
12.			B	A	
13.	B		A		
14.	B	A			
15.				B	A
16.	B				A
17.	A			B	
18.			B		A
19.		A		B	
20.		A	B		
21.		B			A
22.	B		A		
23.		A		B	
24.			B		A
25.	A				B
26.		B	A		
27.				A	B
28.	A	B			
29.			A	B	
30.		B			A

Total number of items circled in each column:

Competing	Collaborating	Compromising	Avoiding	Accommodating

Figure 13.2(b)   Results for negotiating style questionnaire.

Preparation

It may appear self-evident but a well-prepared negotiator is much more likely to succeed in terms of securing a favourable outcome than a poorly-prepared negotiator. Inadequate preparation means that much of the preparation takes place during the negotiation, which is likely to tax the skills and effectiveness of most people.

Preparing implies:

- Being clear about exactly what you want to achieve, namely, your own objectives.
- Research into the other party's interests, motivation and perception, to enable you to form as clear as view as possible of their objectives.
- Thinking through in advance the arguments you will put forward, and the likely rejoinders.
- Considering your fallback position or positions; working out how far, and for what reasons, you would be prepared to make concessions.
- Predicting how much flexibility the other party is likely to show; estimating their fallback position.
- Considering the implications of deadlock, if the negotiating process does not lead to an agreed outcome.

The preparation phase requires:

- Self analysis.
- Research into the problem or issue.
- Research into the other party.
- Creative thinking about the negotiating process.

Dialogue and discussion

In the discussion after presenting their respective objectives, the parties enter into dialogue. Good negotiating skills in the dialogue phase include:

- Careful thinking, to find out as much as possible about the other party and detect signals which might imply willingness to adjust their position.
- Avoidance of 'point-scoring' and defensive argument.
- Testing constructive options, by seeing if the other party is willing to trade concessions.
- Proposing constructive remedies.

Kennedy *et al.* (1986) draw attention to the value of the technique 'If you ... then I ...' in bargaining with the other party, in arriving at an acceptable conclusion. The technique of starting with 'If you ...' lets the other party see clearly the price you expect them to pay for any concession you are prepared to yield.

Closing

The final skill in negotiating is to achieve a satisfactory close. This will entail accurate and detailed summarizing skills, to ensure both parties are in no doubt what has been agreed. Ideally this should take place both orally, and in writing.

Closing will be easier the larger the overlap in the positions of the two parties, as shown in Figure 13.3.

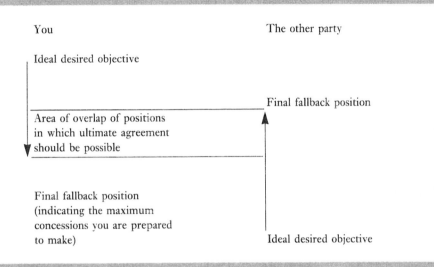

Figure 13.3 Negotiating positions.

Conclusion

Morse (1976) quotes a number of attributes for the ideal negotiation leader or participant:

- Be able to say 'No' effectively.
- Inspire confidence.
- Be a patient listener.
- Be able to 'take it'.
- Have a sense of humour.
- Be able to think in an organized fashion.
- Possess good communication skills.
- Be persuasive.

Kniveton and Towers (1978) stress the importance of training managers in negotiating skills – we cannot expect managers automatically to display the skills required and apply them in negotiations.

ACTIVITY 13.3

▼ Two sisters were arguing over one orange. After ten minutes they compromised and cut the orange in half.

This was not the best solution.

Can you find a better one by:

(1) Separating the people from the problem – arguing got in the way.
(2) Focusing on interests not positions – their position was they both wanted the whole orange.
(3) Creating an option for mutual benefit.

Review of Activity 13.3

▽ The sisters were so busy arguing that they failed to see that the problem was to solve a problem. The people difficulties related to their desire to have the whole orange, which became their position, and which was ultimately yielded by both in compromise. They both won half and lost half.

Once the orange had been divided they retired to separate rooms. The first ate her half and threw away the peel. The second threw away the fruit and kept the skin to make a cake. Their positions were opposed. Their interests, had they been explored, were not.

References for further reading

Kennedy G. *et al.* (1986). *Managing Negotiations*, 3rd edn. Hutchison
Kniveton B. and Towers B. (1978) *Training for Negotiating*. Business Books
Morse B. (1976) *How to Negotiate the Labour Agreement*. Trends Publishing Co

14

Developing one-to-one behavioural skills

In Part Two we have been examining the personal development areas of face-to-face skills. Our awareness of ourselves and others helps us better understand what is going on between us. Self confidence enables us to make effective choices about how we behave and the skills of influencing increase the probability of us meeting our needs without negating the needs of others.

If the aim of our face-to-face contact is to achieve both a positive outcome and good relationships, then the three development areas need to be reinforced by a fourth, behavioural skills.

Behavioural skills are the things we need to do when we are communicating with one or more people, in a sense to capitalize upon our awareness, confidence and influencing skills. It involves doing the right thing at the right time, and doing it well.

There are two skill areas. One is related to the **task**, such as giving, seeking and managing the facts, ideas and opinions which are exchanged in relation to the purpose of the meeting. The other is to do with the **process**, or the feelings and relationships, which affects the climate in which the task is being conducted.

In organizations, managers, supervisors and professionals usually spend most of their time communicating. A great deal of this is face-to-face. Over half is one-to-one and the rest is with several people in meetings of various kinds.

One-to-one: behavioural skills

The more formal and planned one-to-one contacts are often described as interviews, when two people are communicating with a designated organizational purpose, such as recruitment, appraisal, coaching, problem solving, briefing or counselling. More frequent are the unplanned, informal chats which are need driven and which oil the wheels of the organization in pursuit of its objectives. The skills needed to achieve successful task and process outcomes are the same for both types of one-to-one communication.

The general approach, or style, is the pattern of relationship that you try to establish during your communication with the other person. These can be classified as Dominant, Conversational and Counselling (see Figure 14.1). The styles have parallels with the 'influencing' orientations of aggression, assertion and passivity, in terms of control, direction and sharing, but there are differences as well. The counselling style involves encouraging the other person to take the lead and make most contributions to the exchange, but it is an active and deliberate 'passivity'.

Your style choice	Dominant	Conversational	Counselling
Task			
Influence	You use power	Both share control	You listen actively
Time share	You have most	Evenly balanced	You have least
Problem solver	Your role	Both collaborate	Their role
Process			
View of relationship	You are one up	Mutuality	Helper
Feelings	Threat	Amicability	Supportive

Figure 14.1 One-to-one styles.

One-to-one: rapport skills

Success in achieving the aims of the mutual exchange will depend upon the two people's skills in developing and maintaining rapport. It is this which affects the climate of feelings and relationships in which the task will be conducted. As mentioned in Chapter 8, Robert Bales called this *social emotional behaviour* (see Figure 8.2).

Social emotional positive behaviour is part of everybody's interactive repertoire and it has the effect of creating good feelings such as warmth, confidence, supportiveness and a relationship in which both people are comfortable. It becomes a skill when it is spontaneously employed from an awareness that it will be pleasant, as well as helpful to the task to be accomplished. If there is tension, anxiety or bad feeling then investment in social emotional positive behaviour is necessary. Welcoming a stranger with a handshake, friendly words and acts of kindness or boosting the self image of a shy person who has been verbally mugged by an interpersonal bully, are illustrations.

Some people have a strongly dominant task orientation to interaction, particularly at work. They are amongst the ones who are most likely to experience problems of rapport and difficulties in face-to-face relationships.

We can develop social emotional skills by becoming aware of the need and cultivating the behaviours which work for us. In fact we all have them in our repertoire. Skill development often means taking them out more often and practising for improvement.

The other side of this particular skill is recognizing our social emotional negative behaviour. It is probable that much of the behaviour which produces bad feelings and poor relationships is not intended to have that effect, reminding us of the importance of awareness and feedback about our 'blind selves'.

ACTIVITY 14.1

▼ Can you identify verbal and non-verbal examples of social emotional positive and negative behaviour from your observation of others? What impact does it have on the other person and the relationship? Television and video is an ideal way to observe interaction for illustrations of social emotional behaviour.

What about your own social emotional behaviour? Try to assess it at times during your contacts with others. If you are studying in a supportive group, feedback sharing could afford some valuable illustrations and insights.

The four stages of a positive face-to-face relationship

Face-to-face interaction is not static. There are stages that a communication relationship, such as an interview, moves through as it matures. These can be called:

| (1) **Joining** | Getting together and establishing or re-establishing a relationship; discovering mutual expectations and a map of the immediate future; finding out how to work together; getting physically and emotionally comfortable. |
| (2) **Belonging** | Fitting in with each other; accepting each other; |

	feeling mutual commitment;
	feeling the relationship is 'right';
	identifying with what is happening.
(3) **Contributing**	Having an impact on what is happening;
	using valued knowledge and skills;
	feeling a sense of progress.
(4) **Concluding**	Reaching agreement;
	deciding future action;
	cementing the relationship.

The four stages of a negative face-to-face relationship

There is a mirror image of the positive development of a relationship, which is associated with stunting or regression. This would be linked to a climate characterized by social emotional negative behaviour by one or both parties. The four stages are:

(1) **Separating**	Moving away from each other at the outset;
	hiding personal agendas;
	ignoring the other's needs;
	becoming physically and emotionally uncomfortable.
(2) **Disowning**	Unilateral or mutual rejection;
	feeling distrust;
	discounting the other person.
(3) **Withholding**	Not offering help or expertise;
	feeling stuck or blocked.
(4) **Dismissing**	Disagreement, indecision, imposition;
	being dismissive of the other person;
	undermining the relationship.

Social emotional behaviour and relationship development

Relationship Stage	SE+ Climate	SE- Climate
Initial	Joining	Separating
Second	Belonging	Disowning
Third	Contributing	Withholding
Final	Concluding	Dismissing

Figure 14.2 Social emotional behaviour and relationship development.

Movement through to a successful conclusion depends upon the use of social emotional behaviour appropriate to each stage of a relationship (see Figure 14.2). We have personal needs active in our contact with others, and these determine the nature of the four communication phases. It is possible to move from a positive phase across to a negative phase if the climate deteriorates, although the chances of this are reduced if the earlier stages have been negotiated successfully.

Similarly, the pair could move from a negative to a positive phase, but they would first probably need to move back to meet the needs present but blocked at the earlier stages.

Abraham Maslow (1970) identified a sequence of needs that we seek to meet in order to achieve personal development and growth. These are:

(1) Physiological
(2) Security
(3) Social
(4) Reputation
(5) Self esteem
(6) Self fulfilment

These needs could define what we are seeking from our lives in general or, we suggest, from a particular face-to-face event. Subsequently Clayton Alderfer (1979) has proposed a development of Maslow's model, called ERG. He suggests there is a sequence of three needs defined as existence, relatedness and growth.

Our interpretative definition of this personal needs system is as follows:

(1) **Existence**   Physical and security needs, which if not met make our 'existence' feel threatened.
(2) **Relatedness** Social needs of being accepted, feeling that you belong where you are, friendship and fitting in with others.
(3) **Growth**   Having the chance to develop and use our skills, knowledge and our 'self'.

Alderfer suggests that an unfulfilled need will grow in importance. If, and as, an earlier need is met, the next need will emerge to govern behaviour. If this next need is frustrated or blocked, the earlier need will resume its importance and will actually become inflated to dominate an individual's behaviour. This needs system determines the four stages of face-to-face relationships and the appropriate social emotional behaviour needed for progression through them. Any act which affects a personal ERG need active at that moment will be social emotional.

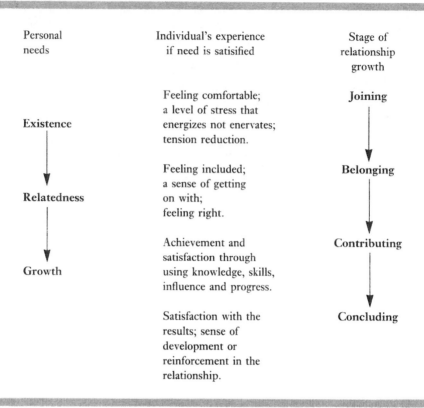

Personal needs	Individual's experience if need is satisfied	Stage of relationship growth
Existence	Feeling comfortable; a level of stress that energizes not enervates; tension reduction.	Joining
Relatedness	Feeling included; a sense of getting on with; feeling right.	Belonging
Growth	Achievement and satisfaction through using knowledge, skills, influence and progress.	Contributing
	Satisfaction with the results; sense of development or reinforcement in the relationship.	Concluding

Figure 14.3   Relationship between needs, experience and relationship growth.

Social emotional behaviour, relationship growth and successful outcomes to face-to-face contacts

The needs, experience and relationship growth model, outlined in Figure 14.3, suggests that social emotional behaviour is positive when it meets a personal need that is active, and that this in turn produces good feelings which help the relationship progress. After the joining phase has been completed, the belonging phase emerges. The duration of these depends upon the needs appetite of the individuals and their success in meeting the other person's needs.

The contributing phase will be the time when the task or business is mostly conducted, but it is not neutral in the social emotional sense. Invitations to offer knowledge and recognition for the contributions are examples of how good feelings are maintained during activity related to this part of the model. If the relatedness or existence needs have not been well satisfied, they may emerge again during the conversation. If they have been poorly met the individual may have difficulty focusing on the task, until sufficient attention has been paid to them.

When the contributing phase has been completed, the concluding phase ensures that neither the task, feelings nor relationships are left unfinished, and the groundwork is prepared for future contacts.

The model indicates that social emotional negative behaviour is anything that one person does which has the effect (not necessarily the intent) of frustrating a need that the other person has related to the interaction at that moment. It will be something which makes them feel bad.

Being made to feel unwelcome militates against the joining phase, and is likely to inhibit movement through to the belonging phase. There may be many responses to initial coldness, hostility or indifference and to its continuation through to the stage where the perpetrator of the negatives may wish to get down to the business.

If the earlier steps have been neglected, the other party may resist commencing the contributions part of the conversation. They may still be seeking reassurance or acceptance, or be concentrating in returning in kind the negatives they perceive they have been sent by the other person. It is possible that some people would still be able and prepared to contribute to the business in hand, but probably in a diminished way, depending upon their needs in the opening phases and the degree of frustration. At the task level they may accommodate the other person by complying, for example if they are very dependent upon them. Another response is to compete and try to show the other who is cleverest or best and in some sense to defeat them. In all events it is unlikely they would reach the concluding phase in its task and feelings/relationship sense.

The effects of positive and negative behaviours on a relationship are illustrated in Figures 14.4 and 14.5 respectively.

Positive behaviour	Needs and relationship growth
You feel welcome, alert, comfortable, refreshed and relaxed as a result of who you are and how you are received.	**Existence**: Joining and then beginning to belong.
'It's good to see you...' Handshake, smiles and warmth. Informal personalized conversation. 'How is ...' 'Would you like a ...' 'I was most impressed with your...' Showing confidence. Displaying humour. 'Do you remember that great...' 'When we last met ...'	The time spent on a phase will depend on the needs appetites of those involved.
	Relatedness: Belonging and preparing to contribute.
You feel accepted, wanted and possibly friendliness.	
'I'd love to hear what you have ...' Display of expressive open gestures.	

145

'That was an excellent job you did...'
'I've heard a lot about...'
Leaning towards. Listening actively.
'Your idea proved very valuable.'
'What do you think about...'
'Will you help us...'
'How would you...'

Growth:
Contributing and
concluding with
a sense of both
achievement and
satisfaction.

You feel valued and feel good at both
what you are doing and how it is
being recognized by the other person.

'This has been very helpful...'
'It all looks most promising...'
'Many thanks.'
Smiles and handshake. Good steady
eye contact.
'I look forward...'
'Good to see you again/get to know you.'

You feel satisfied with the
time spent together.
The task has been progressed
and the relationship has
developed and will start
at a higher level next
time, although you will
both need to rejoin to a degree.

You have shared in the interaction at both task and social emotional levels by **collaborating**.

Figure 14.4 Illustration: positive behaviour and relationship growth.

Negative behaviour

**Needs and
relationship stunting**

You feel unwelcome, confused,
uncomfortable, fatigued and anxious
as a result of what has happened and
how you have been received.

Existence:
Rejected by the other
person.

Cold indifference to open hostility.
No handshake and scowls at one
extreme to impersonal straight
to business at the other end
of the negative spectrum.
'Right. I want to know...'

Most of you will not
want to move to the
next phase. If the
joining has been like
this, neither of you
will expect much from

'What the hell were you up to...'
Rolling eyes upwards into sockets.
Glaring and finger wagging.

You continue to feel rejected,
and uncertain about the indifference
shown towards you.

'I didn't like your...'
Displaying sarcasm.
Aggressive tone and mannerisms.
Ignoring.
Interrupting.
Not listening.

You feel discounted and bad about
what is happening to your
contributions and the lack of
recognition from the other person.

'Now you listen to me...'
Focusing exclusively on the task.
'What needs to be done is ...'
'I'll tell you what I think... '
'The problem appears to be... '
No attempt made to involve you.
Yawns and looks at watch
when you speak.
Puts down your contribution.
'I've got a better idea.'
'Can't you do better than that?'
'How much do we pay you!'
'Well, that's it then. I'm off.'
Departs or turns back on you so that you
know the 'audience' is over.

the next phase. Your
needs, however, will
be what they are.

Relatedness:
Not accepted as
as a person.

Some may persist in
trying to relate to
to the other person.

Growth:
Having failed to get a
positive response to
your efforts to relate
you fall back to self-
defence. Choices are:
(1) Hide – withdraw
emotionally or even
physically.
(2) Comply – nod, agree
and just listen but
contributing mentally
at the 10% level.
(3) Take up arms, by
either showing anger
or trying to show how
good you are. Your aim
is to beat the other!

You feel dissatisfied and the task
has probably not progressed and
the relationship certainly will
have deteriorated.

Your response is to **avoid**, **accommodate** or **compete**.

Figure 14.5   Illustration: negative behaviour and relationship stunting.

Task skills

The social emotional feelings and relationships skills are important in themselves, and provide the climate in which the task can be conducted. They are necessary but not sufficient to produce an effective outcome to a formal interview or a less formal one-to-one meeting. Task skills also need to be developed and applied. It will be noticed that task contributions or interventions also have an effect upon movement through the four stages of development of the relationship outlined earlier.

Effective task behaviour involves:

- Establishing why you are talking together. What is the purpose?
- Identifying how you are going to set about it. What is the method?
- Setting an 'agenda' if it is helpful. Where are you going?
- Agreeing your mutual expectations. What parts will you both play?
- Controlling by the agenda, periodic summaries and questions. Where are we and where should we be going?
- Checking agreement and concluding with agreed action. What has been decided and what next?

Figure 14.6 relates task behaviour to movement through the face-to-face stages.

Stages	Task skills and focus
Joining Getting together and mapping the immediate future.	What is our purpose? What is our method? What is our agenda?
Belonging Fitting in with each other.	What parts will we both play?
Contributing Having an impact and sense of progress.	Where are we and where should we be going?
Concluding Agreement and future action	What has been decided and what next?

Figure 14.6 Task skills and movement through the face-to-face stages.

Both task and process skills help the face-to-face relationship progress through the stages to a satisfactory outcome for both.

Questioning methods

When we are conversing one-to-one, a major need is to seek information. Our method of questioning will determine how successful we are, and will also influence the way our one-to-one style is perceived. We also use questions as a means of control without endangering rapport. For example, many people prefer to be moved on to another area by a question rather than by being told to do so. Question types are related to our one-to-one style as shown in Figure 14.7.

Question	Style
Directive	Dominant
Leading	
Topic changing	
Probing	Conversational
Developing	
Open ended	
Reflecting back	Counselling

Figure 14.7   Questions and one-to-one styles.

A dominant style has a preponderance of direct and leading questions, much like an interrogation, whereas a conversational style would range from topic changing to open ended questions. Counselling would use mainly open ended and reflecting back.

Like questioning methods, active listening was seen as an important task skill in Part One when recruitment interviewing was being considered. Active listening is summarized in Figure 14.8 (see also Figure 10.5 on page 110).

Active listening means:
- Understanding what the other person is saying.
- Detecting non-verbal messages.
- Sensing the other's feelings.
- Encouraging and influencing the speaker.

Active listening involves:

- Reducing distractions, including internal dialogue.
- Suspending judgement.
- Verbal responses – paraphrasing; reflecting back thoughts and feelings; paralanguage (Mmm … Uh huh … etc.).
- Noticing non-verbal responses – facial expression; eye contact; mixed messages; body movement etc.
- Attending behaviour – smiling; asking relevant questions; nodding; looking interested.
- Avoiding non-attending behaviour – yawning; doodling; checking watch etc.

Figure 14.8   Active listening.

References for further reading

Alderfer C.P. (1979). *Existence, Relatedness and Growth*. Free Press
Bales R.F. (1950). *Interaction Process Analysis*. Addison-Wesley
Biddle D. and Evenden R. (1989). *Human Aspects of Management*, 2nd edn. IPM
Honey P. (1988). *Improve Your Skills With People*. IPM
Kakabadse A. *et al.* (1988). *Working in Organisations*. Penguin
Maslow A.H. (1970). *Motivation and Personality*. Harper and Row
Schein E. (1988). *Process Consultation* Vol. 1. Addison-Wesley

15

Developing group behavioural skills

Much of our communication at work is with several other people. As with our one-to-one contacts, these may be formal or informal and planned or spontaneous meetings to achieve both individual, group and organizational purposes. In all types of meeting these various purposes will be met or marred depending upon the behaviour displayed by those involved, and this chapter looks at the skills and insights that can help the achievement of positive outcomes.

There is always the need to avoid the results of the apocryphal committee which met to design a racehorse and instead produced a camel. Indeed, effective groups can achieve that highly desirable and elusive quality known as **synergy**. This is when the group becomes greater than the sum of its parts, the quart does fit into the pint pot and the meeting arrives at outcomes that could not have been reached by the individuals working on their own.

The person who leads or chairs a meeting will have a crucial role in influencing the meeting, but the behaviour and awareness of all members can be critical to its success. There are many leader roles and behaviours and all members can display them. If they do, then the positive outcomes are more likely to be achieved. Group leadership is divisible.

It is useful to spend time prior to a meeting reflecting upon the factors which could affect the task and process. These are listed in Figure 15.1.

Why is the meeting taking place?
Do you have any preferred way of handling the meeting?
What should be on the agenda?
What information will be essential and who has it?
Who is/should be attending?
Do they need briefing/interviewing beforehand?
What personal/departmental interests will be in play?
What are the personal characteristics of those attending?
Will anybody need particular attention?
What decisions will need to be made?
How should they be made?
Will the environment/seating positions/timing be significant?

Figure 15.1   Preparing for the meeting.

151

ACTIVITY 15.1

▼ Think about the one-to-one and group communication you have experienced. Can you identify the similarities and differences between them?

Communication one-to-one and in groups

▽ There are similarities between one-to-one and group communication. For example, the social emotional positive and negative behaviours examined in the previous chapter will affect relationships and feelings at the group level as well. Quite often, meetings can be experienced as a series of one-to-one interactions between different pairs.

Another similarity is that individuals will have the same personal needs of existence, relatedness and growth that were identified in the interview context, only they may be more difficult to meet within the group. Like the one-to-one face-to-face relationship, the group also has positive or negative stages of development.

Compared with a paired communication, group communication has important differences.

Complexity

The more people you have, the more sets of interactions and relationships are mathematically possible. There are proportionately more factors coming into play which affect the dynamics of the group, such as individual verbal and non-verbal behaviour and the range of personal needs. Some specifically group factors exist which do not apply to the pair, such as group norms and pressure exerted collectively.

Conflict

More potential clashes are possible, simply due to the complexity and numbers. There will be more conflicts of needs and interests, more problems of aggression and passivity and the chance of cliques and tribal wars developing. This gives more scope for anger, hostility, discounting and misunderstandings.

Control

Control can mean knowing where you are, where you are going and influencing people and proceedings so that you get there. This is often difficult when you have only yourself to manage. It is much more difficult when several people are involved. People may not be with you, in terms of where the meeting is and what it should be trying to achieve. Influence and control are also things about which people come into conflict. We have already suggested that there is greater complexity, and it is more of a problem noticing and influencing all the things that will affect the task and process of a meeting.

Consensus and decision making

It is not always easy arriving at agreement with just one other person. The problems are compounded when there are several people involved with differing needs and goals.

Group behavioural skills and insights

In the context of group communication, Edgar Schein has made the fundamental distinction between three aspects of behaviour which affect how well a group functions. They are self oriented, group maintenance and task behaviour. This can be interpreted as groups having three needs to be met if positive outcomes are to be achieved.

(1) Individual needs   What an individual needs from the meeting.
(2) Group needs   What is needed for collaboration.
(3) Task needs   What has to be done to achieve the task.

Failure to meet one of the needs will have a negative impact upon the other two. For example, if frustrated an individual may display aggression, thus disrupting collaboration at the group level, and preventing the group from dealing with the task.

Individual needs

A meeting is a temporary group, and whenever it convenes there is a process where the individual fits into it anew. The needs described by Alderfer, which we have defined in an interactive context, relate closely to the needs of individuals in groups identified by Schein. Poorly met needs will have the effect of producing negative individual behaviour.

Schein (1988) suggests that when we join a group we are concerned about **identity**. Who are we going to be in this group? What role will we have and will it fit with our self image or reputation? There is strong uncertainty at this stage linked closely to our 'existence' needs.

He suggests that we will be concerned also about our **acceptance** by the group. This is similar to our relatedness needs, such as feeling we belong and experiencing friendship.

We will also have concerns about **control**. Will we have influence? Who will have power and will their influence be acceptable to us? This is often related to being included or excluded in the task activity by those in control, or gaining recognition from them for ourselves and the quality of contribution that we make to the meeting. These aspects will affect whether we will meet our growth needs.

A fourth factor identified by Edgar Schein which affects our orientation is whether the specific **personal needs** we have at the meeting are part of the group's goals. This will influence how much we invest ourselves in the meeting, and will determine our commitment throughout the proceedings.

The members' contributions to the task and group needs will be limited by the degree to which these four individual need areas are being met.

The group leadership implications of individual needs are given in Figure 15.2.

Identity	Roles and procedures for conducting the meeting should be clarified early in the life of a group. Patience should be shown whilst members work out their roles. This is a reason why new members are cautious initially, and it will take time for them to find their way.
Acceptance	A new group may move from formality to a more relaxed informality over time. Both in these circumstances and in integrating new members, emphasis needs to be placed upon the social emotional process of welcoming, supporting and showing acceptance.
Control	New groups will take time to sort this out and come to terms with the emerging pecking order. It is a part of the group getting to know each other and new members. As with the other needs, the role of leaders is not to eliminate them, but to recognize them as part of the process of all groups, and to act as midwife to them.
Personal needs	Leaders should show interest in the needs of individual members. Schein suggests that time should always be allocated for people to say what they want from a group, so that all are involved and committed to the task.

Figure 15.2   Group implications of individual needs.

Group needs

Groups can move through the same stages of growth or stunting that we saw with paired relationships. Similarly the direction in which they move will be determined by the extent to which individual needs are met and behavioural skills are displayed (see Figure 14.2).

Just as positive behaviour needs to be directed to individuals to meet their needs, so it needs to be aimed at the group to create a climate of collaboration and to avoid blocks and dead-end schisms.

The aim is not to eliminate disagreement. Differences of opinion often form the basis of creativity and development of ideas, effective solutions and decisions. The purpose is rather to create a climate of relationships and feelings within the group where it is possible for differences about the task to be aired, without threat or fear.

The underlying norms are supportive and constructive, with different views being perceived as helpful and the purpose being to integrate the group at both the task and process levels.

Our own work with groups has supported the work of Robert Bales, Edgar Schein and others, that there are clearly identifiable behaviours which help or hinder the meeting of group needs and the achievement of a collaborative climate.

Group needs: positive and negative behavioural skills

Positive behaviour	*Negative behaviour*
Integrating	**Fragmenting**
Getting the group to fit together and accept their differences. Exploring the causes of hostility and dealing with negative behaviour.	Getting the group to split and to clash about their differences. Stimulating hostility between members.

Rules

(1) Emphasize that each member has a contribution to make to the group activity.

(2) Reward collaboration and positive behaviour.

(3) Confront negative behaviour.

(4) Welcome differences and put them in the context of the need for a common solution.

Positive behaviour	*Negative behaviour*
Yielding	**Entrenching**
Encouraging flexibility and a will to compromise.	Stimulating rigidity and digging in to protect a position.

Rules

(1) Remember that threat can lead to digging in.

(2) Encourage and reward a will to yield and 'move towards' the other position.

Positive behaviour	*Negative behaviour*
Sharing	**Hogging**
Ensuring that the 'air time' is shared.	Dominating the 'air time' or reinforcing those who do.

Rules

(1) Spot and bring in the low contributor.

(2) Steer away from the high contributor.

Positive behaviour	*Negative behaviour*

Encouraging
Making the group or individuals
feel their contributions are
valued and welcomed.

Discouraging
Devaluing the contributions
of others.

Rules
(1) Give recognition for contributions, especially for those low in confidence.
(2) Avoid putting people down.

Positive behaviour	*Negative behaviour*

Progressing
Reinforce the group identity
by showing how the group is
working together and moving
forward.

Regressing
Creating a sense of failure
within the group about its
handling of itself and its
lack of progress.

Rules
(1) Emphasize what the group is achieving.
(2) Establish milestones so that the group can measure its progress.

Positive behaviour	*Negative behaviour*

Constructing
Building on others' ideas by
looking for the good in them.
Looking for commonality and
building upon it.

Demolishing
Trying to destroy the ideas
of others. Always seeking
weaknesses and dwelling on
upon them.

Rules
(1) First look for what you agree with in other people's ideas.
    'What I like about that idea is …'
(2) Focus on common interests. Avoid taking positions.

Positive behaviour	*Negative behaviour*

Asserting
Stating your needs and opinions
in a non-threatening way.

Aggressing/withdrawing
Attacking the person rather
than commenting upon their ideas.
Avoiding making constructive
criticism.

Rules
(1) Do not avoid disagreement and necessary confrontation, but do it with respect
    for the other person and their views.

Task needs

Meeting individual and group needs has to be complemented by task skills for the group to achieve its organizational purpose efficiently and effectively. Individuals at the growth stage and groups at the contributing phase are ready to tackle the task.

Three task areas can be identified. They are:

(1) Behavioural skills.
(2) Problem solving phases and synchronization
(3) Decision-making mode.

Task needs: behavioural skills

There are behaviours which need to be performed or prompted if the group is to tackle the task, whatever it may be, whether it is connected to problem solving, decision making or knowledge extension. The areas most frequently identified as significant are:

Starting	The initial task need is to establish why the group is there. What is its purpose? What is it there to achieve? What procedure should the group adopt? How should it set about its task?
Information exchange	Giving – verbal clarity. Seeking – active listening; judicious questioning; noting and absorbing; clarifying and checking understanding.
Developing	Refining and building upon the ideas proposed.
Path finding	Where are we and where are we going? Using summaries and questions to give direction.
Decision making	Helping the group make procedural and concluding decisions.
Action planning	Identifying what action has been agreed, who is to take it and by when.

Task needs: problem solving phase and synchronization

If the group is tackling a problem, it is important that the group is together at the same stage of the process. Much confusion and bad feeling can result from people being scattered across the phases. It is a key task skill to remind the group of these six stages, and where they are at any time.

(1) Awareness   Do we all know there is a problem?
(2) Definition   What is the problem? What are the different angles?
(3) Suggestions   What can we do about the problem?
(4) Assessing   Is that a good idea?
(5) Developing   Can we develop the idea?
(6) Deciding   What has been decided?

Task needs: decision–making mode

It is not only the decisions which are important, but the manner in which they are made. Schein suggests that decision modes can be differentiated by the degree of involvement that all members have in making the decision.

Authority based	The most powerful person makes the decision.
Elite based	A small number make the decision. Perhaps the most powerful, most articulate or most interested.
Majority based	Most of those present indicate their support for the decision.
Consensus	All accept the decision and feel they have had opportunity to influence it, but do not necessarily agree with it.
Unanimity	All agree with the decision.

Many factors influence the mode chosen, including power, convention, interests, personality, expertise and time pressure. As a general rule, broad-based commitment, a significant social emotional factor, increases as the mode moves from authority to unanimity. This affects willingness to contribute to the task and to put energy into subsequent action.

There is a summary of group behavioural skills in Figure 15.3.

Group behavioural skills summary

INDIVIDUAL		GROUP		TASK
Needs		**Stages**		**Skills**
Existence	Identity	*Positive*	*Negative*	Starting
Relatedness	Acceptance	Joining	Separating	Information exchange
Growth	Control	Belonging	Disowning	Developing
	Personal	Contributing	Withholding	Path finding
		Concluding	Dismissing	Decision making
				Action planning
		Behaviour		
		Positive	*Negative*	**Problem solving**
		Integrating	Fragmenting	Awareness and
		Yielding	Entrenching	definition
		Encouraging	Discouraging	Suggestions
		Progressing	Regressing	Assessing
		Constructing	Demolishing	Development
				Deciding
				Authority; Elite;
				Majority; Consensus;
				Unanimity

Figure 15.3 Group behavioural skills summary.

The administration of meetings

In running meetings, or being a participant in meetings, it is important to keep in mind the administrative requirements.

Agendas

An agenda assists in organizing a meeting; by providing an indication of the subjects that will be discussed, members are not only aware of what to expect but can also undertake preparation beforehand. Ideally, therefore, the agenda should be circulated in advance. The agenda in addition clarifies the time and place of the meeting.

Seating arrangements

While the size and nature of the room in which a meeting is held influences the tone of the meeting, the seating arrangements are likely to have a more substantial impact in influencing the flow of information and ideas, and the development of dialogue. For instance, while an arrangement of seats in rows facing the front may be fine for receiving presentations, it is unlikely to be suitable for a meeting aimed at encouraging participation among members. A U-shaped seating plan, where most members can maintain eye contact with one another, is more likely to be suitable for participative meetings.

Minutes

When the meeting has been completed, it is unlikely to be over in that actions agreed will have to be implemented. It is important, therefore, that one member at the meeting undertakes the role of secretary, in recording key points discussed and preparing minutes for subsequent circulation to members. Since they should contain a note of who is expected to do what in a specified timescale, minutes form an important mechanism for follow-up, feedback, control and coordination.

ACTIVITY 15.2

It is suggested that you create an opportunity to illustrate and perhaps use the skills and insights covered in this chapter. Figure 15.3 will provide a guide. You could use the model, or parts of it, to observe a real meeting.

The following Insupply case scenario could be used to develop your own script of a meeting to illustrate the positive and/or negative aspects of group skills.

If you are studying in a group, the Insupply case scenario could form the basis of a role play, or you could perform one in which you could all realistically participate. Observers could divide the Figure 15.3 model into areas for illustration, feedback and discussion.

Insupply case study: Colin Smith's meeting

Colin Smith arranged a meeting on the morning of Bob Armstrong's first day as Administration Manager. His aims were to introduce Bob to his three assistants, to outline his new role and to discuss the challenges and opportunities in the future.

He had in mind the need to help Bob get off to a good start with his staff and to define the tasks of relocation and the introduction of the new systems and technology, in which the Administration Department would have a significant role.

Colin met Bob for 30 minutes prior to the meeting to welcome him aboard, to offer his support whilst he settled into the post, and to brief him about the department.

Colin said that the three assistants were basically sound and reliable, but they each had their small difficulties.

Sally Bullen had been with him for eight years, first as his typing pool supervisor in his old company Buroquip. After the merger with Gloprint her responsibilities expanded in Insupply, where she supervised the pool of administrative staff who worked in different areas. She arranged for the recruitment of temporary staff, from VDU operators to DP Systems Consultants. She was very competent in this aspect and was both interested and able in administrative technology and operation.

She was less knowledgeable in her additional responsibilities for buildings and security, and relied upon Colin, her assistant and outside contractors in this part of her job.

She was articulate and confident in most respects, but Colin felt she made too many demands on his time, especially about buildings. She enjoyed social talk too much in his view, but this was a small price to pay for her enthusiasm and efficiency.

Ekoku Inanga had been recruited to run the PR side of the merger and two years ago added mail, telecommunications, internal communication and quality circles to his role, as Administrative Assistant: Communication. He was well qualified and did his job very competently. The house magazine was highly regarded and he organized and positively influenced the quality circle meetings, which made a real contribution to morale and productivity.

He lacked technical interest and knowledge, which was a handicap in the telecommunication side of his role in Colin's eyes, although Ekoku did not think this was important. He was creative but was rather disorganized and did not manage his time well in Colin's opinion. Sometimes important things were not done on time.

He related well to people generally, but sometimes expressed his frustration aggressively, as he did with Colin over what he saw as lack of discussion over the recruitment process for the new Administration Manager. He was ambitious and would have liked promotion himself, perhaps to that role. Colin had talked with him about a possible promotion into marketing later.

Colin suspected that he would not make life too easy for Bob Armstrong, although his desire for promotion would probably prevent too much obstructiveness, but he did have a short fuse these days.

Peter Paine was the Administration Assistant: Procurement. He purchased all the equipment and supplies needed internally by Insupply, and had an assistant to help in this task.

He was a master with detail and very efficient in his job, but he was a very reticent person. He was reluctant to meet suppliers face-to-face and got his assistant to chase them if they looked like missing a delivery date. He made few contributions to Colin's periodic departmental meetings, through lack of confidence. He was reluctant to get involved in change and seemed afraid of new technology, although he was very adept at using what he had.

Colin felt his diffidence and resistance to change would make it difficult for Bob Armstrong to relate to him, and could pose serious problems in the situation of rapid change which awaited them all in the near future.

The three assistants arrived together at Colin's office where they took coffee and were introduced to Bob Armstrong.

Colin Smith opened the meeting.

References for further reading

Alderfer C.P. (1979). *Existence, Relatedness and Growth*. Free Press

Biddle D. and Evenden R. (1989). *Human Aspects of Management*, 2nd edn. IPM

Kakabadse A. *et al.* (1988). *Working in Organisations*. Penguin

Maslow A.H. (1970). *Motivation and Personality*. Harper and Row

Rackham N. (1977) *Behaviour Analysis in Training*. McGraw-Hill

Schein E. (1988). *Process Consultation* Vol. 1. Addison–Wesley

Tuckman B.W. (1965). Developmental Sequences in Small Groups. *Psychological Bulletin* **63** (6)

16

Developing relationships

In Part Two, we have been looking at how to work positively with others for mutual growth and development, and have focused upon interface skills. This involves doing the right thing well, at the right time, to achieve the right outcome.

Behaviourists consider that we can only act effectively upon what we and others do, and should not try to explain or try to understand people and relationships in terms of what people are like. They feel that attempts to interpret our inner processes will be unhelpful at best and meaningless at worst. This is based on the view that what we can't observe we can't understand. Others, sometimes referred to as the humanistic school, feel that simply because we are human and have insight into our experience, we are able to develop ideas which help us to understand others, and that such understanding can assist us manage our relationships with them.

In many relationships it will be sufficient to rely upon our behavioural skills, yet there will remain some people we find hard work; some we never seem to get on with; others who leave us bemused; and still others who leave us feeling used.

If these people are significant for us we will want to improve our relationship, and this may require that we develop our understanding of ourself and the other person. This chapter will look at some ideas, or models, for understanding what is behind relationships. They can be used as tools to improve or maintain them.

Two types of model will be used

(1) Human needs.
(2) Interpersonal roles.

1. Human needs underlying relationships

In the chapters dealing with behavioural skills, the concept of human needs was introduced as a means of identifying what behaviour would be appropriate for individuals and groups at different times.

Abraham Maslow (1970) suggested a sequence of needs we try to meet so that we achieve personal development. Similarly, Clayton Alderfer (1979) identified three human needs of existence, relatedness and growth which we translated into face-to-face terms. These needs can also be seen as the influencers of the things that people will seek from each other. Lack of awareness of the needs of others could impair relationships.

Edgar Schein (1988) described individual needs in the context of our group membership and relationships. If these needs are not met we have seen the negative impact this can have on both the individual and group development.

Will Schutz (1958) has produced a model which looks directly at the connection between our needs and the relationships we develop with others. The needs he identifies have close similarities to those already mentioned. The distinctive feature is that Schutz defines the needs in interpersonal terms and differentiates between expressed and wanted behaviour.

Expressed behaviour is what we do towards others or they do to us. **Wanted** behaviour is just that – what we want from others or they want from us! Consonance between expressed and wanted means we will get on with each other, dissonance means we will not.

The needs suggested by Schutz that govern our relationships are:

Control   Direction and influencing as opposed to autonomy and independence.

Affection   Showing liking, warmth and closeness.

Inclusion   Expecting and inviting others to join you in your group or be half of a buddy bond.

Figure 16.1 demonstrates the connections between the ideas put forward by Maslow, Alderfer, Schutz and Schein.

Authority	Maslow	Alderfer	Schutz	Schein
Main focus	Individual	Individual	Inter-personal	Group
Needs	Fulfilment	Growth		
	Self esteem	Growth		Acceptance Identity
	Reputation	Relatedness	Inclusion	Acceptance Identity
	Social	Relatedness	Affection	Acceptance Identity
	Security/ Safety	Existence	Control	Control
	Physical	Existence		

Figure 16.1   Human needs models: some connections.

Needs and relationships: Satisfaction and threats

Schutz has described three interpersonal needs which are satisfied or threatened in a relationship. The extent of each need will vary from person to person, both in terms of what we need to do towards others (expressed behaviour) and in terms of the behaviour we want from others (wanted behaviour).

Inclusion

(1) What I do to include you.
(2) What you want me to do to include you.

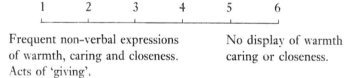

| 1 | 2 | 3 | 4 | 5 | 6 |

Frequent invitations
to join in a work or social
bond. Strong expectations of
loyalty and sense of identity.

No offers to join
in a work or social bond.
No loyalty or
identity expectation.

If we are at widely different positions on the inclusion scale, we will probably experience difficulties in our relationship and possibly dislike each other. If you are '6' and I am '1', you will see me as a threat to your privacy and I will see you as rejecting me.

Affection

(1) What I do to express affection.
(2) How much you want me to express affection.

| 1 | 2 | 3 | 4 | 5 | 6 |

Frequent non-verbal expressions
of warmth, caring and closeness.
Acts of 'giving'.

No display of warmth
caring or closeness.

Widely different positions in our need to express and receive affection would place stress on the relationship. If you are at '1' and I am at '6', you would be disappointed by what you see as my coldness and indifference. I may have no concept of your need and will probably see my position as normal. If I do perceive your need I will probably see it as demanding and even threatening.

If our positions were reversed, you would be embarrassed by the display of affection and would feel awkward in my company, probably avoiding me as much as possible.

Control

(1) What I do to control you.
(2) How much control you want from me.

| 1 | 2 | 3 | 4 | 5 | 6 |

Frequent attempts to direct and
influence.

Encourages autonomy. No
attempts to influence or direct.

If you are at '6' and I am at '1', you would find my interference insufferable. You would experience any relationship as frustrating and repressive. I would see you as awkward, difficult and possibly rebellious or sulky.

Reverse positions could mean that I was seen as unhelpful in your uncertainty, although I might see you as helpless and dependent.

ACTIVITY 16.1

 Visualize situations similar to those outlined above. What could be done to improve relationships?

When behaviour does not match needs: handling the conflict

When a conflict of needs or interests exists, the Thomas Kilman model suggests that each party has a choice of five approaches:

(1) **Accommodation**
This means accepting the other person's position, either by backing off or tolerating their behaviour. You may choose to do this if the other person's need is much greater than your own and it is not very important to you. The problem is that you are denying your own needs and may be encouraging exploitation of yourself.

(2) **Avoidance**
Essentially this means doing nothing about the situation so that the problem remains. One or both parties may avoid contact. If the problem is not serious or there is little need for contact, this approach requires no effort. If it is serious and the conflict is damaging, it is not a good choice.

(3) **Competition**
This involves trying to win. It involves trying to deny the other's needs and interests and maintaining your own position. If you have the power to win you may gain the satisfaction of meeting your needs. How important is this to you? Can you live with your exploitation? Does the relationship not matter? Will you win next time? Do both parties accept the competition?

The following two approaches require both parties to take account of the other's needs and interests. They may examine the needs and consider their respective positions. This may include applying reason and logic, examining feelings, such as fear or threat, and assessing who they are in terms of identity and values.

(4) **Compromise**
Agreeing to move towards each other's position is the essence of this option. The advantage is that the issue is addressed and both have some cause for satisfaction. However, the outcome is not fully satisfying for either person and is usually the result of mutual assessment of relative power, rather than a consideration of each other's position and needs.

(5) Collaboration

This involves exploring mutual positions to try to find a solution that meets the needs of both. It usually requires some trust and an explanation of each other's needs. It also means recognizing the differences that exist between both people and accepting, even respecting those differences. For example,

'I recognize your need to include people in what you do, and you recognize my need to limit what and how I join.'

'I will display affection in ways acceptable to you and you will experiment with accepting it.'

'We will agree boundaries of independence and discuss intrusions when either of us feels the need.'

2. Interpersonal roles

We are unique products of our genes and personal history and we cherish the concept that we can affect what happens to us by making choices.

This book is about enhancing the capacity to choose in relation to the growth and development of ourselves and others. It deals with improving the knowledge and skill required to increase our control over ourselves and the situations in which we live and work.

We often choose without reflection or without knowledge of the alternatives. Mostly we do not choose in a rational sense, but do things from habit and impulse. For most people most of the time this works well enough, but for all of us some of the time it doesn't, and the consequences can be painful. Frustration, anger, recrimination, lack of fulfilment and damaged relationships are some of the consequences of the wrong choice, or not choosing at all but simply reacting to external events.

Sometimes our choices are constrained by ourselves, through our concepts of morality or by others whose views we value and respect. We accept and welcome these constraints. However, we can also feel that we are constrained by influences that we feel are negative, which leave us feeling trapped, repressed or doing things we regret.

Models of the way we form relationships can provide us with insights that can increase our choice and reduce negative constraints. Choice can be improved by understanding the options available to us, developing the skills to implement these choices and increasing our awareness of the consequences. The negative constraints may be reduced by enhanced knowledge about what others may do to influence us in an unacceptable way and how we trap ourselves.

One such model called Transactional Analysis was developed by Eric Berne. The Interpersonal Roles model is derived from Berne's theory and is an adaptation to fit the purpose of this book, in terms of managing to make the most of people.

The six roles that govern relationships

There are six major roles that we can play in our relations with others. We switch into one or other of them for different reasons.

- We woke feeling displeased/happy with the world.
- It is our favourite, and we get into it whenever we can.
- It is a reaction to another person's role.
- It is our gut reaction to the way we interpret the situation we are in.
- We make a reasoned choice about the role that is most appropriate. (Probably the rarest reason!)

ACTIVITY 16.2

You are asked to define each of these roles in your own terms. They will be more meaningful for you that way. You will be able to compare your own interpretation with the authors' description later.

Below are six brief scenarios, one for each Interpersonal Role. You are asked to visualize yourself in each as vividly as possible, perhaps drawing upon a real experience you have had.

For each identify:

(1) Words or phrases which typify your response.
(2) Significant non-verbal behaviour.
(3) What you were feeling and whether you were mainly 'in your head or your heart' – thinking or feeling.

Think of a time when:

(1) You have caught someone red-handed doing something you had expressly forbidden them to do on two previous occasions. It may jeopardize something that is very important to you.
(2) A close colleague who is very vulnerable receives some bad news whilst you are together.
(3) A colleague and you, both having similar expertise, are collaborating to identify a solution to a technical problem.
(4) You are feeling vulnerable and are with a close colleague when you receive some bad news.
(5) Your boss has caught you red-handed doing something you had been expressly forbidden to do on two previous occasions. It may jeopardize something that is very important to the boss.
(6) It is the end of the day. Tomorrow your department closes for a holiday festival. A friend has just heard that he has become a father for the first time.

Descriptions of the six interpersonal roles

The Judge

'I am sitting in judgement and will punish any infraction of the rules.'

Words	Bad; wrong; stupid; ought; improve; rules; guilty.
Non-verbal	Shakes fist; points; glares; shouts; tight lips.
Feelings	Anger; self righteous; dominant; disgust; vengeful.
Thoughts	Tend to reflect and follow the feelings.
Ultimate Role Model	Judge Jeffreys – the Hanging Judge.

The Helper

'I am going to rescue and take care of you.'

Words	That's OK; never mind; tell me all about it; good.
Non-verbal	Smile; caring eye contact; supportive body contact.
Feelings	Concern; worry; sympathy; dominant; protective.
Thoughts	Tend to reflect and follow the feelings.
Ultimate Role Model	Lady Bountiful, Great Earth Mother, or Knight in Shining Armour.

The Thinker

'I am going to analyse, assess and think this one through.'

Words	Correct; how; what; why; amount; analyse; logical.
Non-verbal	Quizzical and thoughtful expression; attentive.
Feelings	Interested; curiosity; calmness; challenge.
Thoughts	Dominant. Feelings neutral or supporting thought.
Ultimate Role Model	The Human Android.

The Fun Lover

'I'm having a great time! Come and join us.'

Words	Fantastic; wow!; whoopee!; I want; let's do it now.
Non-verbal	Laughter; bright eyes; noisy; energetic; bubbling.
Feelings	Excitement; freedom; release; pleasure; elation.
Thoughts	Feelings dominate and freely expressed. Thought is inspirational.
Ultimate Role Model	Mel Brooks or Mick Jagger.

The Defendant

'I've got to get myself out of trouble.'

Mode One: The Appeaser. 'I can turn away wrath.'

Words	Sorry; I'll try hard; please; help me; accident.
Non-verbal	Whining voice; avoids eyes; shuffles; wrings hands.
Feelings	Sad; bad; guilty; fear; manipulative; devious.
Thoughts	Feels strongly and thinks quickly.
Ultimate Role Model	Woody Allen.

Mode Two: The Rebel. 'I can fight my way out of this.'

Words	It's your fault; no!; victimization; don't care.
Non-verbal	Scowl; clench fists; agitation; sneer; pout.
Feelings	Sad; bad; guilty; fear; cornered; defiant; upset.
Thoughts	Tend to reflect and follow the feelings.
Ultimate Role Model	James Dean or Mick Jagger.

The Broken Wing

'I want you to rescue and protect me.'

Words	Hurt; sad; pity; sacrifice; pain; personal problem.
Non-verbal	Pale and wan; eyes full; head in hands; sighs.
Feelings	Sorrow; self pity; dependence; helpless; afraid.
Thoughts	Thoughts and feelings matched and self protecting.
Ultimate Role Model	Pearl White in *The Perils of Pauline*.

The six roles: helping and hindering

Like many aspects of human behaviour, each role can in turn be a strength and a weakness, depending upon the frequency and appropriateness of its use.

The Judge

Helps	*Hinders*
Establishes boundaries and rules.	May produce negative responses in others.
Gives certainty and security.	Can be experienced as oppressive and restrictive.
Maintains order.	Can foster dependence.

The Helper

Helps	*Hinders*
Gives support and encouragement.	May prevent others solving problems themselves.
Protects.	Can inhibit development, in terms of self esteem
Gives warmth and a sense of inclusion.	and fulfilment.
	Can foster dependence.

The Judge and the Helper have in common a sense of dominance, superiority or responsibility at the time for the other person.

The Thinker

Helps	*Hinders*
Applies reason and logic to alternatives and consequences.	Can inhibit creativity. May be seen as boring and impersonal.
Handles the technical side of things.	Unable to form relationships because feelings not
Can reduce strong negative feelings in others.	expressed.

The Fun Lover

Helps	*Hinders*
Develops positive relationships through expressing feelings.	Can be seen as selfish. Can irritate and create negativity.
Can reduce the negativity in others.	Can create disorder and distractions.
The source of creativity through lack of inhibition.	

The Thinker and the Fun Lover have no sense of superiority or inferiority in their contact with others.

The Defendant: Appeaser mode

Helps	*Hinders*
Can help surface relationships with politeness and courtesy.	May be seen as defensive and negative.
Can support orderliness by conformity.	May reinforce the negativity of others.
Can protect the individual from the power of others.	Can inhibit personal growth and problem solving.

The Defendant: Rebel mode

Helps

May cause others to reappraise their attitude and relationships.

Can promote a process of change.

Can protect the individual from the power of others.

Hinders

May be seen as defensive and negative.

May reinforce the negativity of others.

Can inhibit personal growth and problem solving.

The Broken Wing

Helps

Can elicit help and support when needed.

Can help others feel good and form a relationship.

Can protect the individual from the power of others.

Hinders

May be seen as weakness to be exploited.

May be seen as attention seeking and be disapproved.

Can inhibit personal growth and problem solving.

The Defendant and the Broken Wing have in common dependence and inferiority at the time to the other person, and discount their responsibility for themselves.

ACTIVITY 16.3

 Each role has a complementary role. Can you identify the pairs?

Complementary roles

 When we are 'inhabiting' a particular role we target our communication to a complementary role in the other person.

We expect a response from the role at which we have aimed, targeted in return to our own current role. More often than not this is what does happen. We are on the same wavelength.

Judge–Defendant

The Judge is looking for someone to judge, put down and punish. The Defendant is looking for someone with whom to be defensive.

If you are feeling judgemental you are targeting the Defendant in the other person. If you are feeling defensive then you are targeting the Judge.

Helper–Broken Wing

The Helper is looking for someone to help or rescue, while the Broken Wing is looking for just this kind of service. When you are feeling helpless you are targeting the Helper. When you are feeling benevolent you are aiming at the Broken Wing.

Thinker–Thinker

The Thinker is looking for a kindred spirit with whom to think, analyse and be rational. If you are seeking facts or logic, you are aiming at the Thinker in the other person.

Fun Lover–Fun Lover

The Fun Lover is looking for someone to share the fun and be spontaneous. The target will be the Fun Lover in the other person.

Interpersonal role repertoire

We all have the six roles in our repertoire. We are very accomplished at performing some and perhaps not so accomplished at others. We may even prefer some to others, so as far as other people are concerned, a few of our roles may present large targets easy to hit, whereas others may be small and difficult to find.

Because we have preferences and different levels of role performance accomplishment, individual repertoires may vary considerably. This variation partly explains why we get on well with some people and not so well with others.

ACTIVITY 16.4

 (1) Assess your own Interpersonal Role Profile (IPR). What do you think is your most preferred and least preferred role? If you are studying in a group, share feedback about your perceptions of each other's profiles.

Interpersonal role	Estimated % of time in role	
	Self estimate	Others' estimate of you
Judge		
Helper		
Thinker		
Fun Lover		

Defendant – Appeaser

           – Rebel

Broken Wing

(2) Identify somebody you get on with very well.
    (a) What is their profile?
    (b) How does it relate to your own?
    (c) Does it explain why you get on well with them?

Interpersonal role	**Your IPR %**	**Their IPR %**
Judge		
Helper		
Thinker		
Fun Lover		
Defendant – Appeaser		
– Rebel		
Broken Wing		

(3) Identify somebody with whom you experience a difficult relationship.
    (a) What is their profile?
    (b) How does it relate to your own?
    (c) Does it explain why the relationship is difficult?

Interpersonal role	**Your IPR %**	**Their IPR %**
Judge		
Helper		
Thinker		
Fun Lover		
Defendant – Appeaser		
– Rebel		
Broken Wing		

Interpersonal roles: preferences, profiles and relationships

It has been suggested that we may have a preferred, perhaps dominant Interpersonal Role (IPR). This is the one that we slip into most easily. Sometimes we can recognize other people's IPRs more easily than our own, so second opinions may help us check our perception of our own IPR.

When we are in this preferred role, we are targeting a particular IPR in the other person, which we earlier referred to as complementary roles. If the other person has that target role as their preferred role, there is a good chance that the target will be hit, because it is large.

People with complementary IPR profiles will understand each other and find it easy to fall into a relationship which fulfils mutual expectations. As we will see later, this does not necessarily mean that these are 'positive' relationships in the sense of development and growth. It does mean that the relationship will be persistent and easy for both parties to sustain.

For example, the person with a preference for the Judge as an IPR, will find such a relationship with a person with a preference for the Defendant. They will understand each other, will meet mutual expectations and seek each other out.

They will behave in a way which reinforces, even encourages the other's behaviour. The rebellious Defendant goads the Judge. The Judge punishes the rebel, who goads the Judge, and so it goes on unless one or both switch to another IPR. It is a long-term relationship in which they need each other and love to hate each other.

The paradox is that the Judges may rationalize their judgements and punishments as for the good of all and the reform of the Defendants, yet their behaviour towards the others will often produce just the behaviour they are trying to eliminate.

If two people have non-complementary IPR profiles they will find it difficult to hit each other's target roles and will experience problems getting on with or understanding each other, unless one or both make a special effort to find each other's less preferred but complementary roles.

An example would be two people in Helper and Defendant–Rebel roles. They would be targeting the 'wrong' IPRs and not finding them, probably with some confusion and frustration. If this was a regular pattern they would be likely to avoid each other. Again, if one or both switched to less preferred roles which were complementary, the relationship would be different and sustainable. If they switched to Fun Lover roles, for example, they would no doubt laugh at the previous difficulties.

Any two people with IPRs which are non-complementary will have some relationship difficulties with each other, unless they make the effort or have learned how to access each other's complementary roles. If their IPR preferences have very little match, then this will be difficult. For example:

First Person's IPR %			Other's Complementary IPR %
(1) Judge	45%	5%	Defendant
'I want to judge you.'			'I don't like being judged.'

(2)	Helper	5%	20% Broken Wing
	'I don't like helping.'		'I want to be helped.'
(3)	Thinker	30%	20% Thinker
	'I quite like thinking.'		'I like thinking rather less.'
(4)	Fun Lover	5%	15% Fun Lover
	'I don't like having fun.'		'I sometimes like having fun.'
(5)	Defendant	10%	5% Judge
	'I don't like being judged.'		'I don't like judging.'
(6)	Broken Wing	5%	35% Helper
	'I don't like being helped.'		'I want to help you.'

These two people could clash often over the mismatches on (1) Judge–Defendant; (2) Helper–Broken Wing; (4) Fun Lover–Fun Lover and (6) Broken Wing–Helper. There are potential clashes on 55% of their contacts. They would get on only by their skill in hitting small IPR targets, or by concentrating on (3) Thinker–Thinker where they both have moderate and similar preferences.

Complementary roles: implications for long-term relationships

Earlier in the chapter, four complementary roles were identified.

Judge	Defendant (Rebel or Appeaser)
Helper	Broken Wing
Thinker	Thinker
Fun Lover	Fun Lover

When these pairs represent the dominant roles of two people they will form the basis of their long-term relationship and will be the most frequent way they think, feel and behave towards each other. The roles are mutually reinforcing and both will find it easy to relate to the other on this basis. The will target and hit each other's complementary IPR without difficulty.

ACTIVITY 16.5

▼ Our focus is upon positive relationships which stimulate growth, learning and development of one or both people.

How would you assess the four pairs of complementary roles in those terms?

Complementary roles: negative and non-growth relationships

▽ All the roles have a part to play in relationships, but the first two are negative and stultify development and growth if they are the major long-term basis of how two people get on together.

Judge	**Defendant**
'You ought to be different.'	'Why pick on me?'
'You are hopeless.'	'I am, but I do try. Sorry.'

The relationship is self defeating in terms of learning and problem solving. The Judge assumes all responsibility and the Defendant none. The Judge makes judgements and the Defendant excuses, flavoured with lies, manipulation or rows. Neither really listens and the problems are not confronted or tackled. The relationship is a coercive/compliant/aggressive cycle which does not develop and gets nowhere. Neither reason nor creativity is constructively applied to learning.

It would express itself, for example, in a negative appraisal which dealt only with weaknesses as seen by the Judge who would command the Defendant to improve. The Defendant would concentrate on not taking the blame or minimizing the punishment. Awareness of the need, commitment to change and understanding about how to achieve it would be minimal. The appraisee would disown the problem.

Helper	**Broken Wing**
'Let me do it for you.'	'Thanks. I find it difficult.'
'I'll look after you.'	'I'm so grateful.'

The Helper assumes responsibility for the problem and its solution. If this is a permanent feature of the relationship, the Broken Wings will not develop the capacity to take care of themselves and deal with their own problems. They will be overprotected and will not be able to learn and develop the skills and attitudes necessary to function independently.

At work, this will appear in the manager who is unable to trust or delegate and therefore is unable to provide a relationship in which the other person is able to develop and mature. A 'no risk' environment also means 'no learn'.

Both the above complementary interpersonal roles are dominant-dependent relationships. In a sense, it is possible to get locked into them through the IPR profiles and preferences of both people. There will be minimum growth and the relationship will only develop if one or both develop an understanding of what is happening and have the will to change it. Such a change requires patience, often a willingness to take small, secure steps, identification and ability to access more appropriate IPRs and a clear vision of the relationship you want. Applying the IPR model will help the achievement (see Figure 16.2).

We can enhance our personal growth and capacity for developing relationships by:

(1) Increasing our awareness of our own profiles and when we are in particular interpersonal roles.
(2) Being more sensitive to the IPRs of others and the role they are in at a particular time.
(3) Practising and improving those parts of our repertoire in which we feel less skilled and confident, so that we are able to perform them more effectively when appropriate.
(4) Learning to access the IPRs in others that we find hard.
(5) Preparing for potentially difficult encounters by:
    (a) identifying the likely IPR of the other party, and planning and rehearsing the IPR that we would prefer to occupy;
    (b) extending this by thinking about how to access the IPR of the other person that we feel would be appropriate.
(6) Learning how to anchor ourselves into particular IPRs so that we can stay in them, in spite of the pressure from others to switch to an IPR we would prefer not to occupy.
(7) Using the IPR model to analyse relationships with which we are dissatisfied and finding ways to improve them.
(8) Remembering we always have a choice from six roles.

Figure 16.2 Applying the IPR model to develop relationships.

Complementary roles: positive and growth relationships

Thinker	Thinker
'Let's analyse this.'	'Yes. One thought I have is ...'
'What would result if ...?'	'It is probable that ...'

Both people share responsibility for the problems and solutions, applying skills and knowledge, and building on each other's ideas. Both will learn and develop in the relationship.

Fun Lover	Fun Lover
'I've had a crazy idea!'	'That sounds exciting. Amazing!'
'That is hilarious!'	'Let's have some fun with it!'

This is a relationship which is spontaneous, uninhibited and intuitive. Two important outcomes are that it builds and maintains bonds between people and is the source of creativity and inspiration.

Both people are interdependent and equal in each of these two complementary roles. When they are inhabited regularly, reason is combined with creativity in a positive climate within which ideas develop and learning can take place. Other IPRs play a part within relationships, but positive growth occurs only in a climate in which the most important roles are Thinker and Fun Lover. The trick is learning to use them ourselves and to find them in others.

References for further reading

Alderfer C.P. (1979). *Existence, Relatedness and Growth*. Free Press

Back K. and K. (1982). *Assertiveness at Work*. McGraw-Hill

Bales R.F. (1950). *Interaction Process Analysis*. Addison-Wesley

Berne E. (1977). *Games People Play*. Grove Press

Biddle D. and Evenden R. (1989). *Human Aspects of Management*, 2nd edn. IPM

Bolton R. (1979). *People Skills*. Prentice-Hall

Harris T.A. (1979). *I'm OK You're OK*. Pan

James M. and Jongward D. (1971). *Born to Win*. Addison-Wesley

Maslow A.H. (1970). *Motivation and Personality*. Harper and Row

Schein E. (1988). *Process Consultation* Vol. 1. Addison-Wesley

Schutz W.C. (1958). *FIRO. A Three Dimensional Theory of Interpersonal Behaviour*. Holt, Rinehart and Winston

17

Developing a team

In Chapter 15 we looked at the skills which help communication in meetings, when the members are face-to-face temporarily to achieve a particular purpose. The meeting may consist of people who are together on a one-off basis at one extreme, to a group which meets regularly and whose members need to work together frequently. This latter group may be functional, such as a number of specialists brought together for a project, or part of the line structure, when they would be in the same department or section, with a common manager or supervisor. These are recognizable as **teams**. The concept of teamwork applies to any group, but the idea of 'a team' usually applies to those who meet and work together with some frequency and common purpose.

The team factor is **synergy**, with the whole being greater than the sum of the parts. How is this to be achieved? The skills described in Chapter 15 apply to working and communicating within a team. In addition, team leaders need to consider the following:

Characteristics of teams
Complementary team roles
Team assessment
Team development

Characteristics of teams

Successful teams

It is important to establish the characteristics that successful teams have in common. These could be the 'organization as a team', or any team which is a constituent part of an organization. Features which emerge common to several studies, including our own, are:

Goals	Members need to be clear about what they are aiming for. If they feel that the goals are worthwhile, so much the better. Commitment to these goals is an important unifier of the team.

Results	The team needs to be operating in a system where results are an ever-present aspect of the team environment and recognition follows success.
Excellence	The standards which the team sets and by which it judges its results are high.
Skills	Members need to be competent in both technical and social skills in a collaborative climate.
Leadership	The leadership needs to be seen as fair and to have integrity.

Successful team members

In our work with a large number of teams, we discovered that team members themselves rate the following behavioural characteristics as the most important for members to have, if the team is to have a good chance of success.

Goal directed	Behaves and influences in a purposive way.
Enthusiastic	Shows interest and commitment.
Assertive	Pursues own needs but not aggressively at the expense of others.
Competent	Has technical and social skills.
Open	Expresses feelings and conflict, so they can be dealt with.
Flexible	Demonstrates capacity to change and experiment.
Supportive	Displays helpful and friendly behaviour.
Constructive	Looks to build rather than destroy.
Leadership	Leads and accepts leadership with high standards and consensus decisions.

Complementary team roles

Managers are team leaders. When recruiting to a position it is important to assess people not only in terms of their technical expertise fit with the person specification, but also to take into account their likely impact upon the team. We have identified factors above which appear to have commonality, but it is important that we do not fall into the trap of assuming that all members should be identical clones. Effective teams need to have individuals with different characteristics, as well as a sufficiency of the common positive behavioural features of successful team members.

Meredith Belbin (1981), and more recently Charles Margerison and Dick McCann (1990), have identified different roles that need to be performed by different team members if the team is to be effective.

Belbin suggested that the **Chairman** sets the task, guides and coordinates, whilst the **Shaper** shapes the teamwork and makes sure things happen. He also showed the need for a person with ideas (the **Plant**), another who evaluates (the **Monitor**) and the **Teamworker** who looks after the relationships and feelings in the group. Others deal with practicalities, sort out resources and check the quality of the group's work.

Margerison and McCann have identified key work functions of advising, exploring, organizing and controlling which are coordinated by a **Linker**. There are parallels with Belbin's roles. Both sets of ideas seem to relate particularly to teams in problem solving and decision making modes. It is probably true, as they suggest, that individuals prefer some of these roles or functions to others, so if you do not have an appropriate mix, your team may not be successful. However, as we have considered in other parts of the text, we all have a repertoire, as well as preferences. If you have good all rounders in your team, who are able to perform different roles *when they are required*, then it will be successful.

There are connections between these ideas and those of Robert Bales, whose concepts of task and social emotional behavioural contributions were looked at in Chapter 14. We have developed these to show that the team leader needs to ensure that the team has within its number those who can perform the following functional skills (see Chapter 15 for further discussion).

Task	(1) Starting and defining aims and objectives.
	(2) Exchanging or developing information or tasks.
	(3) Path finding for the team.
	(4) Creating ideas and methods.
	(5) Evaluating and decision making.
	(6) Action planning, taking and monitoring.

Social emotional

(1) Looking after individual's needs in the team:

Identity	Working out a role.
Acceptance	Belonging to the team.
Control	Influencing how things are done.
Personal	What is needed from the team.

(2) Looking after the team's needs:

Integrating	Unifying and handling conflict.
Yielding	Helping the group to decide.
Encouraging	Ensuring members feel valued.
Progressing	Showing the team its development.
Constructing	Looking for what is good.

As team leader it is unlikely that you will be able to perform all of these functions skilfully, to the required degree and at the appropriate time. The team needs more than a captain!

You will need to plan to have these skills available to you, develop and encourage them, know when they are needed, and orchestrate their use. This is rather like the Linker role of Margerison and McCann, and Belbin's Shaper, but it emphasizes the need to take responsibility for managing and developing the important individual differences that all successful teams need.

Team assessment

How do you know how good your team is?

There is always the bottom-line test. Is it producing the results efficiently and effectively? However, it is not so straightforward to estimate whether it will continue to do so. Nor is it too easy to diagnose why it is not performing well.

The previous sections offer clues to the kind of things that will explain reasons for success, so you know what to keep doing. They also offer clues about poor performing teams, with ideas about what to develop or do differently.

Teams change, sometimes getting better, sometimes worse. Edgar Schein (1988) uses the concepts of group growth and maturity which can be applied when assessing a team in terms of dealing with its environment, optimum use of its resources, and its capacity to learn and adapt. He considered that a team should have adequate means of getting feedback, both internally and from outside itself. This would enable it to know how well it was doing and what it needed to do differently. It should be flexible in how it does things and have clear communications. Some of Schein's ideas are used, with others we have identified, in the Team Assessment Schedule which will be used to illustrate team development in the Insupply case study as part of the next section.

Team Assessment Schedule

1 Goal clarity

$$
\begin{array}{cccccc}
\cdot & \cdot & \cdot & \cdot & \cdot & \cdot \\
1 & 2 & 3 & 4 & 5 & 6
\end{array}
$$

Unclear goals   Very clear goals

2 Results centred

$$
\begin{array}{cccccc}
\cdot & \cdot & \cdot & \cdot & \cdot & \cdot \\
1 & 2 & 3 & 4 & 5 & 6
\end{array}
$$

Little results focus   Strong results focus

3 High standards

$$
\begin{array}{cccccc}
\cdot & \cdot & \cdot & \cdot & \cdot & \cdot \\
1 & 2 & 3 & 4 & 5 & 6
\end{array}
$$

Low standards   High standards

4 Maximizing the use of team resources

$$
\begin{array}{cccccc}
\cdot & \cdot & \cdot & \cdot & \cdot & \cdot \\
1 & 2 & 3 & 4 & 5 & 6
\end{array}
$$

Poor use   Good use

5   Getting feedback (internal and external)

```
 .     .     .     .     .     .
 1     2     3     4     5     6
Poor feedback            Good feedback
```

6   Flexibility

```
 .     .     .     .     .     .
 1     2     3     4     5     6
Inflexible               Very flexible
```

7   Communication

```
 .     .     .     .     .     .
 1     2     3     4     5     6
Unclear                  Very clear
```

8   Decision making

```
 .     .     .     .     .     .
 1     2     3     4     5     6
No consent               Consensus
```

9   Leadership

```
 .     .     .     .     .     .
 1     2     3     4     5     6
Unprincipled             Principled
```

10   Task skills within the team

Exchanging and developing ideas/materials

```
 .     .     .     .     .     .
 1     2     3     4     5     6
Poor exchange            Good exchange
```

Pathfinding

```
 .     .     .     .     .     .
 1     2     3     4     5     6
Constant confusion       Clear sense of
                         direction
```

Creativity

```
 .     .     .     .     .     .
 1     2     3     4     5     6
Low                      High
```

Evaluation

1	2	3	4	5	6
Ineffective evaluation				Good assessment and evaluation	

Taking action

1	2	3	4	5	6
Poor at getting things done				Good at getting things done	

11 Meeting the needs of individual members (identity, acceptance, control, personal)

1	2	3	4	5	6
Meets needs poorly				Meets needs well	

12 Meeting the needs of the team (integrating, yielding, encouraging, progressing, constructing)

1	2	3	4	5	6
Meets needs poorly				Meets needs well	

Team development

If you assemble a group to work together it will certainly evolve as a result of many factors which include the technical system, group dynamics, the personal characteristics of the members and leadership interventions. It will stabilize eventually at a level of effectiveness related to the team assessment criteria identified above. The level could be anything from highly productive and cohesive to low performing and divided.

Many authorities, including B.W. Tuckman and W. Schutz, have observed that groups move through a number of stages before developing into an effective team. These models of development have been well summarized by A. Kakabadse *et al.*

Schutz describes individuals and groups making three sets of decisions. First, who is **in** or **out**; next, who is **top** or **bottom**; and finally, who is **near** or **far**.

These stages relate to issues of membership, authority conflict and finally the development of team relationships.

Tuckman produced his memorable four stage model of **forming, storming, norming** and **performing**. This sees the group as going through its initial setting-up phase, with its associated uncertainties, to a conflict stage where leadership and membership matters are tested and resolved. Next the group will establish what it is, and who performs the different task, social and leadership roles within the team. Mutual values and expectations, the group norms, are developed. Finally, an effective team will begin the process of collaboration to perform its tasks and achieve its goals.

The common threads to most theories of team development can be summarized by the following four stages:

(1) Getting together.	The members are selected, and begin the process of identifying and assessing each other. It is a time of insecurity and uncertainty. Attention to giving opportunities for the group to get together, with social and task contact, will help move through this stage.
(2) Getting angry.	Groups take time to sort out formal and informal leadership and authority issues. Expertise, personal characteristics and credibility will be mutually explored and tested. Open and covert conflict may occur. Constructive and positive handling of these issues will be necessary and the presence of team members with social emotional skills will reduce the tensions and help the group move through this stage.
(3) Getting ready.	The group will begin to develop an identity and members a sense of belonging. Common expectations and purpose emerge, binding the group. Leaders can facilitate this process; exemplifying by 'modelling' belonging and articulating the norms and the goals of the group can help team building.
(4) Getting going.	The group feel interdependent and are clear about mutual roles. They begin to get going on the task relative to their objectives, more or less effectively.

It is by no means inevitable that groups will evolve through all the phases, but may remain fixed at a lower level. The leader role may well be akin to that of midwife, aware of the stages that groups must go through, and making each one as smooth and painless as possible, helping to overcome any difficulty on the way.

Even if they achieve the final stage of development, there is a wide range of effectiveness possible in relation to all the team assessment criteria scales. The team can assess the degree to which it is performing well and identify directions in which it still needs to develop.

Team building is most effective if it is done *with* the group, rather than *to* it. It is a group process which occurs as a result of the interaction of team members. The leader as midwife is a useful concept, perhaps helping the group to understand its development and share in the assessment of its problems, needs and goals. Skills in building relationships and handling feedback positively will be of considerable value in getting the team to assess where it is on the criteria scales of team development. Involvement creates feelings of ownership and commitment to any plans about team improvement. It is here that the process of team development will begin.

Insupply case study: Developing a team

Insupply had moved to its new site in Midtown Complex some months previously. The move had gone quite well and service to its clients had been maintained. There were many internal stresses and strains, and some frustrations for new and old staff working together in a changed environment and with new systems in place.

Generally the new location was proving advantageous and staff were displaying energy and drive. Bob Armstrong and his department had borne the brunt of the planning and implementation. The Chief Executive Hedi Lindstrom and her deputy Colin Smith expressed themselves well satisfied with the changeover.

Bob's Administration Department was central to dealing with teething troubles, acting as troubleshooters and putting things into place so that Insupply could move smoothly forward. The main operational departments relied crucially upon their performance in providing services in an efficient and co-ordinated way. Colin Smith was aware that this was not happening at the level he expected and he discussed this with Bob during their first appraisal interview (see Chapter 24, 'Objectives and target setting'). Bob knew all was not well in his team and Colin agreed that he should invite a team building facilitator to help.

Bob invited Tim Bild to discuss the problem. Tim was one of his old college tutors who specialized in organizational behaviour and was very experienced in this kind of work.

CASE PROJECT 17.1

If you were Tim Bild what kind of information would you want from Bob Armstrong?

Tim discovered that the team had been under great pressure during the move and all the team had been focused upon the tasks and deadlines rather than their colleagues and relationships. Certainly Bob had had no time for the people side of his role. New people had had to find their own way around to a large extent.

There had been substantial restructuring of the department and changes of staff with movement, transfers in and promotion. Ekoku had moved out to the position in Marketing. Sally Bullen now concentrated upon electronic mail and data processing and had taken over all aspects of internal communication. Her ex-assistant now ran Staffing and her other assistant was promoted to take charge of Buildings and Maintenance. These changes are summarized in the organization chart shown in Figure 17.1.

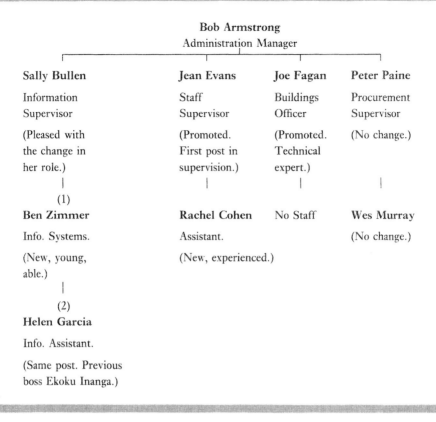

Bob Armstrong
Administration Manager

Sally Bullen	Jean Evans	Joe Fagan	Peter Paine
Information Supervisor	Staff Supervisor	Buildings Officer	Procurement Supervisor
(Pleased with the change in her role.)	(Promoted. First post in supervision.)	(Promoted. Technical expert.)	(No change.)
|	|	|	|
(1)			
Ben Zimmer	**Rachel Cohen**	No Staff	**Wes Murray**
Info. Systems.	Assistant.		(No change.)
(New, young, able.)	(New, experienced.)		
|			
(2)			
Helen Garcia			
Info. Assistant.			
(Same post. Previous boss Ekoku Inanga.)			

Figure 17.1 Insupply Administration Department after the move.

Tim also explored the internal stresses and strains with Bob. A great deal of collaboration was needed between the sections of the department and they were interdependent. For example, Peter needed to purchase and chase delivery on the electronic hardware; Jean had to supply contract staff to Sally and Joe; Sally had to install a new control system for Peter; and Joe had to ensure that the faulty air conditioning was repaired effectively for Jean.

None of these illustrations had worked smoothly.

In the few opportunities Bob had had to get the team together he felt they had achieved little.

- Peter kept quiet.
- Wes got angry.
- Joe made it clear that he was too busy to spend time talking with people.
- Sally looked puzzled.
- Ben and Rachel felt awkward and slightly intimidated.
- Helen said that they all needed to communicate more and that all the others were at fault here.
- Bob reassured them they were a good team and all would soon be well if they worked at it, but he was not sure how they would pull out of it.

CASE PROJECT 17.2

Bearing in mind the framework of this chapter, how would you set about the team building if you were Tim Bild?

How Tim helped the team build itself

Stage One

Tim met all the team members individually for a short chat to break the ice and 'get the feel' of each member and their sense of the team. He explained his preferred approach to Bob and what would be expected of them all. Bob agreed and Tim sat in on their next meeting, and at the end outlined the approach. He emphasized that they would be responsible for the success or failure of the venture more than he would. They all volunteered that they needed each other, but were diffident about how well they worked together. Most felt problems were due to pressure of work but some felt it was more fundamental than that.

It was agreed that the team should meet for three hours on two consecutive weeks to explore the issues and to decide if and how further development should occur.

Tim was sure that he had to reassure each member about himself and the process. It was particularly important that Bob did not feel threatened.

Tim wanted the group to feel that things were not going to be done 'to' them, but that they were all responsible for the process and outcome. The building could only work on the basis of consent and shared responsibility.

Stage Two

The first meeting did not directly focus upon them as a team but upon the characteristics of good teams they had been part of previously. They discussed work teams, voluntary and sports teams and found it easy to agree 'good team' features.

They thought teams needed to know firstly why they were there and what they were aiming for. They needed to know how they were doing so that they could improve and learn. It was also felt that the best teams did not accept second best. Members could be different as long as all had something to offer.

Tim picked up the latter point, and they explored the contributions that individuals could make to a team.

At the start of the second meeting Tim reminded them of the factors they had identified for good teams and good team member contributions. One of the factors was about sharing ideas and giving feedback. Tim spent some time exploring the 'rules' of feedback with them.

He asked them individually to reflect upon themselves in the light of those factors. The group split in two and members exchanged their views about the team before comparing notes in the full group. Each member then was asked to select one feature that they felt helped them make positive contributions and one they felt they could usefully develop. Once Sally and then Bob broke the ice everybody joined in and they found themselves commenting on people's assessments. Rather than being critical of each other they were modifying individuals' self criticisms. Some constructive developmental feedback was exchanged.

Towards the end Bob asked if they wanted a further meeting and suggested that they should try to spend a longer period of time together. Sally thought it would be valuable to meet outside the work environment and the group supported Bob when he proposed a residential weekend to be arranged at a resort two hours away.

In terms of the group's development Tim assessed them to be flitting between 'getting together' and 'getting angry' before the first team meeting. The first activity was a comparatively safe, non-threatening 'there and then' task rather than a 'here and now' focus which would have been risky given the stage they were at. For the first time they experienced together the 'getting ready' and 'getting going' stages of teamwork. In addition they had identified key aspects of good teams and members.

Teams need   Goals; results focus; high standards; skills.

Individuals contribute   Competence; openness; positive ideas; supportiveness; involvement; skills.

The second meeting was able to build on the first by reinforcing the 'getting ready' and 'getting going' experience. It was a simple step to move on to using the criteria the team had developed (and therefore owned) for assessing themselves both as a team and as individuals. Tim had ensured that they were aware of the rules of constructive feedback but did not force the group to do it. This emerged as key individuals took the plunge and thus encouraged others to do so. They were beginning to feel a team and take consensus decisions about their own development. Bob's role in being open, non-threatening and willing to take a risk was critical at this stage.

Stage Three

At the resort the group warmed up with some team exercises which they analysed in terms of the criteria they had established previously. They found this enjoyable and it got them ready.

Tim felt it was time for them to look at how they functioned as a team at work and he chose to do this by asking them to complete a Team Assessment questionnaire as a way into discussion, exchange and development.

The below par average assessments in the Team Assessment Schedule are summarised as follows:

Goal clarity

```
                  *
        .      .      .      .      .      .
        1      2      3      4      5      6
    Unclear goals                 Very clear goals
```

Results centred

```
                   *
        .      .      .      .      .      .
        1      2      3      4      5      6
    Little results                Strong results
       focus                         focus
```

Getting feedback (internal and external)
                    *

      .   .   .   .   .   .
      1   2   3   4   5   6
   Poor feedback   Good feedback

Communication
               *

      .   .   .   .   .   .
      1   2   3   4   5   6
     Unclear   Very clear

Decision making
                         *

      .   .   .   .   .   .
      1   2   3   4   5   6
   No consent   Consensus

Task skills within the team

   Exchanging and developing ideas/materials
                    *

      .   .   .   .   .   .
      1   2   3   4   5   6
   Poor exchange   Good exchange

         Pathfinding
            *

      .   .   .   .   .   .
      1   2   3   4   5   6
   Constant confusion   Clear sense of direction

         Taking action
            *

      .   .   .   .   .   .
      1   2   3   4   5   6
   Poor at getting   Good at
      things done   getting things done

Meeting the needs of individual members (identity, acceptance, control, personal)
                    *

      .   .   .   .   .   .
      1   2   3   4   5   6
   Meets needs poorly   Meets needs well

Meeting the needs of the team (integrating, yielding, encouraging, progressing, constructing)
                    *

      .   .   .   .   .   .
      1   2   3   4   5   6
   Meets needs poorly   Meets needs well

Encouraged by Tim and Bob the group examined each aspect and agreed what they felt were the problems, the extent to which they owned them individually, and what they hoped from each other.

Tim was rather surprised at the group's assessments but he kept this to himself and accepted the feedback as constructive. The team did not blame each other but agreed positive ways forward with a team action plan and one expressed to the group by each individual. Some personal and skill development needs were identified by individuals, which Bob agreed to discuss in the forthcoming appraisal or earlier if it was felt to be pressing.

The team agreed to monitor its progress as part of its monthly meeting and to have a full review with Tim present in three months' time.

The team continued the building process in a positive way encouraged by Bob's leadership, openness and support. They accepted that there would still be problems, but that they had begun to build into the group the means of examining and dealing with them. The team members all took responsibility for developing themselves and had become more sensitive to the needs of the team and other members.

References for further reading

Baker H.K. (1979). The Hows and Whys of Team Building. *Personnel Journal* **58**

Belbin E.M. (1981). *Management Teams*. Heinemann

Davis J.H. (1969). *Group Performance*. Addison-Wesley

Kakabadse A. *et al.* (1988). *Working in Organisations*. Penguin

Margerison C. and McCann D. (1990). *Team Management*. Mercury

Schein E. (1988). *Process Consultation* Vol. 1. Addison-Wesley

Schutz W.C. (1958). *FIRO. A Three Dimensional Theory of Interpersonal Behaviour*. Holt, Rinehart and Winston

Tuckman B.W. (1965). Developmental Sequences in Small Groups. *Psychological Bulletin* **63** (6)

18

Developing the will to work well

So far in Part Two we have looked at the manager's part in developing self and others, in terms of personal, interpersonal and team development. In this chapter focus will be upon developing performance by influencing the individual's will to work well.

'Getting results through people' and 'having a positive effect on the bottom line' are central to the purpose of management. In Part One we examined getting the right person in order to get the results. Part Two has considered ways of developing positive relationships and commitment. Both are necessary to the achievement of individual and organizational need fulfilment, but may not in themselves be sufficient to do this optimally. Apart from the major area of developing the *skill* to work well (Part Three), we need to look at ways of developing the *will* to work well.

The manager's approach to leadership in key areas of influence and relationships is the first aspect. The second is managing motivation, directly influencing the will to work well.

Are there any particular approaches which are more likely than others to have a positive outcome? We will try to draw some conclusions and guidelines from the mass of research, theory and experience in these two areas of leadership and motivation.

The manager's approach to leadership

Leadership dimensions which emerge from the studies in this field in a sense define the choices available to the manager leading staff. As with communication skills, it seems appropriate to see leadership as a repertoire of behaviour which the individual can recognize, develop and from which choices can be made.

Few now argue that there is a single approach that fits all staff and circumstances. As the so-called contingency theory suggests, we should select from the repertoire that set of behaviours which fits the situation.

The three main dimensions of the leader's repertoire are:

(1) Technical–people balance.
(2) Decision and problem solving style.
(3) Relationships style.

1 Technical–people balance

R. Blake and J. Mouton (1981) identified the choice facing the manager between the task and people aspects of the role. They concluded that there should be equally high concern for both. The manager's resources of time and energy are not limitless, so that high concern for one may inevitably mean lower concern for the other, at least in terms of the behaviour of managers, rather than their attitudes and professed values.

P. Hersey and K. Blanchard (1982) looked at the balance between task and relationships behaviour in managers and produced a theory of situational leadership. This suggests that the approach should vary according to the **task development** of the staff, which means their competence and willingness to work with little supervision. When the staff has low task development the approach should be high task and low relationship behaviour, moving ultimately to low task and low relationship when there is high task development. At this stage the staff want delegation and to be left alone to get on with the job!

R. Evenden (Biddle and Evenden, 1989) distinguished between a manager's technical and people priorities. He discovered a 'T-type' bias in 80% of managers which often had more to do with culture, personal motivation and approaches rewarded by the organization than it had to do with a rational choice based upon reflection about the needs of the situation. Perhaps management development should involve helping leaders become aware of their choices. It should also give them encouragement to reflect and guidance about the situational factors to reflect upon. This flexibility and rationality of approach is very unusual although frequently prescribed!

ACTIVITY 18.1

▼ What proportion of your time do you give to the technical side of your role? This is when you are mainly engaged in a functional task.

What proportion of your time do you give to the people side of your role? This is when you are mainly engaged in a people centred activity, such as coaching, counselling, relating or influencing.

Do you feel that this balance between technical and people is appropriate?

What are the factors in the situation which affect this balance? Can you identify those which are appropriate influences on your style balance and those which are not?

▽ The factors affecting our technical–people balance are shown in Figure 18.1.

Job demands	Are you sure it is not something else? This is the usual excuse for technical bias.
Boss demands	Is the boss right? Can you influence your boss?

Culture demands	Are the values right? Organizational values are often inappropriate and stem from another era. If your people are assets and the culture demands you ignore them, change the culture!
Self demands	Are you right? For example, are you holding on to the technical things because you like them, feel safer with them or are frightened to delegate them?
Staff demands	Should you listen to them more? The answer is usually yes.
Time demands	Do you not have enough time for people? Not making enough time for people is probably why you feel time pressure anyway.

Figure 18.1   Factors affecting our technical–people balance.

2 Decision and problem solving style

Power, authority, influence and who exercises them are the central issues for the leader when there are decisions to make and problems to solve. They are also significant for the others in the leader's network in terms of their attitude to the process of decision making and their commitment to its outcome *when the decisions are important to them.*

Power is the weaponry, authority is the right to use it and influence is 'making a difference'. The extent to which this political triumvirate is shared with others is the key variable, whether the leader is relating to an individual on the one hand, or a group or network on the other.

The managerial leader has power and organizational authority vested in the position of manager. Influence will depend how this is used in decision making. It will also depend upon other sources of authority, which stem from knowledge and others' perception of the leader's personal and moral qualities.

One-to-one

On a one-to-one basis, the manager's repertoire ranges from 'dictates' through 'consults' and 'delegates' to 'abdicates'.

Dictates...Consults...Delegates...Abdicates

It is probable that the first and last approaches are unthinking reactions to decision/problem communication. They are the habitual response that some individuals make to meet their own personal needs rather than the demands of the situation.

These extreme positions relate closely to the concepts of aggression and passivity considered in Chapter 12, and usually have a negative impact upon the recipient's motivation. Some managers swing unpredictably between the two, leaving confusion and consternation in their wake. It is possible to justify both in specific circumstances, such as an emergency on the one hand or brainstorming on the other. Although it is common to find frequent users of this part of the repertoire justifying it in terms of staff who prefer it, it is in fact very rare to find a recipient who finds either approach motivating.

Dictatorial managers will always tell you that when they ask for an opinion their staff don't have any; or when they delegate, their staff are frightened of the responsibility. This is much more to do with the dictators' view of the world, and their staff relationship in terms of things like trust, support and development, than it is to do with the staff themselves.

The 'consults' and 'delegates' positions are likely to be a more considered style of decision making and problem solving. They certainly require more skill and judgement in their execution than the extreme fight or flight positions. The recipients of these 'involvement' styles are likely to rate them highly as positive influences upon their motivation, or will to work well.

Consultation involves asking and listening. It should not be confused with 'mock' consultation, when the manager goes through the motions of asking for opinions and ideas, which are then ignored unless they fit the plans and decisions already made.

Delegation is one of the most powerful management skills and one of the most difficult. The leader must be able to trust others to use delegated authority and to give up something that may be personally satisfying. It involves the risk, indeed the probability of mistakes, which need to be treated as opportunities to learn rather than reasons for punishment. It requires investment in communication, skill and knowledge development as well as judicious monitoring of the way the delegated authority is being used. Over-supervision defeats the purpose and lack of reporting can lead perilously close to abdication. Success will produce motivation, bottom-line results and create space for the leader to manage.

The choices and consequences of the four decision-making styles are shown in Figure 18.2.

	Dictates	Consults	Delegates	Abdicates
Means	Telling	Asking	Giving	Hiding
	Dominating	Compromising	Collaborating	Avoiding
	Aggression	Listening	Trusting	Passivity
	Arrogance	Patience	Confidence	Fear
Involves	Coercing	Inviting	Sharing	Distancing
Expects	Acquiescence	Contribution	Results	Nothing
Suits	Short-term emergency	Specific commitment	Long-term motivation	Short-term creativity
Requires	Obedience	Involvement	Development	Hope

Figure 18.2   Decision-making styles: choices and consequences.

Decision making and problem solving in groups

When a group, team, department or network is involved in decision making, there are different ways in which decisions can be made. These range from our old friend the dictator making them to no decisions being made at all.

Dictator...Elite...Majority...Consensus...Unanimity...Indecision

The approach adopted will have a bearing upon:
(1) Commitment to any decision and action to be taken.
(2) Satisfaction with the decision process.
(3) Level of contribution of ideas and opinions.
(4) Subsequent motivation.

During 1970–1990 Robin Evenden explored the experience of several hundred people in relation to the above factors. Almost without exception the four factors depended upon decision-making involvement. Positive group feelings increased progressively as the approach moved from Dictator to Unanimity, decreasing to some extent if the group perceived Indecision.

The process by which groups make decisions is shown in Figure 18.3.

Dictator	One person decides. The others obey.
Elite	A small number makes decisions. The majority have to accept it.
Majority	Most are involved and concur. The minority have it imposed upon them.
Consensus	All consent to the decision, feeling they have had full opportunity to influence it.
Unanimity	All agree with and support the decision.
Indecision	The group are unable to arrive at a decision.

Figure 18.3 How groups make decisions.

Exceptions to the general rule about involvement, influence and positive feelings are if the leader or elite are seen as experts or if there is a shared perception that deadlines are imminent. Similar tolerance occurs if the style is seen as exceptional and the decision makers are trusted.

3 Relationships style

The third significant dimension of the manager's leadership relates to the frequency and the quality of personal contact with staff. At one extreme is the manager who is hostile or aloof and cold, whilst at the other we see bonhomie and friendship. The determining factors are connected with expression of feelings, socializing and showing personal interest (see Figure 18.4).

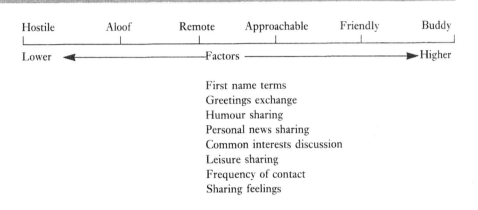

Hostile   Aloof   Remote   Approachable   Friendly   Buddy

Lower ◄————————Factors————————► Higher

First name terms
Greetings exchange
Humour sharing
Personal news sharing
Common interests discussion
Leisure sharing
Frequency of contact
Sharing feelings

Figure 18.4   Relationships style factors.

As with the other style dimensions, there appears to be risk involved in the extreme ends of the repertoire. The Hostile/Aloof style is likely to be at best irritating and at worst demoralizing and demotivating. The Buddy style may be seen as intrusive and lead to bad feeling if favouritism to the 'buddies' is perceived by others. The danger zones are illustrated in Figure 18.5.

Genuineness and naturalness are important or the approach will be seen as insincere or patronizing. However, the dimension should not be seen as the same as introversion and extraversion. Many of the factors are behavioural choices that most people can make.

Hostile   Aloof   Remote   Approachable   Friendly   Buddy

DANGER XXXXXXXXXXXXXXXX   XXX DANGER

************** SAFETY **************
Perceptions and Feelings

Anger	Trust	Liking	Intrusion
Intimidation	Interested	Human	Unfair
Sabotage	Support	Warmth	Two faced

Figure 18.5   Relationships style: safety and danger zones.

The manager and motivation: influencing the will to work well

ACTIVITY 18.2

▼ Taking a managerial viewpoint, what do you believe to be the main motivators of people at work?

Rank the following in order of their motivational importance. (Keep a record of your conclusions for reference later in this chapter.)

Interesting work
Good salary
Social support
Recognition
Loyalty
Security
In the know
Discretion
Personal development
Work conditions

What do people believe motivates

Early theory considered that people at work needed to be controlled by fear of the boss, the tyranny of the machine and the need for money (F. Taylor, 1947). This evolved as industrial society developed socially, economically, technologically and politically so that in the period 1930–1960 management discovered people, welfare and concern for relationships (Elton Mayo, see Landsberger, 1961).

Belonging (W. Schutz, 1958), integration of individuals and organizational needs (C. Argyris, 1957) and leadership (R. Blake and S. Mouton, 1981) subsequently emerged as the means to motivation, hotly pursued by the supporters of growth opportunities (E. Berne, 1977) and the pre-eminence of the relation between the individual and the job itself (F. Herzberg, 1966).

The centrality of the job continues to be presented as a prime contender for main motivator. Tasks, autonomy and performance feedback when linked to individual experience of meaningful work and responsibility for results are cited by J. Hackman and G. Oldham (1980) as the basis of high motivation.

V.H. Vroom (1964) and D. Nadler and E. Lawler (1977) have described the psychology of motivation in terms of 'expectancy theory'. This suggests that individuals will put in effort to perform proportionate to the value they place on the expected reward. It sees us as highly rational beings carefully calculating every action in terms of outcome.

This repeats the fallacy of Economics models based upon assumptions of rational economic man, but it does emphasize that each individual will have their own particular motivational needs which the manager needs to assess.

Individual needs

It would seem that all these approaches have elements of the truth for some people some of the time. The 'need theorists' examined in Chapter 14 suggest that individuals develop different needs, and that the tastes and appetites related to them vary from person to person (see Figure 18.6).

Authority	Maslow	Alderfer	Schutz	Schein
Needs	Fulfilment	Growth		
	Self esteem	Growth		Acceptance Identity
	Reputation	Relatedness	Inclusion	Acceptance Identity
	Social	Relatedness	Affection	Acceptance Identity
	Security/ Safety	Existence	Control	Control
	Physical	Existence		

(From Figure 16.1)

Figure 18.6 Human needs and motivation.

ACTIVITY 18.3

 You are now asked to reflect upon your own experience of motivation.

Think of a time when you were really switched on to perform well. It could be a short period of a few hours or a much longer time.

Concentrate on what was going on. Visualize yourself doing what you were doing; see the other people in the situation and what they did; focus on what happened and what affected the way you felt.

Write down what you were feeling; what was going on inside you.

Write down what was happening outside you which produced those feelings.

You may wish to repeat this exercise by visualizing another situation when you were switched off, again in concrete terms, thinking about people feelings and events.

If you are able, you may want to involve others in this, so that you can compare notes about the feelings and situational factors associated with motivation.

Motivation factors

 Probably your response will fall into the pattern shown in Figure 18.7. Several thousand managers and professional staff have completed the exercise described in Activity 18.3 in the last twenty five years and the response is remarkably consistent.

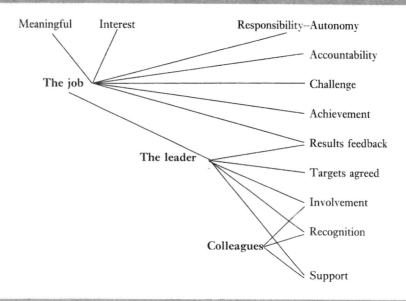

Figure 18.7 The motivation guide.

It suggests to me that at least at the level of managerial and knowledge worker, and probably at other levels from other evidence, Alderfer's *growth* needs, strongly backed up by *relatedness* needs, dominate individual motivation in industrial and post-industrial society. Three or four of the motivators in Figure 18.7 were identified, unprompted, by individuals in almost all personal experiences visualized.

Existence (security) needs are not entirely out of the frame. In recent years one of the authors has worked on development programmes with redundant managers and specialists, those under threat and indeed with those who became redundant during his time with them. The achievement of stability and the positive feelings associated with its attainment, and the desire to minimize the chances of a recurrence, were associated with a high will to perform for the organization lucky enough to employ them.

It is only a matter of time before growth needs reassert themselves and the previous pattern reappears.

This does not mean that the same thing will motivate everybody but that the same *types* of thing will. Appetites and tastes vary. You can't tell without prior discussion what motivational dish a person will choose, but you can bet that the job, the boss and probably significant other people will be on the menu!

How managers and staff see worker motivation

Professor Dan Couger (Couger and Zawacki, 1980) cites a 1986 European study highlighting the difference between managers' and staff perceptions.

Workers' view of workers' *motivation*		*Managers' view of workers'* *motivation*	
1 Interesting work		1 Good salary	(1)
2 Recognition	(1)	2 Security	
3 In the know	(2)	3 Personal development	
4 Security		4 Work conditions	
5 Good salary	(5)	5 Interesting work	
6 Personal development		6 Discretion	
7 Work conditions		7 Loyalty	
8 Loyalty		8 Recognition	(8)
9 Social support		9 Social support	
10 Discretion		10 In the know	(10)

The figures in brackets are from a study by Kenneth Kovach conducted in the United States in the early 1980s. The workers' views and the managers' widest misperceptions are uncannily close in both studies. These studies are neither definitive or comprehensive. For one reason, we can only choose from what is on the list. It does suggest motivation is more than just obvious common sense! How did your responses to Activities 18.2 and 18.3 compare?

Managing motivation

Perhaps the first rule of motivation is not to make assumptions but to find out:

(1) By asking ourselves about our own motivation.
(2) By reminding ourselves about motivational needs.
(3) By observation and most important, asking people.

If you require a map through the confusing, sometimes contradictory landscape of staff motivation, it would seem that the 'developing needs' guides along with the Herzbergian job routes and 'leader behaviour' compass would serve you best.

Influencing the individual's motivation involves leader behaviour and skills, including clarity of expectation, joint target setting, feedback, praise and recognition, support and encouragement, and information and involvement, wherever possible in a positive team climate. This is unlikely to miss anybody.

Variation is likely to occur in the manager's influence in the most potent area: job and individual. It is here that the tools of delegation, coaching and development, creating challenge and scope for achievement, meaning, responsibility, accountability, variety and interest come into their own. We know that money attracts, keeps or loses and that people-blind managers repel, but motivation is what stimulates the will to work well.

References for further reading

Argyris C. (1957). *Personality and Organization*. Harper and Row

Berne E. (1977). *Games People Play*. Penguin

Biddle D. and Evenden R. (1989). *Human Aspects of Management*, 2nd edn. IPM

Blake R.R. and Mouton S.S. (1981). *The Versatile Manager*. Irwin-Dorsey

Couger J.D. and Zawacki R.A. (1980) *Motivating and Managing Computer Personnel*. John Wiley & Sons

Hackman J.R. and Oldham G.R. (1980). *Work Redesign*. Addison-Wesley

Hersey P. and Blanchard K. (1982). *The Management of Organisational Behaviour*. Prentice-Hall

Herzberg F. (1966). *Work and the Nature of Man*. Staples Press

Kakabadse A. *et al.* (1988). *Working in Organisations*. Penguin

Landsberger H.A. (1961). *Hawthorne Revisited*. Cornell University

Maslow A.H. (1970). *Motivation and Personality*. Harper and Row

Nadler D.A. and Lawler E.E.III (1977). Motivation: a diagnostic approach. In *Perspectives on Behaviour in Organisations* (Hackman J.R., Hawler E.E.III and Protek L.W., eds). Mc-Graw-Hill

Schutz W.C. (1958). *FIRO. A Three Dimensional Theory of Interpersonal Behaviour*. Holt, Rinehart and Winston

Tannenbaum R. and Schmidt W.H. (1973). How to Choose a Leadership Pattern. *Harvard Business Review* 51

Taylor F. (1947). *Scientific Management*. Harper and Row

Vroom V.H. (1964). *Work and Motivation*. John Wiley & Sons

Vroom V.H. and Deci E.L. eds (1970). *Management and Motivation*. Penguin Modern Management Readings

19

Developing positive attitudes to change

Managing change

Handling change has become one of the major challenges facing organizations, and those working in them. Managers have a range of issues to consider, in initiating and responding to change. While these issues will vary according to the manager's precise role within the organization, a number of common themes are usually present. It is extremely important that managers should acquire the skills to recognize and handle effectively the problems and issues that are common to situations of change.

Skills in managing change seem certain to grow in importance, with change and a quickening of the pace of change becoming central features of organizational life in almost every sector of business and commercial activity throughout the world.

There is evidence, too, that the nature of the change process facing many managers is altering dramatically, calling for new skills. Handy (1989), one of the major authorities on organizations and organizational behaviour, makes the distinction between continuous and discontinuous change. **Continuous change** is, according to Handy, the more comfortable type of change because it is easier to predict, with the pattern of past trends usually being a reasonably reliable predictor of future change. Handy's view, based on his observations of contemporary organizations is that discontinuous change, a less comfortable and less predictable form of change, is becoming increasingly prevalent. **Discontinuous change** is more dramatic, for example 'where the lines run off the graph paper' and where totally new changes occur. Examples include new technology making traditional skills, which may have been in existence for decades or even centuries, obsolete almost overnight. For a more complete discussion of this philosophy, read Handy (1989).

The modern manager, therefore, requires skills in handling both continuous and discontinuous change.

Handling change framework

In initiating or responding to change it must be kept in mind that a number of elements are likely to interact, as shown in Figure 19.1.

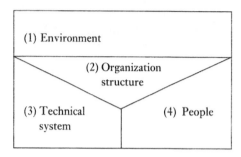

Figure 19.1   Interacting elements affecting change.

ACTIVITY 19.1

▼ (1) What aspects of the external environment can influence change within the organization?
(2) How can changes in the organization structure and technical system affect people in the organization?
(3) Can you recall changes you have experienced? Referring to Figure 19.1, how did changes in organization structure (2) and technical system (3) affect people (4)?

Review of Activity 19.1

▽ A range of environmental aspects can affect change in the organization. These include:

- political factors, for example government policy encouraging certain types of organizations;
- economic factors, for example economic recessions brought about by high interest rates and reduced customer demand, leading to contraction in the size of organizations;
- legal factors, for example changes in employment legislation which may encourage organizations to take on extra employees, or reduce employee numbers;
- social factors, for example more female employees working in organizations.

  At the present time, typical changes in organizational structure include removing layers in the hierarchy, creating flatter organizations. Changes in the technical system are often associated with the increased use of computers.

Both sets of changes are likely to lead to fewer employees being used as core staff. This trend may also be associated with the greater use of bought-in services, and of part-time and temporary employees.

Vision

No matter what size or magnitude of change a manager is dealing with, vision of the desired outcome is an important element. This means that any manager seeking to bring about a successful change must, firstly, have a strong mental image of the final result that is to be achieved.

In the case of specific change (for example, associated with a new project) this element of vision is important not only so that the manager's own thinking is clear, but also to permit the picture of the desired outcome to be tested against colleagues' views, and to be clearly communicated to employees who are going to be involved in implementing the change.

In the case of major organizational change, vision assumes new dimensions and must include a strategic element. Shaping and sharing strategic vision is a key skills requirement, especially for senior managers. It involves developing and articulating corporate philosophy and values, and becomes an essential element of leadership in highlighting future objectives for employees to move towards.

Leigh (1988) provides a clear statement of vision. 'Vision is a sincere expression of what we want. Unlike goals or objectives it is not precise, but it mobilises people to move towards something which has not yet been experienced.'

Vision is about **values** – or what really matters.
Mission is about **purpose** – or what business we are in.
Objectives are about **strategy** – or how we will get there.

Overcoming resistance to change

Any change creates opportunities and risks. All too often individuals focus primarily on the risks and dangers they see associated with change, and become resistant to change. Overcoming resistance to change is one of the major challenges facing managers.

Resistance to change refers to behaviour when the individual attempts to retain the position as it is at present, and opposes forces leading to change. The first skill required of the manager in this area is diagnostic – to identify the source or sources of resistance. Leigh (1988) identifies four principal sources of resistance to change:

- Cultural.
- Social.
- Organizational.
- Psychological.

205

Cultural resistance might occur in an organization which has traditionally had a strong production orientation, placing high emphasis on the technical excellence of its products, and now wishes to develop a market orientation, attaching greater value to identifying the precise needs of its customers and providing high level customer service. Some individuals may be reluctant to go along with the change, preferring to continue to value the technical excellence of products above all else.

Social resistance to change refers to situations where individuals see change as leading to a break up of teams and work groups, owing, for example, to the introduction of new technology or automation.

Resistance to change could be described as organizational when individuals are reluctant to accept a change that involves a change in organizational design or reporting arrangements. The changes bringing about resistance could include the removal of a layer in the organizational hierarchy, or reporting to someone at a less senior level than before. In these cases individuals are likely to see their status threatened.

Resistance to change associated with fear of the unknown and feelings of uncertainty about the future is psychological.

ACTIVITY 19.2

 Think of a situation where you have had to deal with some person at work who was displaying high resistance to change. Are you able to identify the causes of the resistance? Which of the four sources of resistance to change helps to explain the situation?

Strategies for overcoming resistance to change

Strategies for successfully overcoming resistance to change are likely to be associated with:

(1) Accurate diagnosis – ensuring that the source of the resistance to change, and the related fears and anxieties, are accurately identified and understood.

(2) Correcting misconceptions – improving communications where it is clear that the resistance to change is based on some wrong perception.

(3) Minimizing the negative aspects, and maximizing the positive aspects of the expected change – providing individuals with an honest appraisal of the up-side potential and opportunities as well as the down-side risks.

There are no magical formulae that managers can use in dealing with employers who are displaying resistance to change, often because rational responses are closely intertwined with irrational fears and anxieties.

Harvey-Jones (1988) suggests that the best way for a manager to obtain a positive response to change from employees is to heighten, in an open, honest way, their dissatisfaction when they learn they are threatened by superior performance of others – countries, organizations, products, services and individuals.

This implies the importance of:
(1) Keeping people informed about the change process.
(2) Consulting them as far as possible, on the way changes are being handled, to increase feelings of involvement.
(3) Stressing values to which employees attach importance, for example emphasizing that the implementation of changes envisaged will strengthen the organization and lead to more secure jobs.
(4) Avoiding threats – most people will be only too well aware of the possible negative aspects.
(5) Highlighting the opportunities – stressing that most change situations yield opportunities which individuals can grasp, if positively inclined.
(6) Careful consideration of the timing, to minimize threats and feelings of discomfort.

ACTIVITY 19.3

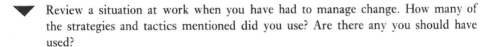 Review a situation at work when you have had to manage change. How many of the strategies and tactics mentioned did you use? Are there any you should have used?

Transformational leaders

Resistance to change can be minimized in the first place if managers adopt appropriate styles of leadership. Modern research evidence suggests that there is no such thing as the 'right' leadership style – it all depends on the situation involved. This view, often referred to as the contingency approach to leadership, suggests that managers should be able to adapt their leadership styles to meet the varying needs of different situations and different groups of employees. This is particularly true during periods of change, when important skills required of the manager are:

• Situation sensitivity – the ability to recognize the particular factors that must be taken into account in any situation (for example, clarity or ambiguity of the tasks to be done; the experience and confidence of the employees) and understand the kind of leadership style appropriate.
• Style flexibility – the ability to adapt, and adopt the kind of leadership style required by the situation.

In recent years several writers have developed the concept of the transformational leader, which is particularly relevant in dealing with major changes. The essential characteristics of transformational leaders are:

(1) The ability to identify and form a clear vision of the changes required, and of the outcomes.
(2) Skill in communicating this vision to employees and in generating their enthusiasm to work towards this new vision of change.

207

Creating employee commitment

Transformational leaders possess the enviable skill of taking others along with them in times of change – in other words they are effective in developing employee commitment towards the achievements of new organizational goals. This commitment implies that employees show interest in, and welcome, changes.

How to generate high levels of employee commitment, creating a positive attitude towards welcoming change, has been analysed by Peter Martin and John Nichols (1987). Their findings highlight three pillars of commitment:

(1) A sense of belonging to the organization.
(2) A sense of excitement.
(3) Confidence in management.

The sense of belonging is important in developing an employee's feelings of loyalty to the organization. This sense of belonging can be built up by managers when they:

- Keep employees informed.
- Involve employees as far as possible in decisions, especially decisions that would affect them.
- Permit them to share in success.

Generating a sense of excitement helps to motivate employees, and to sustain motivation. This is brought about by helping individuals to take pride in their work, by developing good trust levels among employees and managers and by delegating clear responsibilities to individual employees, making them accountable for their own results.

Employees develop confidence in management when managers are seen to exercise their authority, show dedication and display competence.

Insupply case study: Managing change

Insupply planned to move away from its two sites in Hometown, the present headquarters location and Awayville, where the distribution centre is sited, to a new purpose-built factory in a new out-of-town complex, roughly midway between the two present sites.

Colin Smith had responsibility for developing the strategy concerned with the planning and implementation of the move into the new factory. Because it represented a major corporate event, he intended to consult frequently with Hedi Lindstrom, the Chief Executive.

Colin took part in the initial discussions with the developer of the Midtown complex, which led to agreement about a site and leasing terms for the construction of the new factory. After the appointment of Bob Armstrong as the new Administration Manager, with responsibility for planning, coordinating and implementing the move from the present Hometown and Awayville sites to the new Midtown complex in a period of twelve months, Colin and Bob drew up a specification for the new factory and office building. They then invited proposals and presentations from a number of firms of architects, before selecting Smith, Brown and Bevan to design the building. On their advice, GSM Construction was subsequently appointed as the builders.

Colin was eager to ensure that Bob Armstrong, under his supervision, drew up detailed plans including layouts for the factory and office buildings. To do this, Colin and Bob met, on an individual basis, with several department heads and senior managers, to obtain information from them about their space and layout requirements. Bob and Colin were then intending to make presentations to groups of employees, outlining the plans, and inviting their views.

The Awayville weekly newspaper *The Advertiser* published an article, unknown to Colin and Bob, discussing the company's move to the new Midtown complex and speculating about reduction in staff numbers.

Colin and Bob had tried to chat informally with staff at the headquarters in Hometown, to keep them in the picture about the move.

Deputation from Awayville

Colin Smith was surprised to find on his desk, three days after the newspaper article, a letter signed by 40 employees from the distribution centre at the Awayville warehouse. They requested that three of their representatives meet with him.

They said they were seeking:

- guarantees about no compulsory redundancies; and
- reassurance that the distribution activities were not to be disbanded, but run on a contractual basis by buying in services.

They also asked for travel subsidies for those employees who would have longer journeys to work.

Colin called Bob Armstrong into his office to plan for the meeting with the representatives from the distribution centre.

CASE PROJECT 19.1

What would you advise them to do?

CASE PROJECT 19.2

How would you plan the meeting?

CASE PROJECT 19.3

Having undertaken case projects 19.1 and 19.2, reflect on what has happened and indicate in what ways you would have handled things differently from Colin Smith and Bob Armstrong.

Review of Case Projects 19.1, 19.2 and 19.3

A range of options is open to Colin Smith and Bob Armstrong in dealing with the representatives of the Awayville employees.

(1) They could state that there is no way their requests can be met, particularly at this stage while plans are still being formulated; that there inevitably will be savings generated from the move to a new single site, implying that there will be some job losses; and that they are really quite lucky still to have jobs and should not be bothering them with impertinent requests that take up time that could be spent more productively.

(2) They could say that they will consider sympathetically all of the requests made and indicate that they fully understand the need to recompense the Awayville employees for any discomfort caused by the changes.

(3) They could listen carefully to the requests; ensure they fully understand them and how they arose in the first place; explain fully why the changes are taking place, and what they are intended to achieve.

Most people would probably discard option (1) as confrontational and insensitive to the anxieties of employees, though it has to be said that some managers, especially those with autocratic tendencies, may instinctively adopt this kind of approach. There is often a danger in following option (2) that, in attempting to be responsive to the needs of employees, managers appear to make commitments without fully considering the consequences, and can build up expectations among employees which later are not fulfilled.

Option (3) is probably a more realistic approach, in trying to develop a balance between attention to employees' needs and an objective approach to the requirements of the business. In resolving problems it is often useful, for the benefit of all parties, to return to fundamentals and explain the reasons behind the change and what it is intended to achieve.

Colin Smith and Bob Armstrong could probably have avoided the demands from the Awayville employees in the first place, had they held a briefing session, or preferably several briefing sessions, to keep employees informed from an early stage. The dilemma facing Colin and Bob was that they would have preferred greater clarity in their own minds about the changes before briefing and talking with employees. Unfortunately, time (and the newspaper article) did not permit this. They were also less aware of the anxieties of the Awayville employees, since they spent most of their time at the present headquarters at the Hometown site.

Handling change often creates extra pressures and stresses for managers as Colin found out in the case study. Change also generates new pressures and stresses for organizations. The pressures of change can create difficult challenges and apparent contradictions for organizations to handle. These have been well summed up by Rosabeth Moss Kanter (1989). In modern organizations she cites a number of examples of these personal dilemmas that managers must address:

'Think strategically and invest in the future ... but keep the numbers up today.

Be entrepreneurial and take risks ... but don't cost the business anything by failing.

Continue to do everything you are currently doing even better ... and spend more time communicating with employees, serving on teams and launching new projects.

Speak up, be a leader, set the direction ... but be participative, listen well, cooperate.'

The challenges and paradoxes are not necessarily insoluble, but they do highlight the hard choices that managers have often to make in handling change, no matter how far they have developed these skills as outlined in this chapter.

References for further reading

Biddle D. and Evenden R. (1989). *Human Aspects of Management*, 2nd edn. IPM
Drucker P. (1985). *Managing in Turbulent Times*. Harper and Row
Handy C. (1989). *The Age of Unreason*. Arrow
Harvey-Jones J. (1988). *Making it Happen: Reflections on Leadership*. Collins
Kanter R.M. (1989). *When Giants Learn to Dance*. Simon and Schuster
Leigh A. (1988). *Effective Change*. IPM
Martin P. and Nichols J. (1987). *Creating a Committed Workforce*. IPM
Schein E. (1987). *Process Consultation* Vol. 2. Addison-Wesley

PART THREE

The manager as developer: enhancing performance

20

The performance development cycle

Part One explored how to get the right person in the right job. In Part Two positive relationships, leadership and motivation were considered as influences upon the person's commitment and will to work well. Part Three completes the manager's people and performance repertoire by examining how the manager can develop the individual's *skill* to work well. The manager's direct involvement in achieving the growth of appropriate skills and knowledge can be defined in terms of the performance development cycle, which forms the core of the remainder of the book. The cycle is illustrated in Figure 20.1.

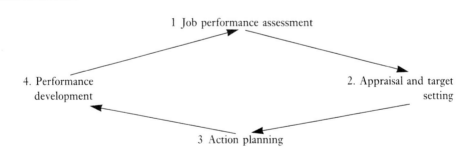

1 Job performance assessment

4. Performance development

2. Appraisal and target setting

3 Action planning

Figure 20.1   The performance development cycle.

1 Job performance assessment

The job description should include an up-to-date definition of the purpose of the job, and the manager should know the objectives for each individual.

It is necessary to define performance in terms of the key areas of the particular job as concretely and precisely as possible. Standards are helpful, not least because then you and your staff will know what constitutes 'good', 'average' and 'poor' performance. Agreed targets and the degree to which they are achieved will form the basis of the assessment.

Evidence and illustrations are important both in making the assessment and for feedback and discussion with the job performer. Evidence can be gained in a number of ways, such as work sampling, observation, identifying significant achievements and difficulties, talking with other people and the person being assessed, and factual evidence about quantity, quality, meeting deadlines and so on.

The focus is on the results and how they were achieved. It is very helpful to keep a private personal file on each member of staff, in order to note these things during the review period, rather than relying on memory. This file could also contain any summaries of discussions, the job description, previous appraisal reports and current action plans.

It is, of course, vital to be seen as fair, unprejudiced and objective. The nature of the human condition means that this can never be the case entirely, but we can get as close to it as possible. Knowing our biases is half the battle. Recognizing the influence of the horns and halo effects contributes to the other half.

Horns means a generalized negative prejudice about all aspects of a person because of one characteristic which is a strong personal pet dislike. **Halo** is the opposite, involving seeing all a person's characteristics through rose-tinted spectacles, because of one feature about them that you greatly admire.

The method of concrete comparison, discussed in Part One in relation to constructing a person specification, is a useful tool in getting to grips with performance and assessment.

Concrete comparison

1 Identify three people doing similar jobs.
2 What does each do better or worse than the other two? This will identify key performance areas.
3 How do you know they are better and by how much? This will give you standards and assessment clues.

2 Appraisal and target setting

Handling appraisal:

(1) **Open sharing** of ideas and feelings has been shown to produce satisfaction with the interview and is more likely to lead to improved performance.

(2) An **encouraging and supportive approach**, which involves listening to the appraisee's point of view, a constructive and shared approach to job problems and giving praise for achievements, increases the chance of a successful outcome. Negative criticism has frequently been shown to have an adverse effect.

(3) **Joint problem solving** which spends time on analysing the real job problems is more likely to be effective than solution-centred appraisals,

especially if the solutions are being imposed by the appraiser.

(4) **Setting specific targets jointly** has a more powerful effect upon subsequent performance than a general discussion about goals. Once more, commitment to the outcome is in direct proportion to the appraisee's feeling of ownership.

(5) **A style** which is helpful, relaxed and friendly is most often linked to successful results.

(6) **Fairness** is seen as an essential ingredient of effective appraisal.

(7) An **agreed action plan**, specifying targets, performance and development plans and steps needed to achieve them, should be the concluding point of the appraisal.

3 Action planning

Assessment and appraisal are only the start of the development process. Every person should have an action plan which is agreed at the end of the appraisal interview, and includes:

(1) Agreed performance targets.
(2) Milestones on the way to the targets.
(3) An agreed development plan, indicating:
  (a) personal development aims;
  (b) means of achieving those aims;
  (c) support and action to be taken, and by whom.
(4) Interim review dates.

4 Performance development

Planning development is one thing, achieving it may be quite another. Development means learning and real learning means change, both of which can prove very difficult. Some of the main responsibilities of a manager are to create opportunities and a climate for learning performance-related skills and to husband and grow the abilities of their staff. This involves skill and commitment in all of the following related areas:

- Appraisal.
- Objectives and target setting.
- Managing the marginal performer.
- The development relationship: coaching and counselling.
- Development methods.
- The manager as trainer.

These will be explored in the remainder of this book.

References for further reading

Argyris C. and Schon D. (1978). *Organisational Learning*. Addison-Wesley

Harrison R. (1988). *Training and Development*. IPM

Stewart A. and V. (1980). *Managing the Manager's Growth*. Gower

21

The costs and benefits of performance appraisal

Performance appraisal: what is it?; why do we do it?

When asked the question 'What do you understand by the term performance appraisal?' most people would probably indicate that it is concerned with monitoring and assessing the performance of employees in organizations, in a systematic way. This is certainly true, but this view describes only one part of the appraisal process – the part that is concerned with looking back at how employees have performed over a particular time period, often the previous six months or twelve months. Increasingly, organizations consider it just as important, or more important, to place emphasis on the forward-looking dimension of performance appraisal, namely that it is also concerned with identifying and agreeing with employees, ways of improving their future performance and developing them, or helping them to develop themselves, as individuals.

You are probably familiar with the concept of performance appraisal, since there is evidence that the great majority of organizations, especially medium-sized and large organizations in most countries, practise some type of performance appraisal which involves periodically (most commonly annually, though time intervals can vary) writing reports about employees, and holding appraisal interviews. Survey evidence in, for example, Britain and the USA suggests that between 75% and 80% of organizations practise some type of performance appraisal. Even if you have not encountered performance appraisal, this topic should still be of relevance, since the issues of assessing and developing employee performance arise in all organizations.

Although this chapter deals primarily with performance appraisal when it is carried out in a systematic written way, many of the points can be applied in situations where performance appraisal is informal and unwritten. While this chapter and the subsequent four chapters focus primarily on the second stage of the performance development cycle discussed in Chapter 20, they examine issues relevant to the other phases of the cycle.

Costs

When organizations decide to introduce systems of performance appraisal, clearly there are costs involved. For example, these costs include the design and development of performance appraisal systems, providing training programmes for managers and employees, as well as the time cost in writing appraisal reports and conducting appraisal interviews. Because of these not insignificant costs, it is important that you should be clear about the benefits that can be gained from performance appraisal.

Benefits

You may find it helpful to consider the benefits from the perspective of the key parties involved:

- the employee, that is, the person being assessed;
- the manager, that is, the person undertaking the appraisal;
- the whole organization.

Unless benefits for the key parties are identified and clarified there is always the danger, as has unfortunately occurred in some organizations, that performance appraisal will degenerate into a kind of ritualistic, paper filling exercise that bears little relation to real life decisions made in organizations.

ACTIVITY 21.1

Please now reflect on the following three questions.

(1) Identify and name at least three important benefits which you feel an employee derives from being appraised.
(2) Similarly, identify and name at least three important benefits for the supervisor or manager carrying out the appraisal.
(3) Imagine you are a member of top management. Identify and name at least three important benefits which the organization as a whole can gain from a well run performance appraisal scheme.

Review of Activity 21.1

(1) A number of important benefits can be gained by employees. These include:

(a) The opportunity to receive feedback from the manager on how the employee's performance is viewed in the organization.
(b) A sound basis for agreeing with the manager a plan for overcoming barriers to performance and developing improved performance in the future.

(c) Gaining an appreciation of the manager's aims and priorities, so that the employee has a better idea of how and where his or her contribution fits in.

(d) An opportunity to communicate views about the job to the manager.

(e) An opportunity for a discussion about career options.

(f) A sound basis for the identification of the employee's training and development needs and for agreeing appropriate action to implement these needs.

(g) Recognition for tasks carried out well and objectives achieved.

(2) The benefits which the manager can receive, in undertaking appraisals are:

(a) The opportunity to learn about employees' hopes, fears, anxieties and concerns relating to both their present job and their future.

(b) A chance to clarify and reinforce important goals and priorities, so that employees can see precisely where their contribution fits in.

(c) Mechanisms for measuring changes in employee performance.

(d) Clarification of areas of overlap or underlap between jobs, which the manager can then rectify, improving the efficiency of the organization.

(e) A sound basis for considering transfer decisions among staff.

(f) An opportunity to motivate staff by recognizing achievements.

(g) A basis for discussing and agreeing upon courses of action to develop employee performance and contribute to overall improved performance in the manager's area of responsibility.

(3) Benefits to the company include:

(a) Assistance with succession planning, in helping to identify those employees who are ready right now, or at some time in the future after acquiring suitable training and experience, to take over from others in key positions.

(b) Help with manpower planning, in identifying those areas where the company has strength in depth or possible weaknesses for particular categories of manpower.

(c) Ensuring objectives agreed for individual employees harmonize with corporate objectives.

(d) Generally improved communications throughout the organization.

(e) Above all, improved performance.

Although the benefits of performance appraisal have been considered in greater detail than the costs in this chapter, the two must be carefully weighed up. In the next chapter, which looks at aspects of performance appraisal in action, further consideration is given to some of the costs and difficulties that can occur in operating systems of performance appraisal.

References for further reading

Anderson G.C. (1986). *Performance Appraisal.* HMSO

Anderson G.C. *et al.* (1987). Appraisal without Form Filling. *Personnel Management* February

Fletcher C. and Williams R. (1985). *Performance Appraisal and Career Development.* Hutchinson

Latham G.P. and Wexley K.N. (1981). *Increasing Productivity through Performance Appraisal.* Addison-Wesley

22

Designing and implementing systems of performance appraisal

Performance appraisal: how do we do it?

In this chapter the focus is very much on the choices to be made in operating performance appraisal, and on the issues that must be addressed in designing and implementing systems of performance appraisal.

Insupply case study: Performance appraisal in action: Buroquip

In Buroquip before the merger, a performance appraisal scheme had been in operation. Simon Smith, no longer in employment with Insupply, was formerly Head of Personnel at Buroquip and he designed and introduced the appraisal scheme. You can see in Figure 22.1 the kind of appraisal document which managers completed for their staff, on an annual basis.

Each Buroquip manager and supervisor held an appraisal interview for every member of staff. Where major disagreements occurred, Colin Smith reviewed and, in exceptional cases, adjusted the appraisal documentation, which was normally submitted to personnel, for filing in personnel records.

CASE PROJECT 22.1

What are your comments on the Buroquip appraisal scheme? How well do you think it worked?

You may have correctly reached the conclusion that neither management nor employees were particularly enthusiastic about this approach to performance appraisal. The managers felt that the appraisal documentation required them to 'play God' in rating employees on a highly subjective set of measures, largely

Buroquip Performance Appraisal Form (applied to all staff)

To be completed by managers for each employee

Please complete the personal details section for each employee, then tick the appropriate number in answering the questions. Managers may show their conclusions to employees, if they wish.

Name of employee: Department:

Name of manager: Duties of job:

	Outstanding	Above average	Adequate	Below standard	Unsatis-factory
1 Drive and energy	1	2	3	4	5
2 Acceptability to others	1	2	3	4	5
3 Appearance & manner	1	2	3	4	5
4 Attendance & punctuality	1	2	3	4	5
5 Ability to inspire confidence	1	2	3	4	5
6 Initiative & innovation	1	2	3	4	5
7 Stability & consistency	1	2	3	4	5
8 Attitude	1	2	3	4	5
9 Judgement	1	2	3	4	5
10 Oral & written communication	1	2	3	4	5
11 Cost consciousness	1	2	3	4	5
12 Job knowledge	1	2	3	4	5
13 Quantity of work	1	2	3	4	5
14 Quality of work	1	2	3	4	5
15 Overall evaluation	1	2	3	4	5

Signature of Manager or Supervisor carrying out appraisal

....

Date ....

Figure 22.1   Buroquip performance appraisal form.

associated with personality characteristics that did not appear to have direct relevance to many of the jobs performed. No training had been given to either managers or employees in performance appraisal and appraisal interviewing; no one was very clear about what the company expected to achieve from the scheme. Most of the employees disliked their appraisal interviews, which they felt provided an opportunity for managers to pick on their faults. Since, however, the completed appraisal forms were sent to personnel for filing, nothing much ever seemed to happen as a result of appraisals! Eventually, about three years after its inception, the scheme was being implemented in a very patchy, unenthusiastic manner – one or two managers and supervisors had stopped doing it altogether! Sally Bullen, who you may recall supervised the typing pool at Buroquip, modified the documentation to suit what she saw as the needs of her staff. She simplified the document, using Questions 10 to 15 only!

Problems associated with the Buroquip performance appraisal scheme

The Buroquip experience highlights a number of symptoms of what happens when things go wrong for a performance appraisal scheme. It may be useful to identify, in a systematic fashion, the source of the main problems.

1 An imposed system – lack of staff commitment

Many of the problems probably originated in the fact that the scheme was seen to belong to Simon Smith, the former Head of Personnel at Buroquip. Others in the company did not have the opportunity to contribute ideas to the design and implementation of the appraisal scheme.

2 Lack of clear appraisal objectives

No one seemed clear what the scheme was expected to achieve.

3 No training/briefing provided

Neither the managers nor supervisors who undertook appraisals, nor employees who were assessed, received any training or briefing. Simon Smith sent a circular to managers and supervisors, which was long and detailed, and remained unread by most!

4 No use made of appraisal findings

The scheme did little to translate appraisal data into practical action plans.

5 Historical orientation

Performance appraisal seemed to apply to the past; as implied in item 4, there was little emphasis on the future.

6 Subjectivity and relevance of ratings

Almost all those involved felt the scheme called for many highly subjective assessments of characteristics, of dubious relevance to job performance.

This criticism applies mainly to Questions 1 to 9 on the appraisal document. In fairness, Questions 10 to 15 are relevant to effective appraisal, but there are weaknesses in the earlier categories. One salesman, who was actually very poor at selling, received 'above average' or 'outstanding' for Questions 1 to 9!

As will be discussed later, this whole approach to performance appraisal, placing emphasis on subjective rating scales of personality characteristics, in the main, is now considered old fashioned, and has been replaced by other approaches, though elements of rating scales, properly defined, can still be used.

7 Fairness

The scheme was seen to be unfair. In situations where disagreement occurred Colin Smith often found himself in a difficult position in having, he felt, to support either the manager's or the employee's viewpoint.

8 Design features

There were a number of flaws in the design of the scheme.

(1) Undefined categories.

For example, instead of simply listing 'Drive and energy' and 'Acceptability', some description of what these terms mean would help appraisers, for example:

    (a) Drive and energy. Is he/she diligent and persistent in carrying out work assigned? Does he/she apply himself/herself with enthusiasm, and with good purpose?

    (b) Acceptability. Does he/she get on with other people? Does he/she command respect and co-operation?

(2) Lack of behaviourial 'anchors' on rating scales.

One modern approach, called Behaviourally Anchored Rating Scales (BARS) requires a behaviourial statement for each point on rating scales, to assist managers making common interpretations of rating scales, and to provide employees being appraised with more useful feedback on how different aspects of their work performance are assessed.

For instance, using Question 9 'Judgment' from the Buroquip form as a illustration, the improved BARS approach would look as shown in Figure 22.2.

JUDGEMENT

1	2	3	4	5
Consistently makes sound decisions even on complex issues	Very sound logical thinker	On the whole, good decisions resulting from logical analysis	Judgement sometimes sound, but errors in judgement do arise	Decisions often wrong or ineffective

Figure 22.2 An example of a Behaviourally Anchored Rating Scale.

(3) Mixed, ambiguous factors.

Factors to be assessed should be simple and undimensional, as far as possible. Examples of mixed, ambiguous factors on the Buroquip appraisal form are shown, for example, in Questions 4 and 10. Question 4 indicates 'Attendance and punctuality' but these are really two separate factors, about which different assessments could be made. Similarly, in including both oral and written communication, Question 10 includes two separate factors.

(4) Absence of descriptive justifications.

Appraisers are not asked to include comment to justify their ratings.

(5) Five point rating scales.

While there is no easy answer as to how many points of discrimination there should be on a rating scale, five point scales are particularly prone to the problems of central tendency (that is, opting for the middle category) and avoidance of extremes (that is, avoidance of points one and five on the rating scales).

(6) Appraisee participation.

The documentation provides little incentive for the employee being appraised to participate actively. For instance, there is no space for appraisee comments, and no requirement for the employee's signature.

Insupply case study: Designing and developing an effective performance appraisal scheme

Many organizations are faced with the problems of designing and developing either a new performance appraisal scheme, or else a modified version of an old scheme. Typically, organizations are involving a wider range of people in this process than before.

Insupply will be used as a case illustration to give you an appreciation of the main steps and issues involved. Hedi Lindstrom, the Chief Executive of Insupply, came from a company where performance appraisal made an effective contribution to the management of people, and she felt that developing a new performance appraisal scheme should be a priority for Insupply. While being aware that Buroquip had a rather negative experience of this, and that Gloprint had none at all, she asked Colin Smith, Company Secretary and Deputy Chief Executive of Insupply, to take responsibility for this project, especially as she knew Colin appreciated the importance of performance appraisal and wished to avoid the mistakes that had been made at Buroquip.

Defining appraisal objectives

The first step in establishing any performance appraisal scheme is to agree on what the objective or objectives of the scheme should be. Typically, appraisal schemes serve a number of objectives, so clarification is needed. One starting point that has been used in some organizations is to agree on a list of possible objectives, and then ask the senior team (for example, the directors) or a wider group, including employees from different levels and functions, to place them in order of importance.

Colin Smith and Hedi Lindstrom decided to enlist the help of an external consultant to conduct a survey of employee attitudes towards appraisal in general, and appraisal objectives.

The main findings from the survey (not untypical of the kind of results in other organizations conducting this type of survey) were:

- Most employees welcome the idea of regular performance appraisal.
- Most felt its objectives should primarily focus on improving employee job performance, and on identifying training and development needs to assist employees in developing themselves.
- There were mixed views on whether performance appraisal should be linked to decisions on pay and rewards, and whether it should be used to identify employee potential for promotion purposes.
- Most employees sought active involvement in the scheme, and felt it should assist in communicating their views to management. Their main concerns were that appraisals might not be totally fair, because of the possibility of subjective assessment being made and managers adopting inconsistent standards (for example, they felt some managers might be hard markers, others soft).

Colin Smith and Hedi Lindstrom asked the consultant to present a summary of the survey findings before the board of directors, so that decisions could be taken on what objectives the performance appraisal scheme should serve, and on other key issues that would help to define the parameters and broad shape of the performance appraisal system.

The seven directors then completed the document shown in Figure 22.3, having reduced the range of possible objectives to seven, and put them in rank order. The results are shown also in Figure 22.3.

Appraisal objectives	Rank of importance assigned by 7 directors						
	1st	2nd	3rd	4th	5th	6th	7th
To review past performance	–	3	2	2	–	–	–
To make decisions on pay	2	–	1	1	–	1	2
To improve future performance	4	2	1	–	–	–	–
To strengthen communications	–	–	1	2	3	1	–
To identify employee potential	–	–	1	1	1	2	2
To identify employee's training and development needs	1	2	1	1	1	1	–
To help succession planning	–	–	–	–	2	2	3

Figure 22.3 Ranking of appraisal objectives by Insupply directors.

These results highlight the value of the process in making views explicit, as you can see the range of different views. On whether to link appraisal and pay, the directors are clearly divided.

On talking through the issues and their differences of viewpoint, the directors agreed on the following objectives:

(1) The main objectives of the appraisal scheme are:

    (a) To improve the current and future performance of employees.

    (b) To help employee to develop, through identifying their training and development needs.

    (c) To review past performance.

(2) Additional objectives the appraisal scheme should achieve are:

    (a) To strengthen communications.

    (b) To help succession planning.

It was agreed that once the performance appraisal scheme had been established, and run for at least one year, the Board would revisit the question of whether to link appraisal to pay decisions, and to the evaluation of employee potential.

ACTIVITY 22.1

What are the arguments for and against linking appraisal to pay decisions? What do you think?

Review of Activity 22.1

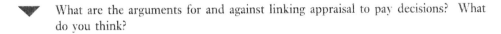

The arguments in favour are:

(1) Many employees perceive appraisal as a fair basis for pay decisions.
(2) It provides higher rewards for the better performers, and encourages the development of a positive performance culture in the organization, in which it is seen as legitimate to reward high performers and give less to poor performers.
(3) All parties will take performance appraisal seriously.

The arguments against are:

(1) The pay issue will tend to overshadow all other aspects of appraisal.
(2) If the performance appraisal scheme is not seen as fair, employees will feel dissatisfied.
(3) If jobs are highly interdependent, some form of group reward may be more appropriate.

Insupply case study: Developing the parameters of the appraisal scheme

Key questions that must be addressed are:

- What categories of employees should be appraised?
- How many variants of the appraisal scheme are needed?
- What criteria should be used to evaluate performance?
- What kind of documentation should be used?
- Who should be the appraisers?
- Should the contents of appraisal reports be freely shown to employees?
- Should employees make an input into their own appraisals?
- What should be the nature of the performance appraisal cycle?

The directors of Insupply decided to consult widely before finalizing answers to these questions. All managers attended a 1½ day seminar to discuss the issues involved. A working party consisting of Colin Smith, two managers, three employees and the consultant was set up to produce recommendations, which were then considered by the directors.

The decisions reached were as follows:

(1) All three hundred employees to be covered.
(2) Two variants of the scheme needed – one for supervisors, managers and directors, another for all other employees.
(3) The achievement of objectives to be the main criterion for the managerial scheme; performance and behaviourial criteria for non-managerial staff.
(4) Documentation to be kept as simple as possible.
(5) The immediate manager normally to be the appraiser, with appraisals being reviewed by the appraiser's manager.
(6) Employees to see their appraisal reports, and to be asked to sign them.
(7) All employees to be encouraged to complete a self-assessment document.

Clearly, the shape of a very modern appraisal scheme was being developed. A summary of the appraisal cycle is shown in Figure 22.4.

1 Central Personnel issues appraisal documents to all managers who are to be appraisers.

2 Managers distribute self-assessment documents to staff, and arrange appraisal interview dates.

3 Employees complete self-assessment documents and return them to their managers.

4 Managers prepare for interviews, study employees' self-assessment forms and consult reviewers (that is, their managers).

5 Managers conduct appraisal interviews.

6 Managers complete appraisal documents, employees insert comments if they so wish; both sign the documentation which is passed to reviewers.

7 Reviewers call meetings with appraisers to discuss the consistency of ratings; sign documents, and transmit to central personnel, with copies returned to individual managers and employees.

8 Managers and employees consider action points agreed at the appraisal interviews.

9 Central Personnel discusses with managers employees' training needs to organize, where appropriate, company-wide programmes.

Figure 22.4 Performance appraisal cycle.

The new appraisal document for managerial staff is shown in Figure 22.5, the document for non-managerial staff in Figure 22.6, and the self-assessment document in Figure 22.7.

Please study these documents before moving on to the next activity.

CASE PROJECT 22.2

How soundly based do you feel is the new Insupply performance appraisal?

Comments on Case Project 22.2

These appraisal documents are fairly typical of many modern schemes currently in use. There is no such thing as perfect appraisal documentation; many options are available, each with positive and negative aspects. It is important that appraisal documentation is developed to meet the needs of a particular organization. While you can probably identify some deficiencies in the paperwork, the important issue is to what extent the appraisal documentation reflects the needs and philosophy of the company, as previously described.

CASE PROJECT 22.3

What other conditions should Insupply fulfil to ensure its performance appraisal scheme is effectively launched?

Review of Case Project 22.3

It should ensure that all the key parties – employees, appraisers and reviewers – receive adequate training.

Employees require briefing on the scheme, guidance on self-analysis for completion of the self-assessment document, and an appreciation of the skills they need to participate in the appraisal interview.

Appraisers have similar needs, plus the need for skills in planning for, organizing and conducting appraisal interviews.

Reviewers require briefing on their responsibilities, in ensuring that appraisals are fair, objective and accurate.

Confidential

NOTES FOR APPRAISERS

The overall objective of the performance appraisal is to review the performance of each employee over the last period.

Establish if targets have been met and in areas where they have not, establish a plan to address any shortcomings of an individual nature.

You are expected to agree and plan targets for the next period and discuss career aspirations of the interviewee.

Prior to your meeting with your staff member you should have received from them the self-appraisal form in order to allow you to prepare for the meeting.

1   NON-CLERICAL STAFF

PERFORMANCE REVIEW INTERVIEW

Name of Appraisee: .... Period Under Review: ....

Job Title: .... Department: ....

Please insert comments under each heading. If additional space is required, please attach separate sheets.

Describe the main purpose of the job in the space below.

To what extent does the job holder have sufficient technical knowledge for the job?

Comment on the business know-how of the job holder.

2

Comment on the analytical skills of the job holder.

Comment on the written and verbal communication skills of the job holder.

Comment on direction/control skills.

Comment on interpersonal skills.

3

Setting Objectives

Comment on performance over the last 12 months in relation to objectives/tasks.

4

Setting Objectives (Continued)

Please set down agreed objectives for the next twelve months, stating clearly the measures/criteria to be used.

5

Performance Summary

Performance summary including areas of performance that need to be addressed and outlining in what ways this will be done.

Please include action points at the end of the performance summary.

6

Development Needs

Comment on individual's personal development needs by completing the table below. State in what areas action is required and by whom: (a) internally by the manager; (b) by internal training; (c) by external training.

Training and Development Plans

Action	Purpose	Training

Appraisee's Comments

Signature of Appraisee: .... Date: ....

Signature of Appraiser: .... Date: ....

Signature of Reviewer Manager: .... Date: ....

Figure 22.5 Appraisal document for managerial staff.

Confidential

NOTES FOR APPRAISERS

Please complete this form for each member of non-managerial staff in your area of responsibility.

1
Complete only as applicable

PERFORMANCE REVIEW INTERVIEW

Name: .... Period Under Review: ....

Job Title: .... Department: ....

Appraiser to circle the appropriate rating for each category and for overall performance. Please also indicate why you made this rating.

Rating scale for each category and for overall performance

Volume of Work	1	2	3	4	5	6	7	8

How does the amount of work done compare with the amount required by the job?

Below Expectations   Meets Expectations   Exceeds Expectations

Why did you make this rating?

Quality of Work	1	2	3	4	5	6	7	8

Comment on the quality of this person's work.

Below Expectations   Meets Expectations   Exceeds Expectations

Why did you make this rating?

Participation	1	2	3	4	5	6	7	8

Comment on and rate the level of participation this person makes to departmental objectives.

Below Expectations   Meets Expectations   Exceeds Expectations

Why did you make this rating?

2

Job Knowledge	1	2	3	4	5	6	7	8

Below
Expectations

Meets
Expectations

Exceeds
Expectations

Does this person
have the knowledge
to do the work
satisfactorily?

Why did you make this
rating?

Dependability	1	2	3	4	5	6	7	8

Below
Expectations

Meets
Expectations

Exceeds
Expectations

How well does this
person follow
procedures?

Why did you make this
rating?

Teamwork	1	2	3	4	5	6	7	8

Below
Expectations

Meets
Expectations

Exceeds
Expectations

To what extent does
this person perform
as a team member in
the department?

Why did you make this
rating?

Attendance	1	2	3	4	5	6	7	8

Below
Expectations

Meets
Expectations

Exceeds
Expectations

How does this
person's attendance
record meet with
Company expectations?

Why did you make this
rating?

3

Punctuality	1	2	3	4	5	6	7	8

Below
Expectations

Meets
Expectations

Exceeds
Expectations

To what extent is
this person punctual
in arriving/departing
and at break periods?

Why did you make this
rating?

Communication	1	2	3	4	5	6	7	8

Below
Expectations

Meets
Expectations

Exceeds
Expectations

To what extent does
this person's verbal
and written skills
meet the needs of
the job?

Why did you make this
rating?

Overall Performance	1	2	3	4	5	6	7	8

Below
Expectations

Meets
Expectations

Exceeds
Expectations

Comment on why
you made this rating.

Other Comments: e.g. (no rating scale necessary)
Identify training needs agreed.

4

Appraisee's Comments:

Signature of Appraisee: .... Date: ....

Signature of Appraiser: .... Date: ....

Signature of Reviewer Manager: .... Date: ....

Figure 22.6 Appraisal document for non-managerial staff.

Confidential

NOTES FOR EMPLOYEES

STAFF APPRAISAL
SELF-APPRAISAL

The attached form is to help you collect your thoughts together about your job. It should also help you to think about what you want to achieve during the next period in:

(a) your job

and

(b) in terms of your personal development

Consider the targets you had for the last period and whether or not you had achieved them. Consider any factors outwith your control which hindered you. Be prepared to discuss tasks/targets with your Supervisor and also be prepared to plan for the next period.

If you have any suggestions which may help you in your job, be prepared to share them with your Supervisor when you meet.

It is also an opportunity to consider if there are any career moves you want to make.

Please complete the form and hand it to your Supervisor two days before Appraisal Interview and be prepared to discuss it with your Supervisor.

1   NON-CLERICAL STAFF

PERFORMANCE REVIEW INTERVIEW

Name of Appraisee: .... Period Under Review: ....

Job Title: .... Department: ....

Please insert comments under each heading. If additional space is required, please attach separate sheets.

Describe the main purpose of the job in the space below.

Which aspects of your job do you feel you have done well in during the review period?

Describe any difficulties you may have had and how you overcame them.

2

Describe internal/external factors outside your control which may have affected you doing your job.

Which areas of your job performance do you feel could be improved by you or with the help of your manager? Please state actions which you feel should be taken, and by whom.

What work objectives would you consider to be important to achieve over the next year?

3

Does your job fully utilize your abilities? If not, how could your skills be used more fully?

List any additional qualifications you have achieved during the review period, and any courses you have attended.

In what way would you like to develop over the next year?

4

What personal development would you hope to achieve:

(a) during the next year?

(b) in the longer term?

5

Any other constructive comments?

Signature: ....

Date: ....

Figure 22.7 Appraisal document for self-assessment.

Clearly, as explained in this chapter, managers should take an interest in how appraisal schemes are designed and planned, to ensure they have a good understanding of the performance appraisal process, what it attempts to achieve and how it should be implemented.

The next chapter focuses on the skills required to handle the interpersonal situations when appraisals are discussed with employees.

References for further reading

Anderson G.C. (1986). *Performance Appraisal*. HMSO

Anderson G.C. *et al.* (1987). Appraisal without Form Filling. *Personnel Management* February

Mohrman A.M. *et al.* (1989). *Designing Performance Appraisal Systems*. Jossey-Bass

23

Developing appraisal interviewing skills

Appraisal interviewing: An introduction

The appraisal interview is seen by most organizations as the key feature which will determine the success or failure of the performance appraisal scheme.

The appraisal interview is one of the most difficult forms of interview which you will undertake because:

- the interview can prove to be extremely unpredictable, especially the discussion over matters relating to areas of deficient performance and the weaknesses of the individual;
- you must display a wide range of interpersonal skills in conducting effective appraisal interviews;
- appraisal interview skills cannot be readily learned from watching other managers in action, since, because of the confidential nature of the appraisal interview, it is unlikely that you will witness anyone else in the role of the interviewer except your own manager.

Who should conduct the appraisal interview?

Most organizations have adopted the view that the employee's line manager should undertake the responsibilities of writing appraisal reports and conducting appraisal interviews since these tasks are an integral part of the management process, and since he or she should, through close working contact and through directing and controlling the employee's activities, be in a better position than anyone else in the organization to evaluate the employee's strengths and weaknesses and level of performance.

How much time is devoted to appraisal interviews?

The effectiveness of interviews cannot obviously be judged according to the amount of time devoted to them, but the data in Figure 23.1, derived from the IPM 1977 and 1986 surveys, highlights wide variations in practice.

Time	Percentage of organizations	
	1977	1986
Up to half an hour	19	3
Half an hour to an hour	34	27
One hour to two hours	26	53
Over two hours	7	15
Not known	14	3

Figure 23.1   Time devoted to the appraisal interview for managerial staff.

Clearly this data must be interpreted with caution, since it was impossible for respondents to know exact times for their organizations, and the length of interview is likely to vary both with the organization, and even for the same interviewer. In addition, some of the organizations involved in the survey did not feel able to answer the question.

If appraisal is carried out with conviction and commitment, it is likely to make considerable demands on managerial time, and the evidence suggests that in some organizations substantial amounts of time are devoted to appraisal interviews.

What the appraisal interview can achieve

The appraisal interview can serve a number of objectives, which should relate to the overall objectives which the organization expects its performance appraisal scheme as a whole to achieve. In an appraisal interview you should aim to achieve the following.

(1) Let the employee know where he or she stands.
   This is most readily achieved in an open appraisal system when you are frank with appraisees, and they have ready access to their appraisal reports.
(2) Discuss the employee's job performance over the period under review.
   This is most readily achieved by a two-way exchange of information, when you explain and amplify the contents of the appraisal report, and let employees put forward their point of view.
(3) Agree action to improve the performance of the employee.
   The discussion of performance can lead readily to the consideration of career prospects in the organization, the employee's ambitions, and training and development required to realize the employee's potential, as well as focusing on new targets to achieve better performance.

Links between formal appraisal interviews and informal appraisal

A common line of argument often put forward by managers and others who are sceptical about performance appraisal is to stress that appraisal interviewing on an informal basis is an integral part of day-to-day management and supervision. Good supervisors and managers will therefore be regularly monitoring the performance of subordinates, indicating defects that call for correction and providing encouragement to build on strengths. Formal appraisal interviews are consequently superfluous and time-consuming.

This type of view runs counter to research findings which show that the more managers talk over subordinates' work with them, the more likely it is that managers will conduct appraisal interviews that are perceived as having positive effects on job performance and job satisfaction. This seems to contradict the view that if we have good communications the rest of the time, we do not require appraisal interviews. These research findings help to demonstrate the importance of regular, informal appraisal counselling sessions involving manager and employee, not as a replacement for, but in addition to, formal appraisal interviews.

Preparation

Any appraisal interview held without planning will at best waste time and money, at worst it may lead to a decrease in productivity. Poorly planned appraisal interviews are likely to have damaging effects on employee morale and motivation.

In the planning stage both appraiser and appraisee need to reflect on the goals the appraisee has been trying to achieve during the review period.

You may find it helpful in analysing each goal of a member of your staff to use four criteria:

- Was the goal too easy, too difficult or too vague?
- What did the employee do that contributed to the goal being achieved or missed?
- What did you contribute?
- What external factors have altered, influencing the probability of achieving the goal?

The ensuing stages of preparation require consideration of the following questions:

- In what way has achievement or non-achievement of the goal affected the employee, the organization and yourself?
- Has anything happened to change the employee's duties or business objectives from now on?

253

- What will the employee have to do to achieve maximum effectiveness in future?

This approach to planning – if carried out by both parties – should permit both you and the appraisee to enter the appraisal interview with provisional answers to three questions:

- How effective is the employee's job performance?
- What are the factors influencing this performance?
- What changes should be made?

Styles of conducting appraisal interviews

A wide variety of styles considered appropriate for conducting appraisal interviews have been discussed in the literature. Probably the best-known classification of appraisal interviewing styles has emerged from the work of the American industrial psychologist, Norman Maier (1976). Maier put forward the proposition that three main styles of appraisal interviewing can be identified.

The tell and sell approach

This style is likely to be adopted by interviewers who have an authoritarian approach to management. The main features of this approach are that interviewers concentrate on telling employees the evaluation that has been made of their performance, and then attempt to convince the employees of the fairness of the assessment, and the need for them to accept whatever follow-up action is recommended. Maier considers the main deficiency of their approach to be the defensive responses which this style is likely to evoke from employees, and the consequent difficulty of securing their commitment to the follow-up action which the appraisers attempt to impose upon them.

The tell and listen approach

Interviewers still attempt to convey their evaluation to subordinates, but, in this second style, some attempt is made to develop two-way communication by encouraging employees to express their views and respond to the evaluation made of their work performance. Maier sees this as an improvement on the 'tell and sell' method, but considers it still suffers the drawback that employees may feel forced into a defensive position on hearing how the appraiser has evaluated their performance.

The problem-solving approach

Under this approach, the appraiser commences the interview by encouraging the employee to identify and discuss problem areas and then consider the development of solutions. This approach means that the subordinate plays an active part in analysing problems and suggesting solutions, and the evaluation of performance emerges from the discussion at the appraisal interview, instead of being imposed by the appraiser upon the employee, as in the case of the other two approaches. Maier indicates a preference for this third style, and under the problem-solving approach the emphasis is less on what went right or wrong with performance in the past and more on ensuring that steps are taken to improve performance in the future.

Guidelines for appraisal interviewing

In the literature many prescriptive lists of suggestions have been put forward. A summary of what are most frequently seen to be key elements in effective appraisal interviewing is set out below. These guidelines must be interpreted with caution, since a high degree of flexibility is likely to be shown by good interviewers in dealing with the widely differing problems and needs of individual employees.

(1) Begin the interview with a clear statement of purpose.
    This will help to generate a purposeful interaction, and remind both parties in what ways the formal appraisal interview, as a key part of the performance appraisal process, can be differentiated from informal appraisal and counselling sessions.

(2) Attempt to put the employee at ease, and establish rapport.
    This process will be assisted if a high degree of mutual trust and confidence characterizes superior–subordinate relationships. Rapport will be more readily established if adequate informal counselling and guidance on performance are provided, so that the employee is confident that no surprise issues will be raised, and that the formal appraisal interview will be used to review achievements and problems previously discussed informally.

(3) Discuss the main tasks and responsibilities undertaken by the employee and invite comments.
    In situations where the employee completes a self-appraisal document, it may be useful for you to initiate the discussion by reviewing the employee's comments concerning job objectives and key tasks.

(4) Ensure a balanced discussion takes place.
    This requires not only that praise be given for good work, but also that areas of deficient performance be frankly faced up to and discussed. Where possible, it is desirable that praise and criticism be related to expected

standards of job performance, and that comments on personal characteristics and personality traits be minimized, except in so far as these have a major impact on job performance and future potential.

(5) Encourage the employee to talk freely about any frustration in the job, and about problems areas.
Probing questions asked by yourself assist the employee to identify underlying problems and to generate possible solutions.

(6) Encourage the employee to develop self-analysis and self-discovery. If you avoid a spoon-feeding approach, you can attempt to encourage employees to think through points for themselves, helping them to develop a better understanding of the areas where change and improvement are required.

(7) Consider the year ahead, including action to develop performance.
In encouraging employees to talk about career expectations, you can assist them to relate their ambitions to likely organizational opportunities.

(8) Bring the interview to a close with a summary and plan for future action. This permits both parties to clarify what action is expected of them following the interview.

Issues of appraisal interviewing and appraisal follow-up

You are asked to read the article *Nurse Appraisal in Practice*, which reports on and discusses the findings of a research study investigating the effectiveness of appraisal interviews in a particular occupational setting.

NURSE APPRAISAL IN PRACTICE

Effective management of people in all branches of the National Health Service has never been as important as it is now. Pressure on resources means that new ways have to be found to improve productivity and employee satisfaction.

Because of the labour intensive work in the health service particular interest focuses on improving people's effectiveness within the organization. Commitment, not compliance, and competence are the keys.

And despite suggestions that the health service's climate has been undesirably altered in the pursuit of economic effectiveness, the need for performance appraisal schemes is increasingly recognized in the NHS and elsewhere in the public sector.

In view of this it may be helpful to consider experience of using a staff appraisal and development system for a number of years.

The present formal approach to assessing employee performance was introduced for nursing staff in Scotland in 1977. The nursing staff development programme's principal objectives are to give employees feedback on their performance and the opportunity to discuss any relevant aspect with their senior officer at a formal appraisal interview, held annually, as well as to develop employee skills and performance.

We carried out a study to review the effectiveness of appraisal interviews among all specialties and grades of nursing staff in a selected Scottish area health board in 1985. This study was based on questionnaires completed by nursing staff.

Performance appraisal is regarded by many as a problematical area, and there is a lot written about the problems and pitfalls organizations encounter. Appraisal interviewing is a particularly crucial part of performance appraisal.

Handled well, it can make an important contribution to improved staff management in terms of achieving the scheme's objectives. If mishandled, it can clearly have extremely damaging effects on work relationships and performance levels.

Consequently, we felt it was appropriate to raise fundamental questions about the nursing staff development programme, as it has been operating in many parts of Scotland for the past eight years.

Questions include: how the appraisal interview is viewed by those interviewed, as well as conducting appraisals; what the main problems and issues of appraisal interviewing in nursing are and what evidence there is that it makes a contribution to improved patient care standards.

These and other related questions were investigated. Three hundred and seventeen questionnaires were completed representing a response rate of 83%. Participants in the survey were drawn from all the major nursing functions and each level in Fife health board. The largest representations were from community and general nursing and there were substantial responses from teaching, midwifery, geriatric, psychiatric and mental handicap staff.

A number of highly positive findings from nursing staff emerged about performance appraisal. The three most significant were satisfaction with the conduct of the appraisal interview; perceived fairness and enhanced motivation; and the setting up of a wide range of actions to develop staff performance.

One of the most encouraging findings of the survey was the general positive set of employee responses towards the way appraisal interviews, in general, are handled. The majority of participants (54 per cent) reported that they found their senior officer's attitude at the appraisal interview highly supportive, and a further 25 per cent found it slightly supportive. Most of those involved in the survey indicated that they enjoyed considerable freedom in putting forward and discussing their ideas and feelings at the appraisal interview.

The majority of survey participants indicated that their senior officer's assessment of their performance was extremely fair. Further still, the majority indicated positive links between the appraisal interview and motivation, stating that, on the whole, they felt encouraged at the end of the interview.

Many activities planned were implemented

A major positive finding is that a wide range of actions to develop performance were agreed by staff with their managers at the appraisal interview. Encouragingly, a substantial number of the activities planned were subsequently implemented (Figure 23.2).

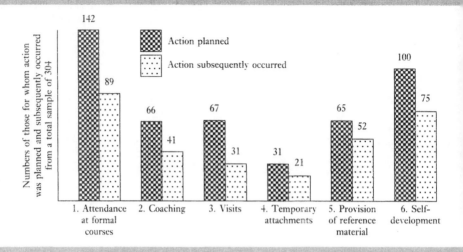

Figure 23.2   Action to develop performance.

Although attendance at formal courses elicited most mentions, an interesting feature is that in many cases alternative approaches to employee development were planned and implemented, in particular self-development, coaching, temporary attachments, visits to other nursing units and the provision of reference materials all gained considerable mention. While inevitably some of the planned activities did not take place, more than 50 per cent did except in the case of visits to other nursing units, where the success rate was lower.

Several mixed, and less positive findings emerged, in particular 'lack of perceived importance and relevance to patient care standards' and the short duration of appraisal interviews.

Respondents' views towards the appraisal interview's importance and its perceived relevance to improved job performance and better healthcare standards are much more problematical. In this area of the survey a mixed pattern of responses emerged. Only 47 per cent of respondents rated the appraisal interview as being of reasonable or substantial importance to them.

Views on the interview discussion's relevance to improving nursing service/patient care standards were extremely mixed – 47 per cent indicating either some or substantial relevance, but 40.8 per cent saw only slight or no relevance.

Service staff who have discussed these findings consider that the individual staff member being the focus of attention may account for the lack of perception of the discussion's relevance to patient care.

Indeed, this may be reflected in the response to the question on benefits of the programme – 'at last, time for me'. This could be a timely reminder to managers faced with falling standards of morale.

More disturbingly negative are a sizeable group's (50.4 per cent) views that their performance has improved only slightly or hardly at all because of the appraisal interview. And just under a fifth 'didn't know' whether their performance had altered because of the appraisal. This suggests a need for informal counselling as a key part of the staff development.

A disappointingly large number (33 per cent) estimated that their most recent appraisal interview was of less than 25 minutes' duration. It seems most unlikely that meaningful, in depth discussions reviewing a whole year's work and planning for the year ahead could take place in such a short time. A further 32 per cent indicated between 25 and 40 minutes as the length of their appraisal interviews.

This data compares unfavourably with the findings of a recent national Institute of Personnel Management study covering a wide variety of organizations' appraisal practices. This showed that most appraisal interviews of management staff lasted for between one and two hours. To avoid a totally unfair comparison, it should be noted that under 50 per cent of our sample could be classified as holding managerial positions.

The survey responses reveal a small group (5–7 per cent) aggrieved about most aspects of the appraisal interview. They felt that they were unfairly assessed; felt discouraged after the appraisal interview; and saw few opportunities to express their views at the interview.

It is disturbing to find so many people with such a negative approach to appraisal interviewing.

The most striking feature of the senior nursing staff appraisers are their generally positive views towards the appraisal interview, and commitment towards its success. A high degree of conscientiousness is indicated by the substantial amounts of time devoted to preparation for appraisal.

The majority (52 per cent) of those in the sample who conduct appraisal interviews devote between a half and one hour to interview preparation, for each member of their staff. A substantial number (31 per cent) indicated they spent between one and two hours in preparation for each interview.

Appraisers saw interviews as a two-way exchange

The great majority of appraisers perceived the interview as a two-way exchange of views in which the employee being interviewed plays a full and active part. Few (only 17 per cent) admitted to encountering difficulties in planning for, or conducting, interviews. They also, generally, recognized the value of the review form as an aid to planning and conducting appraisal interviews.

In view of the fact that 65 per cent of appraisees used the pre-interview, self-assessment form and overall found it an aid to discussion, increased benefits may have arisen had more time been devoted to the actual interview.

A desire to further develop their appraisal interviewing effectiveness can be seen in the fact that though many have undergone various forms of training, a large proportion recognize the need for further training.

The percentages of those who have already received appraisal process and interview training and those who want further training are shown in Figures 23.3 and 23.4.

Appraisers identified the need for training in the areas of interviewing techniques and coaching skills in particular. This highlights a new dimension to the training issues involved in performance appraisal not revealed by either the line management study or by the 1976 review of nursing staff appraisal.

That so many appraisers recognize the need for training in coaching skills shows they are increasingly aware of the importance of the connection between regular coaching which goes on at the place of work and the formal performance appraisal programme.

The central conclusion appears to be that although nurses mainly have positive views towards the appraisal interview processes, there is not universal and

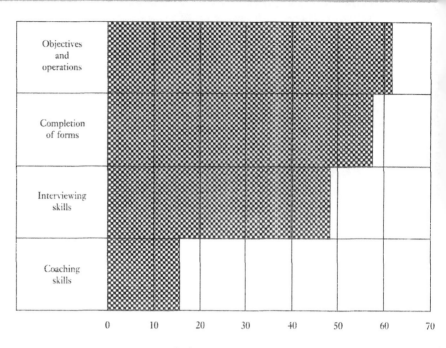

Figure 23.3   Percentage receiving training before conducting interviews.

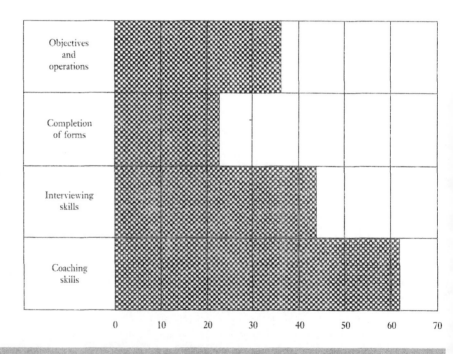

Figure 23.4   Percentage requesting further training.

wholehearted commitment to the importance and relevance of the appraisal interview to improving job performance and organizational efficiency.

Many nurses see appraisal as being principally concerned with the development of careers and preparation for promotion, rather than with the improvement of performance in the present job. It may be the case that the survey's main finding is that the mechanics of performance appraisal are working reasonably well, but more must be done to communicate the formal appraisal programme's objectives to all involved.

The analysis highlights some apparent paradoxes: the substantial amount of preparation carried out by many appraisees and appraisers, and yet the apparent shortness of most appraisal interviews; the very mixed views on the individual and organizational importance of the appraisal interview despite the fact that a wide range of useful actions are planned, and in many cases, carried out; and few appraisers admitting to problems yet many expressing the need for further training.

A number of training implications have emerged from this. They include the need to communicate the objectives of the nursing staff development programme more effectively to everyone; organizing follow-up activities to ensure actions agreed in the appraisal interview take place; periodic training to reinforce the effects of earlier training to ensure that people are reminded of what is involved in achieving effectiveness in appraisal interviewing. And training appraisers in coaching skills as an extension of traditional approaches to performance appraisal training is vital.

(Anderson G. C. and Barnett J.G. (1986). Nurse appraisal in practice. *The Health Service Journal*, Vol. 96, No. 5023, October.)

ACTIVITY 23.1
▼

Identify from the article:
(1) Important challenges any appraisal interviewer must address and
(2) The kind of follow-up action that is required after appraisal interviews.

Review of Activity 23.1
▽

(1) Important challenges for appraisal interviews identified in the article include:

- Ensuring adequate preparation.
- Allocating sufficient time.
- Making the interview a two-way dialogue.

(2) A wide range of follow-up actions can be agreed, including:

- Attendance at formal courses.
- Coaching.
- Temporary attachments.
- Visits to other units/departments.
- Self-development activities.
- Provision of reference material.

Working positively for growth and development

As pointed out in Part Two, how effective and committed a manager is in carrying out performance appraisals will enhance or retard the development of the skills and knowledge of each individual who reports to that manager.

The face-to-face skills described in Chapter 8 are critical both in carrying out effective appraisal interviews and in setting the right climate for performance appraisals through less formal discussion on performance and development issues as and when the need arises throughout the year. Important skills for any manager in conducting appraisal interviews with staff include the ability to recognize and use the distinctions between task and social emotional behaviour and between social emotional positive and negative behaviour. It would be a good idea at this stage to review and refamiliarize yourself with the concepts discussed in Chapter 8 because of their high level of relevance to appraisal interviewing. Robin Evenden's research findings on meetings, that positives should outweigh negatives in the ratio of 2:1, are equally applicable to appraisal interviews. Indeed some American authorities (for example, Mohrman) go even further, recommending, in the context of appraisal interviews, a ratio of four positives to every negative on the part of the manager conducting the interview.

If we accept that one of the important measures of success of the appraisal interview is getting employees to accept the need for change, whether in terms of improving their current performance or developing themselves, the importance of behaviour skills, defined in Chapter 9 as 'doing things that improve our strike rate in getting a positive response from others' and 'doing the right thing well, at the right time' become extremely important for managers in conducting appraisal interviews.

References for further reading

Anderson G.C. (1986). *Performance Appraisal*. HMSO

Anderson G.C. *et al.* (1987). Appraisal without Form Filling *Personnel Management* February

Maier N. (1976). *The Appraisal Interview*. University Associates

Mohrman A.M. *et al.* (1989). *Designing Performance Appraisal Systems*. Jossey-Bass

24

Objectives and target setting

Why set objectives and targets?

The appraisal process can be enhanced by using the interview as an opportunity to agree objectives and targets for the coming review period. Staff have two priority 'wants' from their manager:

(1) 'Tell me what you expect from me.'
(2) 'Let me know how well you think I am doing.'

Objectives and targets can:

(1) Provide clarity, realism and precision for staff in these areas.
(2) Help both parties focus upon the assessment in terms of the same criteria and thus increase the possibility of agreement and reduce the scope for disagreement.
(3) Motivate, if handled as a basis for recognition and development rather than an opportunity for blame and punishment.

Reasons for setting targets are summarized in Figure 24.1.

To help the organization
- Achieve its objectives.
- Improve performance.
- Communicate.
- Appraise and motivate its staff.

To help the individual
- Achieve objectives.
- Improve performance.
- Know what is expected.
- Identify how they are doing.
- Work out the priorities in their job.
- Be motivated by a sense of progress and achievement.

Figure 24.1   Reasons for setting targets.

How does appraisal and target setting affect performance?

Appraisal, including objectives and target setting, is a continuous process which has a periodic review and planning interview. There are four performance factors to be considered in an appraisal (see Figure 24.2).

The appraisal can identify technical factors which are constraints and problems affecting an individual's performance. These can usefully be noted, but it is important not to develop a technical discussion, detracting from the main purpose of talking about the individual, their job performance and plans for the future. However, if important issues are raised, it is essential that you both agree to focus on them another time.

A major role for appraisal is to consider the person's ability in relation to the job they are doing and to their future career. Aspects such as skill, knowledge and experience should be explored, and one area to try to agree is the gap between what they have and what they need. If a gap is identified it is important to discuss how the gap can be removed. It is futile identifying performance shortfalls and targets if necessary development is not agreed, planned and achieved.

Appraisal is the time to establish the lowest limits of performance that are tolerated, if this is necessary.

The fourth aspect of influencing performance by appraisal is through the potential motivation impact.

	Upper limit set by:
Performance High	
	1 Technical factors 2 Ability (skill, knowledge, experience)
	Position between the limits owing to: 3 Motivation (Why people work well)
Performance Low	4 Tolerance level

Figure 24.2   Performance factors.

ACTIVITY 24.1

▼ Reflect upon the motivating impact of appraisal and target setting, in relation to either work or study. How many sources of motivation can you identify?

Review of Activity 24.1

▽ See Figure 24.3.

Motivation from appraisal	How can objectives and targets help meet the motivator factors?
	(Objectives – things to achieve. Targets – how well and when.)
Purpose	Discuss priorities and where job fits in.
What is expected from me	A chance to find out.
How I am doing	You will know all the time.
Challenge	Targets should be a realistic challenge.
Achievement	Continuous opportunity, especially if targets are stepped or progressive milestones.
Job satisfaction	Can aid job interest.
Recognition	Chance for self esteem and praise.
Responsibility	Increased. Responsible for agreeing and achieving targets.
Advancement	Increased for good performance.

Figure 24.3 Getting appraisal to motivate by setting objectives and targets.

Guide to key areas and objectives – What are they?

Key areas	*Objectives*
These are the main tasks that need to be done in a job, so that effective contributions can be made to departmental and through them, company objectives.	Objectives are what needs to be achieved in a particular key area in general terms.
	Examples: Where a special effort is needed.

You need to identify the tasks which have the biggest impact on departmental success.

Where there are time factors.

Where previous successes need to be repeated.

Another way to identify the key areas is to ask yourself what would be missed most if the job was not being done.

Where shortcomings need to be avoided.

Key areas can usefully be ranked in order of importance during appraisal, so the appraisee can identify job priorities.

Where the job has changed to give new things to achieve.

Where results could be improved.

Standards and targets

When you specify different levels at which a key task objective could be performed in terms of quantity, quality or time, you are setting **standards** by which you can assess how well the objective has been achieved. If you identify a specific standard for a person to aim at, you are setting a **target**.

Standards/targets may be

- descriptive and verbal, for example good/bad;
- ranking, for example always...never;
- numerical ranking, for example 1–6;
- quantitative, for example 10% increase.

If you are setting standards it may be helpful to identify at the time the constraints external to the individual which may affect achievement, for example technical problems.

Targets need to be realistic and are most effective if they are agreed by both parties and not over-optimistic.

Target setting: definitions

(1) Key area – main tasks in a job as defined, for example, in the job description. An example might be 'Manage staffing'.
(2) Objectives – what needs to be achieved in a key area.
This is broadly what individuals need to achieve in their own specific

circumstances. It may not apply to everybody doing that job. These personal objectives are what would be discussed in an appraisal to focus upon what the person was aiming to achieve last year and to identify broadly what he or she should aim for next year. It is to achieve these that targets are set. An example might be 'Reduce staff turnover'.

(3) Standards – specification of different levels of achievement of objectives. For example, 50% staff turnover is poor; 5% is excellent.

(4) Targets – identifying a standard to aim at. It should be something specific to achieve which will help to meet a personal objective. For example, to reduce staff turnover from 30% to 15% during the next year.

You would then discuss specific ways of achieving this reduction.

Ground rules

- Do not set too many.
- Should be set jointly by the manager and individual.
- Should be related to agreed personal objectives.
- Should be reviewable and not too rigid.
- Try to make them measurable and quantifiable. At least establish ways of knowing if they have been achieved.
- Clear, unambiguous, concrete and challenging.
- They need to be realistic and achievable in the light of constraints, such as ability, potential and resources.
- Note constraints which may affect achievement.
- Targets should relate to improvements in quality, quantity, time, cost.
- Identify time scales, review dates and milestones on the way.
- Link target setting into the appraisal and action plan.
- Agree how you will both know how well the targets have been achieved.

Format

Targets should be specific, agreed and written down clearly.

For example:

To ... (do something measurable, quantifiable or at least concrete, definable and assessable.)

By ... (date; update review; milestones.)

So that ... (something challenging and realistic is achieved in relation to a personal objective.)

Archery analogy: key areas, objectives, standards and targets

Job objective	To get a high score.
Personal objective	To improve your score.

Standards
Miss – 0
Outer – 1
Inner – 2
Bull – 3

Key area   Archery field

Personal target	To average a score of five with three arrows in three months. (For a beginner. A more skilled and experienced person would have higher targets to achieve.)
Action plan	To practise and be coached twice a week. To enter a novice competition in six weeks. To average a score of three in one month. To average a score of four in two months. To review and update the plan every month.

Preparing for the performance review: setting targets and objectives

(1) Review and gather relevant information, such as the job description; previous reports; the results of listening to others who work with the appraisee; systematic observation and work checking; or the current action plan.

(2) Refer to your confidential personal file. This could include job documentation; summaries of previous reports and plans; objectives and targets that are current; achievement of results and development; and significant aspects of the appraisee's work during the period.

(3) Review the tools. Is the job description still valid? Will the key areas be the same?

(4) Assess performance during the review period. Identify appropriate evidence and illustrations.

(5) Provisionally produce realistic objectives and targets for the coming period.

(6) Make summary notes but consider not completing the appraisal review form until after the interview, so that the action plan is genuinely a jointly developed and agreed document.

Handling assessment and setting objectives and targets jointly

(1) Once you have established the basis of the review and discussed how the interview will be conducted, check the key areas, objectives and targets agreed at the last appraisal review.

(2) If this is the first appraisal, check your mutual understanding of the key areas.

(3) For each key area and its related objectives and targets, first ask the appraisee for their self-assessment and reasons. Explore these as appropriate, noting explanations for below par performance.

(4) Being as positive as possible, feed in your own assessment. If you differ, it is sometimes a good idea to offer your evidence before giving your assessment for discussion. If you are unable to agree, clarify where you disagree, and defer this item until later in the interview.

(5) Try to organize the interview so that good points and agreement occupy the early part. This makes it easier to handle later disagreement.

(6) As you complete each assessment item, encourage the appraisee to translate this into objectives and targets for the following review period. Also discuss how the person will achieve them, with deadlines and milestones, so that you are building up the action plan as you progress.

(7) Note significant things that emerge which require attention. These could be factors hampering performance such as technical aspects or personal/domestic matters. Agree to pursue these *outside* this interview. There could also be things for you to do, such as coaching, making training plans or job changes.

(8) Refer back to areas where agreement has not been reached and review them. Explore thoroughly the reasons given for lower than expected performance. Try to evaluate them objectively and focus upon what it is reasonable for that person to have achieved. Even if you can't agree, it is important for the person to believe you have really listened to their point of view.

(9) Conclude by summarizing, checking agreement and understanding of the assessment and future action plan.

(10) Regardless of the 'official' form, a written note of the key points of the performance and development action plan will be important for you both, and should assume its place in your private personal file.

Example interview questions: review and setting targets

(1) What would you say is the overall purpose of your job?

(2) What key area shall we discuss first?

(3) What were the main things you aimed to achieve during the review period, broadly speaking? (Objectives)

(4) What specific things were you trying to achieve? (Targets – quantity; quality; time.)

(5) What do you feel quite pleased at having achieved?

(6) Are there any disappointments?

(7) Are the same things at the right level for next time? If not, how would you see them?

(8) What exactly can we agree that you will be aiming for?

(9) What could get in the way and how could we avoid barriers?

(10) Are you going to need any help? What? From whom?

(11) What are you going to have to do yourself to get there?

(12) Can we summarize what we have agreed and make a note of it?

You do not have to keep mentioning the tools. Just use them!

This question sequence suggests ways of reviewing an area and then directly translating it into plans for the future. This affords clarity and continuity.

The question–led approach increases ownership and commitment to the process and the action plan, but does not preclude the appropriate injection of your own opinions.

Development action planning

The point of the appraisal and objective-setting process is that something should happen as a result. The end point should not be the completion and signing of the appraisal form to be filed away until the next time.

It is usually helpful to both parties to have a reference to their agreement, probably independently of the formal document. It could be referred to as a Development Action Plan which may be an informal written note outside the formal system.

The plan should be about development of the person and performance, the creation of opportunities and tackling of problems. The action specified should be what is to be done, by whom and by when. It should be a clear summary of the objectives, targets and standards agreed and the personal development to be undertaken. Time-scales and progress milestones are valuable inclusions.

In most current environments, plans are overtaken by events well before the next formal review is due. This is not an argument against planning, but a reason for reviewing and updating plans periodically.

The plan and action should be 'owned' by the appraisee. Ideally the appraiser should merely be a supporting reference point.

Insupply case study: appraisal and target setting

Colin Smith appraises Bob Armstrong

After full consultation, Insupply had introduced a new appraisal scheme (see Chapter 22). Its main aims were:

- To improve current and future performance.
- To help employees develop.
- To review past performance.

It was the first time that Colin Smith, Insupply's Deputy Chief Executive had appraised the Administration Manager, Bob Armstrong, who had been with the organization almost one year.

Insupply had recently relocated from Hometown to Midtown. Bob was responsible for the move, and for ensuring that the organization settled down smoothly.

Bob got on well with people and had a good working relationship with Colin Smith, who had recruited him for his organizing ability, good nature and capacity to welcome change.

Bob's department had been restructured around the time of the move and there had been staff changes. Senior management felt the move had been handled well, but that there were some team teething troubles in Bob's department causing difficulties.

Bob Armstrong, Administration Manager: Job description summary

Purpose	To provide efficient and effective administrative support for the Executive and departments to help Insupply achieve its corporate objectives.
Key Areas	1. To manage the department's objectives, planning, control and coordination within budget.
	2. To liaise effectively with the Executive and other departments to meet their needs.
	3. To develop new administrative systems, with special reference to technology.
	4. To manage sections and be responsible for communication, temporary staff resourcing, information systems, buildings management, and purchasing.

Colin Smith's appraisal of Bob Armstrong.

This was their first appraisal and a new scheme, so Colin felt a little tentative. He was convinced that a periodic semi-formal discussion, pulling together things that had been done during the year, was a good idea, particularly if Bob felt it was a joint activity. He hoped they would agree and that one or two difficulties would be resolved. He was not clear about the problems or solutions.

Colin had prepared thoroughly, and had thought about all the areas of the review form (see Chapter 22). He had plans and ideas, but only intended to complete it after the discussion when things had clarified and crystallized. He would welcome Bob's input.

As this was the first appraisal there had been no objectives nor targets set, except in general terms. Colin planned to see if they could identify some common retrospective ground here, and planned to set objectives and standards for the coming year.

CASE PROJECT 24.1

Referring to the Insupply case study, especially the move and the subsequent situation, as described below in an extract from Chapter 17:

(1) How would you handle the interview?
(2) What would you hope to achieve?

Insupply administration department after the move

Insupply had moved to its new site in Midtown Complex some months previously. The move had gone quite well and service to its clients had been maintained. There were many internal stresses and strains, and some frustrations for new and old staff working together in a changed environment and with new systems in place.

Generally the new location was proving advantageous and staff were displaying energy and drive. Bob Armstrong and his department had borne the brunt of the planning and implementation. The Chief Executive Hedi Lindstrom and her deputy Colin Smith expressed themselves well satisfied with the changeover.

Bob's Administration Department (see Figure 24.4) was central to dealing with teething troubles, acting as troubleshooters and putting things into place so that Insupply could move smoothly forward. The main operational departments relied crucially upon their performance in providing services in an efficient and coordinated way. Colin Smith was aware that this was not happening at the level he expected.

A great deal of collaboration was needed between the sections of the department and they were interdependent. For example, Peter needed to purchase and chase delivery on the electronic hardware; Jean had to supply contract staff to Sally and Joe; Sally had to install a new control system for Peter; and Joe had to ensure that the faulty air conditioning was repaired effectively for Jean.

None of these illustrations had worked smoothly.

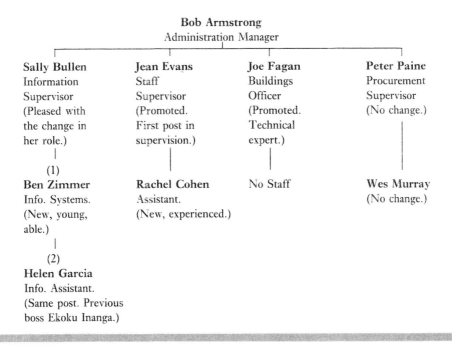

Bob Armstrong
Administration Manager

Sally Bullen	**Jean Evans**	**Joe Fagan**	**Peter Paine**
Information	Staff	Buildings	Procurement
Supervisor	Supervisor	Officer	Supervisor
(Pleased with	(Promoted.	(Promoted.	(No change.)
the change in	First post in	Technical	
her role.)	supervision.)	expert.)	

(1)

Ben Zimmer	**Rachel Cohen**	No Staff	**Wes Murray**
Info. Systems.	Assistant.		(No change.)
(New, young,	(New, experienced.)		
able.)			

(2)

Helen Garcia
Info. Assistant.
(Same post. Previous
boss Ekoku Inanga.)

Figure 24.4   Insupply Administration Department after the move.

In the few opportunities Bob had had to get the team together he felt they had achieved little.

- Peter kept quiet.
- Wes got angry.
- Joe made it clear that he was too busy to spend time talking with people.
- Sally looked puzzled.
- Ben and Rachel felt awkward and slightly intimidated.
- Helen said that they all needed to communicate more and that all the others were at fault here.
- Bob reassured them they were a good team and all would soon be well if they worked at it, but he was not sure how they would pull out.

Colin Smith had detected from other departments that there were difficulties and he already picked up from Bob himself that he wasn't happy with the way his new team were settling in. Bob felt there were teething troubles that would disappear soon enough. He had said that he hoped they could chat about it during their appraisal the following month.

Extracts from Bob Armstrong's appraisal

Colin had set the scene and checked that Bob was clear about the nature of the discussion and had had a chance to do some thinking himself about the past months and the coming year.

They agreed that it had been one of the busiest periods in their careers and that by and large they both felt they had reason to be satisfied, though not complacent Bob emphasized.

CS: *What would you say is the overall purpose of your job?*

BA: *You mean what might not happen if I wasn't here! Well we all like to think we are indispensable. I suppose it is keeping the organization's wheels oiled. Making sure that things get fixed before folk know they are broken, and that we are ahead of the game with our systems. Looking after matters which are 'indirect' to other departments so that they can get on with their main tasks.*

CS: *The job description says 'efficient and effective admin support ... to help achieve our corporate objectives.' I think you put it better.*

They agreed the main parts of the job and examined the introduction of new administrative systems, which was progressing very favourably. Resourcing and target dates were reviewed and Bob felt that he should spend more time on Ben Zimmer's induction to the organization. It was agreed when and how this could be done.

CS: *What key area shall we discuss next?*

BA: *I think we need to look at the department's liaison with other departments to meet their needs. It ties in with my coordination and management of my sections to an extent.*

They clarified what Bob meant by this with some concrete illustrations.

CS: *What were the main things you aimed to achieve during the review period – broadly speaking?*

BA: *The main objective was to get us to Midtown in good shape, fully resourced and continuing to meet client needs. Once we were here, the need was to get us up and running, so you could scarcely see the join between Hometown and Midtown. How can we assess this? I suppose by seeing how the others feel their admin support has been.*

CS: *Let's boil this down then. What specific things were you trying to achieve for Insupply as a whole? Then let's look at individual departments.*

They talked about the logistics of the move; its cost against estimates; deadlines; problems faced and how well they had been overcome. The service to each department was assessed in turn. They noted the success and explored what they could learn from the aspects which had gone less well.

CS: *What do you feel quite pleased at having achieved?*

BA: *Getting us here and getting us going. The negotiations with Planning and the construction people were difficult, as you know. I think getting building completion on time pleased me most.*

They discussed other aspects of the move and developments of new systems which they both felt were good achievements. Colin was very pleased with the way Bob's organization had enabled Distribution to maintain deliveries on time without a hitch.

CS: *Are there any disappointments?*

BA: *Well, I guess you know what is currently on my mind. My new team is not settling down. Everybody seems to be operating only for themselves. Of course, we are all still under a great deal of pressure ... But that is not really the issue. When people work only for themselves there are going to be problems ... work problems.*

They examined how each team member was performing and how the sections were failing to meet each other's task needs. One outcome was that some new computer control systems for Procurement had been delayed and this had implications for efficiency and quality of service, as well as profitability.

CS: *Matters are obviously not right. How would you see them improving? What can you do differently?*

BA: *Spend more time with them and get them to spend more time with each other. See if we can find out what is going wrong and do something about it. The trouble is that when we get together people are ill at ease with each other ... and me.*

Colin Smith and Bob Armstrong spent some time talking around the situation. It began to resolve itself around Bob's team leadership and the way his team were relating to each other.

CS: *What exactly can we agree that you will be aiming for?*

BA: *Improving the team and my part in helping them work together. Getting them to clarify what they need from each other. Helping the new members to feel at home. Maintaining the service standards we had until recently. These are my objectives in this area.*

They specified targets for Bob to aim for. This included, for example, response times to building maintenance requests and deadlines for several new systems installations.

CS: *What could get in the way and how could we avoid these barriers?*

BA: *Could we discuss how we are going to improve teamwork? If we don't do this I doubt these targets will be possible.*

CS: *Are you going to need any help?*

BA: *I don't feel I can do this on my own. In a sense I am part of the problem. That has become clear to me as we have talked it through. I would like to invite somebody to spend some time with me and the team.*

They discussed the idea of a team-building process, and options that could arise. Colin was clear that he wanted things to get better quickly, and they agreed that Bob should invite a facilitator, known to him, to meet Colin and himself within the next ten days. The aim would be to discuss this with the team shortly after and begin the activity within six weeks. It was agreed to review this after the initial meeting with the facilitator.

CS: *So we agree that you have to develop yourself and the team. What are you going to have to do yourself to get there?*

BA: *Swallow a little pride! Listen and help the facilitator help us establish what we all have to do differently. I think it is important that I don't give the team the impression that I am blaming them. At this stage it is down to me.*

CS: *I think we are making real progress. There are some ideas here that we might want to extend to other parts of Insupply. Can we summarize what we have agreed and make a note of it?*

They summarized and built into the action plan the objectives discussed above, the specific quantitative and time targets they had agreed as realistic, and they were clear about what they were looking for in the qualitative aspects of team building.

Bob Smith felt pleased with the interview. He had had good recognition from Colin, whom he respected, and was clear in his own mind what was expected from him in the coming review period. The plans and targets he felt were his, and he was reassured that he was doing a good job and that he was getting the support he needed from Colin Smith. The action plan would be a focused guide for his next year at Insupply.

Example of the format for objective and target setting

Extract from Bob Armstrong's appraisal report

- To ... (do something measurable, quantifiable or at least concrete, definable and assessable.)
  To arrange a team-building process for the Administration Department.

- By ... (Date; update review; milestones.)
  By ten days from this date CS and BA will have met a facilitator and in six weeks we will begin so that within three months ...

- So that ... (something challenging and realistic is achieved in relation to a personal objective.)
  ... so that within three months the team will be working together more effectively to meet its own needs and those of other departments.

The outcome can be read in Part Two: Chapter 17, 'Developing a Team'.

References for further reading

Anderson G.C. (1986). *Performance Appraisal.* HMSO

Anderson G.C. *et al.* (1987). Appraisal without Form Filling. *Personnel Management* February

Fletcher C. and Williams R. (1985). *Performance Appraisal and Career Development.* Hutchinson

Latham G.P. and Wexley K.N. (1981). *Increasing Productivity through Performance Appraisal.* Addison-Wesley

Maier N. (1976). *The Appraisal Interview.* University Associates

25

Managing the marginal performer

Managing staff who are very able and highly motivated is relatively easy. Conversely, if an employee is performing so badly that disciplinary action must be taken, it is reasonably clear what a manager should do. Often the more difficult and less clear-cut, though equally important, situations which a manager must undertake are to manage marginal performers. One way to define marginal performers is by reference to Figure 25.1. Marginal performers are those who are performing at, or just above, the minimum acceptable level of performance, as shown in the figure.

There is often a temptation for a manager not to intervene with this type of employee, since they are at least performing to minimum acceptable standards. There is, however, a substantial waste of unrealized potential, if staff are performing well short of the level of which they are capable.

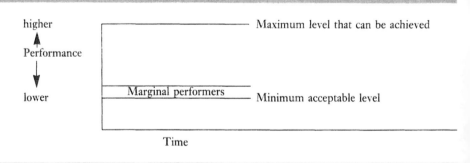

Figure 25.1   The challenge in managing marginal performers.

Because the marginal performer does not infringe the lower limits acceptable to management, managers may lack a sense of urgency in addressing problems and issues relating to marginal performers. Nevertheless the possibilities for improvement are such that managers should address the problems of developing the marginal performers.

The importance of diagnosis

The starting point should be the accurate diagnosis of factors causing the relatively poor level of performance, or holding back improvements, before strategies for dealing with marginal performance can be formulated.

ACTIVITY 25.1

▼ What are the main reasons explaining why an employee performs in a marginal way, failing to realize their full potential? Note as many reasons as you can think of, drawing, where possible, on your own experience of working with others, or supervising staff.

▽ The list is probably longer than you suspected. Assess how many match the following range of factors which, operating either individually or in some combination, may be responsible for the barely adequate level of performance.

Poor selection decisions

It may be that a poor selection decision has been made, leading to the appointment of a person whose skills, motivation and experience do not match well with the requirements of the job.

The induction phase

No matter how good the selection decision-making process has been, any new job-holder has the challenge of coming to terms with many new issues, and will normally undergo a rapid learning period. Managers should recognize that new starters may often perform initially in the marginal area, and need special help during the induction phase.

Unidentified training needs

The performance of individuals may be constrained by failure to train them, and managers should recognize that they have training needs which, if fulfilled, would enhance their work performance.

Loss of motivation

The marginal performer may possess the skills and abilities to work productively but is demotivated or has suffered a loss of motivation. The causes need to be probed.

- Boredom and monotony.
- Lack of, or reduction of, interesting job content.
- Lack of recognition.
- Failure to understand role.

Irritations or dissatisfaction with work

If the employee experiences strong feelings of irritation or dissatisfaction with:

- the physical environment at work,
- the style of supervision,
- the organization culture, or
- the fairness of rewards,

these feelings can build up blockages which impede the achievement of high performance.

Loss of self image

If a member of staff possesses a poor self image, or has suffered a loss of confidence, they are likely to be in a state of mind incompatible with high performance.

Illness

Ill health, which can take a wide variety of forms, some of which may be undetected by managers, can be the main factor bringing about marginal performance.

The aging process

Irrespective of health problems, some individuals age faster than others, in terms of diminishing physical and mental powers.

Personal problems

Difficulties associated with personal relationships, marriage break-up, drugs and alcohol can be important contributory factors, especially if the problem is one of changing and deteriorating levels of performance.

Non-work activities

Work performance may be constrained by alternative competing objectives which the individual is striving to achieve outside work. Such objectives can be associated with, for example:

- the attainment of qualifications on part-time basis, such as taking a degree by part-time or distance learning study;
- the achievement of goals in sports;
- the pursuit of hobbies;
- political and social activities – for example, holding office in political or voluntary organizations.

Poor time management

A cause of marginal performance may be poor personal organization and an inability to assign priorities and manage time effectively.

Stress

A limited amount of stress stimulates performance; there is increasing evidence that beyond a certain level stress inhibits performance as well as causing individuals considerable personal distress – often unrecognized, or unappreciated, by managers.

Overload

Excessive work load, leading to dissipation of effort and energy in too many directions, reduces work performance.

Unacceptability to peers/others in the organization

An important blockage to high performance can take the form of poor interpersonal relations and reduced cooperation from others.

Poor delegation and control

When problems of marginal performance emerge after a promotion, especially if the individual has previously been a high performer, a likely cause is their inability to delegate effectively and achieve a balanced control of the work of others.

Unclear, confused objectives

The problems of marginal performance may lie more with the manager than with the employee if objectives and priorities have not been agreed and clarified.

Inadequate coaching

Managers may lack the skills and inclination to coach their staff on a regular or periodic basis, leading to reduced performance.

Actions for helping and developing the marginal performer

Face up to the problems

The first step, and in some ways the most important, is for the manager to address the problems facing the marginal performer, and to engage in a candid and frank dialogue with the member of staff. It is all too easy for this important first step not to be taken by the manager. If the member of staff in question is performing at, or a little above, the minimum acceptable level of performance required, the urgency in facing up to problems that would be apparent in the case of a totally unsatisfactory employee is unlikely to exist. Yet unless the problems facing the marginal performer are addressed, there will remain a major missed opportunity for improving productivity.

The marginal performer may experience feelings both of relief and of enhanced motivation if the manager has the confidence to face up to the problem areas, and talk over ways of overcoming them.

Using the performance appraisal system effectively

Systems of performance appraisal can assist in a variety of ways:

- By encouraging the manager and the employee who is a marginal performer to talk.
- By providing mechanisms to assist in measuring and monitoring changes in the employee's level of performance.
- In some systems of performance appraisal, provision is made for increasing the frequency of reviews with those employees performing in a marginal way, or worse. (For example, in an organization where performance appraisal on an annual basis is the norm, marginal performers may be subject to an appraisal every six months, or even every three months until there is evidence of performance improvement).

Problem identification and problem-solving meetings

The manager needs to meet with marginal performers not only at formal performance appraisal interviews, but also on a regular, on-going basis, by holding meetings to identify problems and barriers to improvement and to undertake problem solving.

Key skills required of the manager in conducting meetings of this type include:

- Sound questioning techniques, implying the ability to use a range of types of questions, including open questions, probing questions and reflective questions.
- Good listening skills.
- The ability to define problem areas accurately and to generate a range of possible solutions.

Giving and receiving criticism

An important element in the formulation of actions to help the marginal performer is likely to centre around giving and receiving criticism. To ensure that feelings of trust and mutual respect are generated between the manager and the marginal performer, it is imperative that the manager possesses good skills in giving and receiving feedback, and a high level of awareness of the problems and issues that can readily occur. The principles of giving and receiving feedback have been discussed in an earlier chapter. As far as possible feedback should be specific, factual and constructive. Any criticisms should be made of behaviour or approaches to work tasks, and not directed towards attacking the individual.

Preserving and building self esteem

Closely linked to skills in handling feedback is the need for the manager to develop a style of dealing with the marginal performer that will preserve and build the latter's self esteem. Often the marginal performer will be experiencing feelings of threat and insecurity – indeed these may be a contributory factor to marginal performance – and the manager can play a significant part in creating a situation that will encourage improvement by showing that the marginal performer is someone whose services are valued, and who could be making a potentially valuable contribution.

Secondment and transfer

The manager should recognize that a range of options is available. If the diagnostic phase in exploring the reasons for marginal performance highlights, for example:

- wrong selection decision,
- staleness in the job,
- inability to relate effectively to colleagues, customers or suppliers,

then the options of secondment or transfer should be seriously considered. Transfer assumes the existence of job opportunities elsewhere in the organization, and implies a permanent change. Secondment is of a temporary nature and assumes that a change of function for a limited period will assist in remotivating the individual and/or help to overcome the barriers that have been impeding performance.

Training and development

Another option is to provide training and development for the marginal performer. One of the dangers is to assume that training and development represent a panacea; there are unlikely to be any easy short-cuts to better performance.

To be effective, training and developing the marginal performer must be based on an accurate assessment of training and development needs. The manager can assist the training and development process by the provision of support, coaching and counselling, and through organizing, where appropriate, on–the–job training.

Self analysis and self development

Dealing effectively with marginal performance involves bringing about change; whether the required changes take place will depend to a large extent on how committed the individual is to the courses of actions discussed with the manager. The greater the extent to which the individual is encouraged to undertake self analysis of the problems, and to embark upon self development, the greater the likelihood of sustained performance improvement. The manager therefore requires skills in involving the individual at all stages, in avoiding imposed solutions or solutions that are perceived as being imposed, and in fostering self analysis and self development.

Insupply case study

Bob Armstrong, the Administration Manager, recruited a young graduate, Mary Jones ten months ago, as a graduate trainee. Bob has planned a one-year training programme for Mary, in which she will spend three months with each of the four supervisors in the department, before being placed in a definite job.

The four supervisors are:

Sally Bullen, Information Supervisor
Jean Evans, Staff Supervisor
Joe Fagan, Buildings Officer
Peter Paine, Procurement Supervisor

As well as giving Mary good all-round knowledge of the department, Bob feels that by the end of the year he should be in a better position to judge Mary's abilities and interests and to assess exactly where she could contribute best to the department.

Summary profile of the graduate trainee

Name	Mary Jones.
Age	23 years.
Status	Single.
Qualification	BA Honours (II) in Economics and Psychology.
Work Experience	One year in Personnel Department of large retail company; 10 months with Insupply as graduate trainee.
Personality	Quiet, but self confident.

Graduate training programme

1st three months: Sally Bullen's section

2nd three months: Joe Fagan's section

3rd three months: Peter Paine's section

4th three months: Jean Evan's section

Performance issues

Mary seemed to fit in well during her periods with Sally and Joe. Bob Armstrong became aware of some difficulties during her spell with Peter Paine. In talking recently with Jean Evans, with whom Mary was now working as the training period moved into its final stages, Bob realized that problems with Mary's performance had continued to increase.

The evidence

Mary started coming in late occasionally during her third training period with Peter Paine; she began to show less interest in what was going on, and made it clear to all she did not like working for Peter. (Peter is a reserved person; so this did not totally surprise Bob.)

Jean Evans now reported that Mary had made several careless errors, for example, sending out information about job vacancies to the wrong applicants; failing to undertake an analysis of salary movements in the prescribed time-scale; and being rude to several colleagues. She had also been absent, without explanation, on at least two occasions.

What should be done

Bob Armstrong was planning to appraise Mary formally after twelve months, as part of the company's performance appraisal scheme. He felt, however, that he should meet with her now, as he felt her performance had deteriorated in the last two or three months and was now barely acceptable – very much, in his view, in the category of being a marginal performer.

ACTIVITY 25.2

▼ How should Bob Armstrong conduct the interview with Mary? Briefly sketch out a plan for conducting the interview.

Comments on Activity 25.2

▽ Bob did the right thing in deciding to discuss matters with Mary now, rather than waiting till the formal appraisal interview.

The interview plan should follow the lines advocated in this chapter – emphasizing especially the diagnostic aspects, finding out through probing and reflective questions what factors are affecting her performance, and then evaluating the various courses of action that can be taken.

Postscript

Bob Armstrong found that at first Mary was reluctant to admit to any problems. As she became convinced the aim of the interview was to help rather than to punish her, a whole host of points, unknown to Bob, emerged:

- difficulties in relating to Peter Paine's supervising style;
- problems over a shift of accommodation;
- break-up (in the previous month) of a personal relationship;
- worries about what would happen to her at the end of the one-year training programme.

In terms of immediate action, Bob decided that nothing of a major nature needed to be done immediately, except that, with Mary's permission, he agreed to brief fully Jean Evans, her supervisor for the final element of her training programme, about the contents of their discussion. Mary said she felt much better having had the opportunity to discuss her problems; she indicated to Bob that she wanted to work to the best of her ability, and looked forward to the appraisal interview with him in two months' time.

References for further reading

Anderson G.C. (1986). *Performance Appraisal.* HMSO

Anderson G.C. *et al.* (1987). Appraisal without Form Filling
  Personnel Management February

Biddle D. and Evenden R. (1989). *Human Aspects of Management.* IPM

Clark N. (1991). *Managing Personal Learning and Change: A Trainer's Guide.*
  McGraw-Hill Training Series

Herzberg M. (1966). *Work and the Nature of Man.* Staples Press

Latham G.P. and Wexley K.N. (1981). *Increasing Productivity through Performance Appraisal.* Addison-Wesley

Maier N. (1976). *The Appraisal Interview.* University Associates

Munro F.A. (1983). *Counselling. A Skills Approach.* Methuen

Pedlar M. *et al.* (1986) *A Manager's Guide to Self Development.* McGraw-Hill

Singer E. (1981). *Effective Management Coaching.* IPM

Stewart A. and V. (1980). *Managing the Manager's Growth.* Gower

26

Development relationships in learning organizations

Development involves enhancement, maturing, growing, and improving what is already there. It can relate to any aspect of the individual that is capable of change and progression. At work we think of this often in terms of the 'hard' skill and knowledge development directly related to the technical aspects of the job. Part Two suggested that it is also useful to consider personal growth as a very important part of this process. Thus development can include personal factors like increasing understanding and self awareness; learning skills; perceived responsibility for self development; confidence; and self image. These 'soft' personal factors not only affect the acquisition of the 'hard' skills, but directly influence motivation, commitment, and capacity to make choices and achieve personal goals.

Responsibility in the development relationship

Development does not take place in a vacuum. Learning and growth occur as a response to the environment in which the individual lives and works. The organization and its representative, the manager, are a major part of the learning environment. They have a massive influence upon the nature and direction of an individual's development, or indeed, whether an individual grows, stagnates or even regresses. The manager has a responsibility for the learning and development climate.

Individuals are responsible for their own learning. If development takes place through a process of choice, it is because individuals choose to learn and change, not because the manager chooses that they should. The managers, however much they may try and wish to, cannot do the learning for others.

The organization may offer opportunity and incentive. The manager may appraise, assess and agree purpose, direction and objectives. The means of development through coaching, counselling, experience and courses may be made available. This is the organization and manager's side of the psychological contract and development relationship. It is too often poorly honoured.

Of course, people can learn and do things differently under coercion. This is compliance rather than development, and the scope and impact is likely to be limited, to say the least.

Learning new skills and acquiring knowledge of any complexity and substance requires effort and investment upon the part of the developing person. This is even more true of the kind of personal development mentioned earlier. It is the individual's responsibility to learn through this commitment. Without the taking of this responsibility, and the 'ownership' that goes with it, effective development will be limited. This is the individual's side of the development relationship.

Anything that a manager can do to encourage the individual's development ownership and responsibility will promote real learning and growth. The manager should accept a good measure of responsibility for the learning environment and opportunities, and the learner responsibility for the learning.

By action and attitude it is possible for the manager to assume responsibility and ownership of the other person's learning as well. The effective development relationship requires that the manager is careful to avoid usurping the individual's responsibility but active in encouraging and supporting it.

It is possible to characterize the manager as having three modes of values and behaviour in the development relationship. These modes represent different but related aspects of the development interface between manager and individual.

One mode can be defined as **Usurper**, because the manager attempts to take over fully the individuals' responsibility for their development. There can be a need for this kind of dominance as an initial phase of some people's learning. It can be argued that immature, inexperienced individuals with low learning competence benefit from this mode. The low level learning syndrome will still apply, but with suitable awareness on the part of the manager, this could be seen as a temporary transitional phase, moving on to the second mode when the individual has grown sufficiently to take advantage of it.

The second mode is **Supporter/Sharer**, where the two parties maintain a constructive dialogue on development and both have different development responsibilities. The manager provides the opportunities for development and the individual the responsibility for taking and using them. The two parties share and discuss development needs and the means of meeting them, in relation to organizational and personal requirements. This is the development interface that is likely to benefit both parties in terms of learning, ownership, motivation and 'complementarity' of needs. The scope here is similar to the consults/delegates dimension of the manager's leadership style (Part Two, Chapter 18).

The development relationship could move to a third stage, the **Abdicator**, where the manager abandons the interface. Indeed, managers who have this as a general approach to leadership may well begin in this mode, irrespective of the needs of the situation and the individual concerned.

This could have numerous effects. If the individuals already take responsibility for their own development and there are resources available, then the autonomy may increase ownership and enhance development. This is the essence of self-managed or self-directed learning. However, it is possible that the development may not match organizational needs. It is also likely that individuals, unused to this kind of autonomy and climate, may fail to take responsibility for their development.

The three development relationship interface modes are summarized in Figure 26.1.

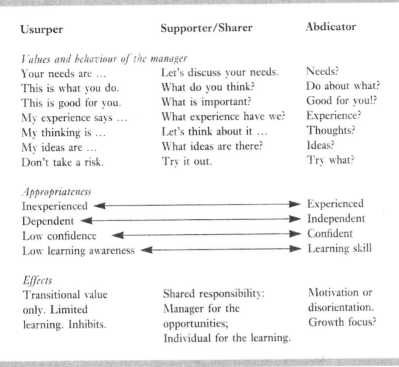

Usurper	Supporter/Sharer	Abdicator
Values and behaviour of the manager		
Your needs are ...	Let's discuss your needs.	Needs?
This is what you do.	What do you think?	Do about what?
This is good for you.	What is important?	Good for you!?
My experience says ...	What experience have we?	Experience?
My thinking is ...	Let's think about it ...	Thoughts?
My ideas are ...	What ideas are there?	Ideas?
Don't take a risk.	Try it out.	Try what?
Appropriateness		
Inexperienced		Experienced
Dependent		Independent
Low confidence		Confident
Low learning awareness		Learning skill
Effects		
Transitional value only. Limited learning. Inhibits.	Shared responsibility: Manager for the opportunities; Individual for the learning.	Motivation or disorientation. Growth focus?

Figure 26.1 The three development relationship interface modes.

How people learn and develop

David Kolb has indicated that learning is cyclical and involves moving through four stages of a learning cycle.

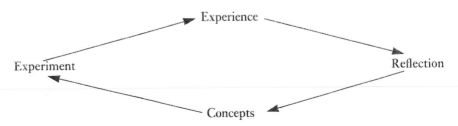

Experience   We can learn by having experiences, being part of things happening. Doing things.

Reflection   We stand back and think about our experience, mulling it over, analysing it.

Concepts   We then develop ideas based upon our experience, about how things relate to each other. We establish guidelines.

Experiment   We test our ideas and guidelines to see if they are true, or work, or need changing.

Most people appear to prefer some parts of the cycle to others and we all have a learning profile. This has implications not only for our own learning, but how we help others learn.

ACTIVITY 26.1

▼ Think of a time when you felt you had learned a great deal. Visualize how you learned, so that you can recall vividly what you were doing.

Give each of the four stages in the Learning Cycle a rating out of ten according to how significant it was in the learning experience you visualized. Is this representative of the way you think you usually prefer to learn?

Assess how you think others learn, or if you are able, get them to assess themselves.

Compare yourself with others:

- What are the strengths and weaknesses of the different approaches?
- What are the implications for your own learning?
- What are the implications for helping others learn?

Helping learning

▽ A well-rounded learning cycle, drawing with equal facility on experience, reflection, concepts and experimenting, means that we can find many different learning opportunities in many types of circumstance. Our learning is likely to be well integrated and effective.

If, as is true of most of us, we have a bias in one direction or another, it means that our learning opportunities are fewer and we may find ourselves less effective in some areas and more effective in others. If we can recognize this in ourselves we may be able to develop our capacity to learn by improving those aspects we choose to ignore or do not use well.

For example, the person who never reflects but always rushes headlong into action, experimenting and experiencing, may fail to make sense of what they have done for future reference. On the other hand, the person who never experiments does not try out the ideas produced 'in the head'. One results in 'action fraction', the other in 'analysis paralysis'!

We can help others develop by encouraging them to learn in new ways, and perhaps by helping them to recognize how they stop themselves from learning. However, as learning habits are often deeply ingrained, it may be more productive to recognize and play to their strengths.

Usually we assume that the way we prefer to learn is normal and that most people learn like we do. This means that when we try to help others learn, we use the approaches *that appeal to us*. If this doesn't work, there is a risk that we may assume the learner is slow to learn or uninterested, when it probably means that we are not using the methods that suit that individual.

ACTIVITY 26.2

 If you are learning in a group whose members have assessed their learning styles, ask them individually to identify the way they feel they can best learn *at work*. Identify different approaches for each of the four preferences:

Experience
Reflection
Concepts
Experiment

Figure 26.2 shows how to fit learning opportunities to learning preferences.

Preference	Learning opportunity
Experience	Focus upon experience and concrete events and feelings in discussion with them. Encourage involvement in a variety of tasks. Delegation. *Challenge* Get them to reflect on their experience and produce ideas with which to experiment.
Reflection	Encourage them to reflect upon events. Give them reflective activities such as planning and analysis and discuss them. *Challenge* Get them to turn their reflections into ideas to test out and experience the outcomes.
Concepts	Focus on ideas and guidelines. Explore relationships and the links between what they do and the results they achieve.

Explain and seek explanations.

Challenge Get them to put their ideas into practice and reflect upon the experience of doing it.

Experiment

Give them things to check out.

Encourage experimentation and risk taking by not blaming for failure.

Ask them to observe the consequences of things they need to learn about.

Challenge Get them to think carefully about the results of the things they try out and to draw some conclusions.

Figure 26.2 Fitting learning opportunities to learning preferences.

Unblocking learning

▽ Learning involves change and doing things differently. Frequently people resist and have a range of things which prevent them from learning. These have been described by D. Biddle and R. Evenden (1989) as:

Closed Mind	–	blinkered.
Normative	–	'how to learn' beliefs and prejudices.
Emotional	–	lacking confidence.
Relational	–	too selective in who to learn from.
Motivational	–	no interest in learning.

Many who are attempting to help others learn are themselves frustrated by the blocks they see from the learner. They will often assume a confrontational approach to the blocks and try to dynamite them away. Perhaps we should see, as Neil Clark suggests (1991), that resistance is something a person shows as a protective device. It is important to respect and acknowledge the basis of the resistance rather than to deny or dismiss it.

Neil Clark recommends that rather than trying to force people through their resistance, a more effective and perhaps more moral approach includes:

(1) Accept explicitly the resistance.
(2) Encourage self support and exploration of the resistance.
(3) Provide support and show concern.
(4) Get the person to examine reality – what would be the worst thing that could happen if you learn/change/develop?
(5) Give them time, your time and encouragement.

The learning organization

Learning and development are about changing and dealing with change (A. Toffler, 1980). In organizational terms it is about adaptation and survival in the face of turbulence and unpredictability.

T. Burns and G.M. Stalker (1961) identified organizations that could cope with change and innovation and those that couldn't. They described the former as 'organismic' (organic) and the latter as 'mechanistic' (mechanical).

(1) Organic Organizations.

These rely on spoken communication, make decisions through expertise, not status or power, and don't have rigid boundaries and demarcation between roles. They absorb, indeed create, innovation and thrive on turbulence. They are not very efficient at doing standard things in a standard way on a repetitive basis. They are flexible, creative and effective in dynamic situations.

(2) Mechanistic Organizations.

These are formal, rely on written communication and make decisions through position in the hierarchy. Roles are clearly defined and there is strong demarcation. An alternative label is 'bureaucratic'. They are unable to cope with change. When faced with it, Burns noticed that they were likely to respond in what he described as a pathological way. That is to say, they would make themselves even more mechanistic, and even more unable to cope with the change situation they were in.

They do large-scale, repetitive, standard things efficiently. Mechanical organizations are inflexible and are effective in static situations.

What Tom Burns described so graphically were the parents of what is currently called the **learning organization** and the **non-learning organization**.

ACTIVITY 26.3

 (1) Can you identify organizations within your experience that have mechanical or organic characteristics?
(2) Do they have different approaches and aims for the development and learning of their staff?
(3) How do they respond to change:
   (a) technical;
   (b) organizational;
   (c) external factors which affect them?
(4) What do managers need to do to create a learning organization?

The mechanical organization is usually good at training people to perform the technical tasks which have to be repeated without modification and initiative. It is not, however, a learning organization as much as an instructional organization,

293

because it and its members experience limited development and growth. They are instructed to fit into a fixed pattern and structure rather than developed to learn and exercise judgement and choice.

It is not good at learning new things and it is not good at learning itself. New experiences are rejected, there is no time for reflection built into the managers' roles, and traditional concepts, rules and guidelines are not subjected to testing in the light of new circumstances.

Organic organizations, rare birds, are there usually to create, innovate and seek out change. There are vast differences in the attitudes and values prevalent in the two organizational types. Organic elements sometimes exist within largely mechanical organizations. Examples of this can be effective research and development departments, creative design, and in the days before they became part of the bureaucracy themselves, computer and systems departments. Both parts have great difficulty in relating to each other, because of their differences.

Large organizations tend to be mechanical. In the climate of change and turbulence, or dynamic situations, many giants are trying to learn to dance (R.M. Kanter, 1989). For example, Civil Service Departments in the United Kingdom are attempting to become more flexible, with role discretion and judgement being exercised at lower levels. Terms like 'delegation', 'innovation', 'autonomy' and 'people initiatives' are being used. For these giants to move towards a more organic state they will need first to become learning organizations.

The transition will need strategic vision and massive determination from those guiding the organization. It cannot simply be willed. People who have been reared in instructional or non-learning organizations will find it difficult to cope with the demands of learning and change.

Organizations function through formal procedures (for example appraisal, discipline and operational procedures) and informal norms and values, which maintain the culture from generation to generation. Those at the top need to change the formal aspects to develop the organization; more importantly, the significant members need to influence the norms and values, by word, deed and not least, investment. The creation of a responsive organization, with organic characteristics, will not be achieved by statements of intent, but by rigorous pursuit of the learning organization (C. Handy, 1989).

The Learning Organization (LO) is built upon the development relationship, and real investment by all managers and staff in the learning and development psychological contract mentioned earlier. It evolves out of a genuine commitment to shared responsibility, starting with induction and moving through appraisal, jointly-set targets, agreed action planning and development.

Recognition of the learning procedures, such as appraisal, by top level participation in them, is one example of building the LO from the top down. Recruiting thrusters and allowing them to thrust through development, rather than continuing to take on sleepers and letting them sleep, is a way of building the LO from below.

Helping managers to learn how to promote the development of their staff, and rewarding and recognizing success in achieving this through appraisal and promotion, is how to develop the LO from the middle out.

Survival and effectiveness in turbulent environments require responsiveness and flexibility within organizations. Essentially, this means having people who are supported and encouraged to learn, develop and change.

The learning organization has managers at all levels who:

- Actively pursue the development relationship.
- Conduct appraisal as a joint activity.
- Agree action plans for performance and development.
- Allow staff to 'own' their own development.
- Seek to create learning opportunities.
- Encourage experimentation and risk taking.
- Believe that mistakes are to be learned from.
- Invest in development.
- Base decisions on expertise not status.
- Take pleasure from the success of others.
- Make people management a high priority.
- Show real concern for individuals.
- Are responsive to individual differences.
- Are open to development and learning for themselves.
- Share the present and the future with their staff.
- Help those who have difficulties with development and change.
- Transmit the LO values to new and temporary staff.
- Encourage and use ideas from all sources.
- Evaluate ideas on merit not the status of the source.
- Invest time and skill in coaching and counselling.
- Work at achieving development through the job.
- Have a constant and creative involvement in staff development.
- Expect their own staff to be committed to others' learning.

References for further reading

Argyris C. and Schon D. (1978). *Organisational Learning*. Addison-Wesley

Biddle D. and Evenden R. (1989). *Human Aspects of Management*. IPM

Burns T. and Stalker G.M. (1961). *The Management of Innovation*. Tavistock

Clark N. (1991). *Managing Personal Learning and Change: A Trainer's Guide*. McGraw-Hill Training Series

Handy C. (1989). *The Age of Unreason*. Arrow

Kanter R.M. (1989). *When Giants Learn to Dance*. Simon and Schuster

Kolb D.A. *et al.* (1974). *Organizational Psychology – an experiential approach*. Prentice-Hall

Schein E. (1987). *Process Consultation* Vol. 2. Addison-Wesley

Toffler A. (1980). *The Third Wave*. William Collins

27

Development skills: coaching, counselling and job-related growth

The development relationship between manager and staff is a shared responsibility. The staff member needs to be encouraged to actively pursue self development; the manager should be a stimulating and effective resource for the individual. Both parties should take initiatives in the relationship, and steps taken need to be mutually agreed for them both to feel ownership.

As a manager you can become an effective trainer, enhancing the skills and knowledge of a group of staff. This is the focus of the next chapter. There is also a key developmental role for the manager with individual members of staff, which will be examined in this chapter. The three one-to-one aspects are:

(1) Coaching.
(2) Counselling.
(3) Job-related growth.

1 Coaching

Coaching involves systematically and deliberately helping another person develop skills and knowledge. It may involve personal development in terms of attitudes and motivation. The effective coach gets satisfaction from the development and success of others. Time needs to be invested in the role, which has elements of appraisal, support, communication and motivation.

It is important that the coach recognizes that people learn in different ways. Some prefer to learn by experience; others by reflection; or by ideas and guidelines; and many by testing things out. Coaches should not assume that everybody learns as they do themselves, but need to accept that learning preferences vary. So part of the job is discussing with the individuals how they best learn.

Part of the approach could include developing the learning skills of the developer. This may mean encouraging them to seek new ways of learning about the job they are performing. (See pages 289–90.)

Performance coaching means that the manager works with staff in a systematic way, so that in turn they:

(1) Become aware of problems and needs – experience.
(2) Think about performance and development – reflection.
(3) Develop clear ideas and guidelines – concepts.
(4) Try out new skills and approaches – experiment.

The role of the coach is summarized in Figure 27.1.

The role of coach is an amalgam of four other roles:

Appraiser	Agrees what development is needed, what standards to aim for, and how to get there; development action plan.
	Observes and assesses
Supporter	Creates opportunity.
	Provides support, services and resources.
	Counsels and helps with problems.
Communicator	Gives balanced and constructive feedback.
	Offers advice and suggestions.
	Develops positive relationships.
	Is clear and informative.
Motivator	Encourages.
	Gives recognition.
	Challenges.
	Exhorts.
	Has expectations.
	Understands the developer.

Figure 27.1 The coaching role.

Coaching opportunities

An action plan agreed at appraisal may need to specify the means by which development is to be achieved. This may involve the two parties establishing a coaching relationship and identifying opportunities when the manager can intervene directly in the individual's learning.

Experiential coaching

This takes place when the coach is observing or sharing the individual's on-the-job activity. The coach can guide the work performance, encourage, give feedback and 'model' the appropriate skill.

Reflective coaching

The coach asks questions about the individual's performance in the development area so that the key aspects of the experience can be recalled and thought about. This may produce new angles and insights for the person being coached. It can often produce 'Eureka' leaps forward in learning.

Guideline coaching

This approach involves the coach in explanation or in giving rules and guidelines. It is the instruction element of coaching.

Trial coaching

The coach gives the individual the chance to try out a new skill. Both parties will manage the degree of risk in the trial. It is an opportunity to test and experiment in relative safety, as a preparation for the real thing.

Coaching as preparation for learning

If the individual is to have a development opportunity in the near future, the coach can help maximize the learning by discussing it beforehand. If the person is about to attend a course, for example, the coach manager should spend time checking what learning they both would like to occur. It will help learning motivation for the manager to share hopes, enthusiasm and expectations.

Coaching as learning reinforcement

New learning needs reinforcement and the coach can be instrumental in helping achieve this. If the individual returns from the course with new skills and knowledge, for instance, it is vital for the coach to discuss it. Together they can check what has been learned, what else needs to be done, how the coach can support the development and how much of their plan has been accomplished. Opportunity to practise is essential. What you don't use you lose.

The coach needs to be able to use different styles of coaching with different people, or even different styles with the same person at different times. Effective coaches have developed these as part of their repertoire. They are directly related to the five interpersonal roles identified in Part Two, Chapter 14.

Interpersonal role	Coaching style	
The Judge	**Tough**	Pushes hard; challenges: makes demands; critical.
The Helper	**Protective**	Takes care not to hurt; kindly; reassuring.
The Thinker	**Calculator**	Calm; dispassionate; logical; questioning.
The Fun Lover	**Whoopee**	Everything is 'a ball'; creative; exciting.
The Defendant	**Manipulative**	'Winds you up'; provokes; teases; cajoles; humours.

ACTIVITY 27.1

▼ Reflecting on coaching you have given or received, what are the advantages and disadvantages of each of the coaching styles?

The effects of each coaching style is summarized in Figure 27.2.

▽ Positive		Negative
	Tough	
Can push through difficulties, when the going is hard.		Can produce rebellion. May lead to bad feelings.
	Protective	
Can lift up a person when they are low.		Can stunt development by being over-protective.
	Calculator	
Can help you find solutions and help you work it out.		Can be seen as impersonal and distant. All head and no heart.
	Whoopee	
Can motivate by energy and enthusiasm.		Can be seen as frivolous. May avoid tough issues.
	Manipulative	
Can energize and influence.		May produce anger and feelings of betrayal.

Figure 27.2 Effects of different coaching styles.

299

Insupply case study: Coaching

> Bob Armstrong assessed the staff in his department in terms of how he saw them as people and the way they approached the job, other people and learning. For each of them he reminded himself of the performance and development targets they had agreed at appraisal.
>
> He was committed to supporting their development and thought about the individual coaching style that each would need. Bob worked out the approaches he would try out and was prepared to modify them in the light of experience.

CASE PROJECT 27.1

Bearing in mind Coaching Roles and Styles, what approach would you adopt to Bob Armstrong's staff, if you were him. Bob's staff are profiled below.

(1) Personal Profile — **Sally Bullen**. Information Supervisor.
Responsible for two staff, Helen and Ben.
Information Systems and Communication.

Learning Style — Good with concepts and ideas.

Personal Details — Good ideas and plans well.
Efficient.
Seems to need frequent discussions and reassurance, yet enjoys thinking about and using new equipment and systems.
Often seems detached from what is happening around her.
Not sensitive to the needs of others.

Agreed Performance and Development Targets — To translate plans into action more often and more rapidly.
To spend more time influencing her staff.

(2) Personal Profile — **Jean Evans**. Staff Supervisor.
Responsible for temporary and contract staff.

Learning Style — Experiments and likes to be active.

Personal Details — Very sociable.
Gets on well with others and has a lively sense of humour.
Good relations with clients and suppliers.
Can get muddled and spread confusion.

Agreed Performance and Development Targets — To plan more effectively and to assess better client needs.

(3) Personal Profile — **Joe Fagan**. Buildings Officer.
Responsible for maintenance.

Learning Style — Practical experience and challenge.

Personal Details — Very tied up with his job.
Has little time for people, literally and figuratively.
Appears brusque and offhand.
Not a good team person.

Agreed Performance
and Development Targets — More planning and coordination of maintenance and new work.
To improve his personal relationships.

(4) Personal Profile — **Peter Paine**. Procurement Supervisor.
Responsible for meeting supply needs.

Learning Style — Reflects on things at length.

Personal Details — Avoids issues. Will not confront tardy suppliers effectively.
Shy.
Lacks confidence.
Technically very sound.

Agreed Performance
and Development Targets — To meet and speak more frequently with clients and suppliers.
To improve delivery time of supplies by 10%.

(5) Personal Profile — **Ben Zimmer**. Information Systems Officer.
Responsible to Sally Bullen for IS.

Learning Style — No real preference. Seems to learn many ways.

Personal Details — Very rational and logical approach to his job.
Has ideas and anxious to implement them.
Still new to Insupply.
Needs to get to know the functioning of all departments.
Seems to have good relations within the team, but keeps a little in the background.

Agreed Performance
and Development Targets — To get to know internal clients and their system needs in the next three months.
To recommend a systems development and modification plan within six months.

Bob Armstrong's approach to coaching

(1) **Sally Bullen** — Manipulator approach with Calculator backup. Bob felt that he would meet Sally frequently and briefly in the Manipulator mode. He coaxed and cajoled her in these brief contacts and would teasingly enquire about her success in relation to her targets. She enjoyed this attention and seemed reassured by it. It also brought her down to earth and reminded her to do things as well as develop ideas.
Each week, initially, Bob would have a long meeting with her in Calculator mode, when they would analyse her situation and results. Bob assessed that this was helping her develop in the agreed direction.

(2) **Jean Evans** — Whoopee approach. Bob decided to relate to Jean in coaching through fun and humour, thinking this would get them on the same wavelength. Although humour

was strong in her relationships, this style did not work with her when discussing her performance and development. She felt Bob was not taking her seriously so he rapidly and successfully switched to Calculator backed up by Protective.

(3) **Joe Fagan**

Tough approach. Bob decided that with Joe respect would only be gained by initial confrontation and a firm, judgemental approach. It worked and Joe accepted there was a problem and expected to be pulled up if he was seen by Bob as backsliding. However, Bob also soon used the Calculator style when analysing Joe's planning and showing him ways of being more effective. He got Joe to *experience* the process of planning and see the results.

In addition, Bob used the Protective style when they were together with others, supporting and encouraging positive contributions from Joe. He rightly suspected that Joe's brusque manner hid a lack of confidence in dealing with 'clever' people. It helped.

(4) **Peter Paine**

Bob decided to try the Protective style in the medium term. He made helpful suggestions and was anxious to appear non-threatening. Peter was encouraged to monitor his own progress and report about it. Bob attended the more frequent client and supplier meetings to give support.

There were signs of progress and Bob hoped to switch to a less active Calculator mode as Peter gained confidence.

(5) **Ben Zimmer**

Bob used the Calculator approach with Ben most of the time. He spent time with both Ben and Sally looking at the Insupply system needs. Ben related to the analytical, logical methods that Bob brought to these meetings and the encouragement to get things done and take the odd risk.

Bob used these meetings not only to get the results he wanted from Sally's section, but also to enable the pair of them to learn from each other. Sally was encouraged to get things moving by Ben, meeting her 'action' focus needs. She provided Ben, in turn, with insight into Insupply functions and systems and included him in her meetings with their internal clients.

Bob Armstrong was pleased with the successful development of his staff. His approach was different for them all and he monitored the effects of his coaching carefully. He found valuable his initial reflection on the approach to use. If it worked it became an almost spontaneous part of his relationship although it was clear to him that it was part of a planned and agreed development and coaching strategy. He came to use a dominant style with some and a flexible mix with others.

2 Counselling

Counselling is a tool, difficult to use well, but rich in returns for the person being counselled if it is successful. It should not be confused with giving advice. The art of counselling is to enable individuals to discover what advice to give themselves.

All counselling can be seen in some sense as developmental. It serves to help the individual become aware of problems, to reflect upon their nature and to identify choices and perhaps solutions for themselves. In itself this is a growth process but the removal of blocks or difficulties is also developmental. If a person is stuck, feeling trapped or stunted by a personal issue, counselling may provide them with the way out and onwards. Issues may include fear, lack of confidence, inability to cope, emotional crises, shortage of skill, difficult relationships, lack of clarity, confusion and any other personal problem which is holding a person down.

Counselling can't be imposed on others. All you can do is to be aware that the other person is troubled and to make an offer of your time, support and your ear. If your offer is accepted, be clear with yourself what your role is to be. If you think you are the Judge as described in the chapter on developing relationships, you may make the situation worse.

Similarly, if you see yourself as the Helper, rather than hoping to be helpful, you will probably try to take over the person, the problem and the solution. Lady Bountiful and Knight in Shining Armour beware. Similarly, a psychologist, therapist or welfare expert self image is not a helpful orientation, unless you happen to be one such professional. If you can see yourself as a reflective, supportive, sensitive Thinker or an intelligent sounding board with humanity, you may have a good chance of success.

Of course, many people may *ask* for your advice in these situations. Perpetual Broken Wings do this all the time. If you judge it to be a counselling need, and want the individual to own and take responsibility for the problem and its solution, resist the temptation. If not, you will end up owning the problem and it is unlikely to get solved.

Apart from an appropriate orientation to counselling, which will transmit your attitude to the person who may seek your assistance, a successful outcome depends upon how you handle it. The essential skills are being a good and active listener, who asks questions well and creates a supportive non-judgemental climate. You need to be able to give time and attention to a person who needs somebody to help them think through a situation in which they find themselves.

Insupply case study: Counselling

CASE PROJECT 27.2

Reflect upon the five people with whom Bob Armstrong has a coaching relationship, as described earlier in the chapter:

Sally Bullen
Jean Evans
Joe Fagan
Peter Paine
Ben Zimmer

(1) Which of them do you feel would benefit from a counselling relationship?
(2) In which areas do you feel that counselling would help?
(3) Can you visualize how you would handle each case?

If you are studying as part of a group, you would find it helpful to undertake counselling/coaching role plays using the Insupply scenarios. Give feedback on how the interviews were handled, perhaps in terms of Figure 27.3.

- Be sensitive to a person's need for counselling rather than advice.
- Find an opportunity when you can have privacy and ample time.
- Reassure about confidentiality and that you are interested in listening to them.
- Listen actively:
    - Ask open questions.
    - Show you are attentive.
    - Summarize.
    - Reflect back their thoughts and feelings.
- Show you are human:
    - Reveal things about yourself but don't dwell on them.
    - Make supportive comments and sounds.
- Be a sounding board:
    - Don't be judgemental or express opinions.
    - Don't take over the problem.
    - Don't smother with sympathy.
- Problem solving:
    - Establish facts and clarify.
    - Identify choices.
    - Help them find solutions for themselves.

Figure 27.3   Effective counselling skills.

Counselling and development

Self assessment of attitude and performance is a powerful prerequisite for learning. Counselling is the means by which individuals can be encouraged to do this.

Training and development needs can best be established by the individuals themselves. With counselling and informed steering they are in the best position to identify what is required when a performance or potential need has been established. It is the case that counselling modules form an intrinsic part of the appraisal process and interview.

Attitude influence and change is a part of personal development. Coercion is not likely to achieve this and even if the manager can produce some modest change by being a respected 'significant other' or role model, some may regard this as unethical manipulation. If the attitude is critical, for example, a casual approach to safety or a negative approach to clients, counselling on the issue may lead to the individual unearthing the nature of the difficulty and selling themselves the solution and attitude change. Ownership is once again a key ingredient.

Development plans can often be elicited effectively from the individual by a counselling approach, particularly if the learning is in sensitive areas, such as personal skills.

Development blocks constrict ability and limit potential and are a major retardant to growth and learning. Counselling is often the only way to uncover these and enable the individual to begin the process of removing them.

Learning blocks	Stuck in a 'learning style'. Analysis paralysis. Long on ideas; short on action. Takes unevaluated risks. Experience not used for learning.
Value blocks	Beliefs about 'right' and 'wrong' ways of learning. 'It is essential to make sure I am never wrong, so I take no chances.' 'It is only possible to learn from experience.'
Feelings blocks	Emotional barriers to learning. 'I am no good at this kind of thing.' 'I can't do this on my own.'
Rewards block	Development seen as valueless.

3 Job-related growth

Development is needed in order to:

- Learn for a new or changed role
- Improve performance in a current job.

Skills are improved with practice and perhaps the best way to learn about a job is to do it. The manager who wishes to make the most of people should make full use of on-the-job learning, and do so in a planned, systematic and creative fashion. This involves using the staff development action plans and linking them with the tasks and responsibilities available within the manager's scope.

Job experience and related coaching is a major route to competence and confidence in terms of skill, knowledge and responsibility. Motivation is not only important for performance but also for learning and development. It is clear that the job itself is one of the most powerful motivators (F. Herzberg, 1966) and a strategy of stretching or challenging through the design of a person's job is a potent means of development.

The manager and the developing individual need to be clear which job components are going to be the focus for learning and growth. Job components are:

Technical skills	Range of tasks.
	Level of complexity of tasks.
People skills	Nature and significance of the people component.
Responsibility and accountability	For what and to whom.

Development by design

Joint planning of job experience for learning purposes could design an individual's development using the following methods.

(1) Assignments.
(2) Delegation.
(3) Working with a model.
(4) Peer learning.
(5) Temporary roles.

1 Assignments

If the requirement is to develop a person beyond their current job limits, special projects and assignments which have real purpose and developmental objectives can be very effective. Too often they are used to give new staff with potential an aimless Cook's Tour of sundry departments when time is occupied in mundane tasks which have no connection with the individual's development. Nobody coordinates or has accountability for the project, which may result in good talent being lost rather than grown. Assignments need designing and managing to ensure that developmental objectives are met.

> *Insupply case study: Ben Zimmer*
> **Agreed performance and development targets:**
> To get to know internal clients and their system needs in the next three months.
> To recommend a systems development and modification plan within six months.

Bob Armstrong arranged for Ben's supervisor, Sally Bullen, to organize an assignment that would take him into a different department for two days each week. He was to identify and analyse their work systems and procedures from scratch, by observing and interviewing key staff. Each department was to allocate Ben to a mentor to support his activities and help him learn what he needed.

Bob spent time with Sally and Ben, clarifying both the job and the developmental purpose of the assignment. He also dovetailed Ben's job-related growth activity with that of Sally herself.

2 Delegation

Skilled delegation is organizationally efficient and motivating, carrying with it messages of trust and challenge. It is also one of the most powerful developmental instruments in the manager's toolkit.

This is not the delegation of the chore dumper or the abdicator, but the planned and prepared devolution of authority to do, to decide and to act, within the boundaries agreed and understood by both parties.

If the delegated scope is tailored to the capacity and potential of the recipient, and designed to increase as that person grows, skills will be developed, experience acquired and responsibility shouldered, so that performance is not only enhanced in the current job, but preparation is made for the next.

Like most things, delegation does not work well if it is imposed. If it is the product of collaboration and agreement, it is likely to succeed; if it is part of a development plan, it is very probable that growth will be achieved.

Many managers are afraid to let go. The risks are low if it is handled well and mistakes that are made are minimized by monitoring and are themselves a source of learning.

Insupply case study: Sally Bullen
Agreed performance and development targets:
To translate plans into action more often and more rapidly.
To spend more time influencing her staff.

Bob would usually have organized Ben's assignment himself, because of the level at which decisions needed to be made and liaison maintained. He decided that he would delegate the management of the project to Sally, Ben's supervisor.

Bob talked with Sally about the scheme and her development plan. They both felt that the planning aspect would play to her strong suit, but that the learning benefit for her would come from getting results and managing Ben and his development.

They decided that Bob should be kept informed of plans and progress in the early stages. Sally would accept Bob chatting to Ben about the assignment, although she said she would prefer to be present if possible. Bob would inform his own manager of the plan. (Delegation to his team was part of his own development plan. Nobody escaped the net in Insupply.) He would also let the other department heads know what was happening, and seek their cooperation.

Sally was apprehensive. Bob reassured her that she could discuss it at any time. It could be part of their coaching 'contract'.

Another source of uncertainty was the resource implications. Her budget had been set before the assignment was decided upon and she was not sure how it would be affected. Bob did not think this was an important factor, so they did not spend time on it.

Bob had a long chat with Sally, agreeing the ground rules and discussing how she would handle the management aspects. He asked her to lead a meeting with the two of them and Ben.

After the first two weeks Ben was behind schedule, although he had put a great deal of his own time into the project, which he found very challenging. However, he was becoming frustrated at not achieving his time targets.

Sally took the problem to Bob, who questioned her about the problem and helped her to analyse it. She concluded that she should examine with Ben the number of interviews he was holding and the help he was getting from his mentor. It emerged that Ben was duplicating many of his interviews, a problem which was ironed out when the needs were clarified with the mentor.

The assignment was a success but the budgetary vagueness caused problems for them all and the project was overspent. Both Bob and Sally learned from this.

CASE PROJECT 27.3

Review the way Bob handled the delegation of the assignment with Sally. How does it fit with the way you think delegation should be handled?

A checklist for handling delegation is given in Figure 27.3.

1 Check to establish the individual's current work load. Can the delegated tasks can be reasonably carried out?
2 Communication: offer; listen; clarify; explain; check understanding; agree.
3 Specify the areas of delegation and the amount of authority and resources available.
4 Competence and confidence. Provide training/coaching support.
5 Be available and interested.
6 Let go. Do not oversupervise but agree monitoring and consulting arrangements.
7 Phase your withdrawal to match the individual's growth.
8 Give support if mistakes are made. You are accountable for them. Both learn from them and share the success.

Figure 27.3 Handling delegation.

3 Working with a model

Modelling ourselves upon respected other people is a key learning method. Skill and attitude development is influenced by those who work in close proximity. It could be the manager or work colleague who transmits the information which is copied by the individual.

Learning by modelling and copying will happen whether it is planned or not. However, it can be made more powerful if steps are taken to harness this potent development force. If the role model is identified and is developed *as a coach*, so that the influence is transmitted in a positive and focused fashion, the learning is likely to be more effective.

This 'sitting by Nellie' school of learning has always been the informal standby of staff development. Controlling and planning this 'working with a model' would build upon the model's strengths and reduce the chances of copying their weaknesses. It really involves bringing modelling explicitly into the coaching framework by recognizing 'Nellie' and managing the process. Of course, as manager, you may well be 'Nellie' yourself.

Copying a model can enhance skill, knowledge, judgement and confidence in handling both the people and technical side of jobs. Ensure you have positive not negative models.

Insupply case study: Peter Paine
Agreed performance and development targets:
To meet and speak more frequently with clients and suppliers.
To improve delivery time of supplies by 10%.

Bob had diagnosed that Peter's difficulties stemmed from low interpersonal confidence. He spent time counselling him and they agreed on a coaching relationship. It transpired that Peter admired Bob's apparent ease with people. Bob suggested that what he did when meeting others was a matter of some skill, a deal of practice, self management and confidence reinforcement.

He agreed to meet some internal clients and external suppliers with Peter, to provide support and to discuss the meetings as a basis for feedback and coaching. He was also able to give recognition for success as a positive reinforcement. He resisted showing off and lecturing Peter, who was encouraged to assess his own performance.

Peter also chose to attend an assertiveness workshop, run by Tim Bild, who was responsible for the Administration Department's teamwork activities. Bob was able to help him practise what he had learned. They agreed that progress had been made towards both development targets.

4 Peer learning

As well as copying role models, people develop a great deal from the ideas and methods they learn from their peers. This has elements of modelling, but involves discussion, listening and colleague support. In many cases, individuals will admit and discuss difficulties with their peers much more comfortably than with their managers, or even with 'equals' who are formally recognized as mentors.

If the peer group is functioning as a team, in the sense that it is supportive, collaborative and sensitive to the needs of its members, it can provide a lot of impetus to individual development.

The manager's role is to facilitate team building and to create the awareness of the value of peer learning as a significant element of teamwork.

Insupply case study: Joe Fagan
Agreed performance and development targets:
More planning and coordination of maintenance and new work.
To improve his personal relationships.

During the Administration Department's team workshop, Sally Bullen was told privately by Joe about what he regarded as his uncomfortable appraisal. Sally found planning easy, and was able to provide ideas and subsequently some periodic support.

Joe's distant attitude to the team was picked up as an issue during the team workshop. The facilitator, Tim Bild, ensured that he was not attacked for what was seen as his negativity. Effort was made to help him join the group and he began to relax with them socially. He exchanged work support with team members and they recognized his positive qualities as valuable.

Joe learned much about himself and his relationship with his peers, and there is no question that the people side of his job improved from this point. He found that this assisted his task activity because he found it easier to exchange information with his 'clients'.

5 Temporary roles

There is often a need for staff to stand in for others during absence. Rather than seeing this as fire fighting or plugging a gap, the manager can use it as a deliberate activity to meet development needs.

Systematic rotation through jobs related to your own may not only be motivating, but can also help you perform your interface role more effectively. There is also the clear acquisition of wider skills and experience.

If you are keeping a personal 'appraisal and development' file on your staff to help your people management, a record of job-covering experience is worth noting. Plans for future temporary task allocation can be designed into individual plans. So rather than using temporary role cover as an expedience, it could become part of your people development strategy.

One of the most problematic aspects can be the assessment of leadership and management potential. It is also difficult to prepare individuals prior to promotion, because there is no substitute for having responsibility for learning how to handle it. Planned and systematic 'temporary role promotion and upgrading' can be used to great effect to achieve this kind of development, especially when allied to coaching.

Insupply case study: Jean Evans
Agreed performance and development targets:
To plan more effectively and to assess better client needs.

The Recruitment Officer was shortly to take maternity leave. She was responsible for recruiting permanent junior staff and providing a service to management in selecting senior staff. Jean was responsible for taking on temporary and contract staff.

Bob suggested that Jean should take over some of the Recruitment Officer's responsibility as career development for herself, and to use the experience to meet her development targets in her current post.

She was encouraged to spend time preparing her assistant, Rachel Cohen, to take on more temporary responsibility and to develop a plan to achieve it. Rachel was anxious for this and made sure that it happened.

Bob mentioned the new system of job descriptions and person specifications used for recruitment by Personnel. He suggested that Jean should familiarize herself with these and see if she could make use of the method in her permanent job. She was able to use her experience in her temporary role to devise an effective and simple 'Contract Staff Specification' form, which her 'internal' clients came to use when seeking such staff. Jean found out about the needs of the departments by working with them on recruitment.

She attended a Recruitment Skills course prior to the attachment to Personnel and subsequently Bob supported her when she began a course of study for membership of the Institute of Personnel Management.

The development relationship begins with recruitment and induction; progresses with assessment and appraisal; is focused by the action plan; and is consummated by the manager's active role in assisting learning by coaching, counselling and designing creative job-related growth.

The manager can add substantially to the development of relevant skills and knowledge by acquiring training skills.

References for further reading

Argyris C. and Schon D. (1978). *Organisational Learning*. Addison-Wesley

Barker D. (1980). *TA and Training*. Gower

Clark N. (1991). *Managing Personal Learning and Change: A Trainer's Guide*. McGraw-Hill Training Series

Clutterbuck D. (1987). *Everyone Needs a Mentor*. IPM

Grant D. (1984). A better way of learning from Nellie. *Personnel Management Journal* December

Harrison R. (1988). *Training and Development*. IPM

Herzberg M. (1966). *Work and the Nature of Man*. Staples Press

Munro F.A. (1983). *Counselling. A Skills Approach*. Methuen

Pedlar M. *et al.* (1986) *A Manager's Guide to Self Development*. McGraw-Hill

Schein E. (1987). *Process Consultation* Vol. 2. Addison-Wesley

Singer E. (1981). *Effective Management Coaching*. IPM

Stewart A. and V. (1980). *Managing the Manager's Growth*. Gower

28

The manager as trainer: the people side

Managers are responsible for the development of their staff. In the previous chapter we explored the approaches that can be adopted in the one-to-one relationship. Increasingly the manager will be expected to help groups learn skills, develop knowledge and achieve personal growth. This is the manager as trainer.

External courses can be expensive and sometimes remote from individuals' needs, which can best be met in the work context in most cases. In-house courses run by internal or external resources may be a partial answer to the need for relevant and job-related learning and development, but if managers are able to develop confidence and competence as trainers themselves, they will have the cost effective solution in their own hands. With tight budgets, and internal training support often restricted to advice rather than provision, many managers may find that doing it themselves is the only option.

This chapter and the next explore approaches that the manager can try out and learn from, so that training skills can be added to the people management repertoire. As with all other parts of this book, the content and methods have been tested and proven by the authors' work with managers. Practice and development can be a solo activity, but if possible work through the ideas with others with similar interests. The ready-made courses in Appendix B may be a practical help.

Some reflections on learning and training

We have seen from earlier chapters that we learn in four ways:

Experience	– being involved 'here and now'.
Reflection	– standing back and thinking about experience.
Concepts	– developing or studying guidelines and ideas.
Experiment	– testing out those ideas in practice.

Some people make equal use of all the different ways to learn and can respond effectively to a wide range of training methods. However, most will have distinct preferences. Many prefer reflection and concepts, the traditional approach to education through books, learned discourse and academic lectures. Others prefer learning by doing and from experience, the practical approach to knowledge and understanding.

Learning styles: Some implications for trainers

(1) It can be helpful to discuss the way people learn at the outset of a course, probably in connection with the methods you plan to use. It helps to encourage members to be open minded about learning methods, and to be prepared to try them all.

(2) Remember when thinking about your training approach that many people in the group will have a different learning style from your own.

(3) Try to include a wide range of approaches to any course. The variety will assist learning motivation and ensure that everybody has a chance to use their favoured approach, perhaps also discovering other good ways to learn.

(4) Don't discount people. The difficulties that some people appear to have may be due to the lack of fit between your methods and their way of learning, rather than problems of ability or attitude.

(5) Try to 'round out' your own learning style, possibly by trying different training approaches from those you regard as your preferences.

Confucius probably said

(1) Wisdom can't be taught.

(2) The best teachers don't. They help others learn.

(3) I hear and I forget.
I see and I remember.
I do and I understand.

Trainer styles and methods

As in most things, we have choices as trainers. The pattern follows closely the dichotomies we have seen in other aspects of communication and relationships, of which training is just one special form. They relate to:

- who is responsible;
- who has ownership; and
- whose needs are being met?

The styles of training range from directive and structured, through shared, to non-directive and unstructured. Usually trainers make the choice on the basis of the approach with which they are most comfortable. Perhaps it *should* be based upon the nature of the subject matter, the level of the trainees, whether we are training for rote skills or fine judgement, and the degree to which we believe motivation to be significant. (Note the parallels with coaching styles.)

In the directive/structured approach, the trainer would dominate all aspects of the training and training decision making. The timetable and content would be cut and dried before the training commenced. The oppposite style would give the trainer the role of facilitator/resource, acting almost as catalyst, helping the group to define their needs and determine methods and content. There are, of course, points in between these two extremes. Trainer styles and methods are shown in Figure 28.1.

| Directive/Structured ....Shared ....Non-directive/Unstructured |

The Trainer
Defines the need.
Prepares the timetable.
Takes full responsibility.
Is the 'expert'.
Makes most contribution.
Assesses and evaluates.

The Trainees
Define the need.
Decide time use.
Take full responsibility.
See trainer as a 'resource'.
Make most contribution.
Assess and evaluate.

Methods related to style

Instruction – Lecture	–	Discussion	–	Involvement Activities
Question and Answer		Syndicates		Cases; Role plays;
		Buzz groups		Simulation;
				Trainee-chosen events

Figure 28.1 Trainer styles and methods.

Handling the training group

It is useful to see the trainer as a leader of a team with the aim of learning. The ideas considered in Part Two, Chapter 15 'Developing group behavioural skills' and Chapter 17 'Developing a team' have particular relevance. These looked at the ways teams develop; the needs that individuals and groups present for satisfaction; and the problems that arise if these needs are not met. It is important to examine these aspects in the context of the trainer as team leader of a learning group.

Group factors

When we come into contact with a newly formed group, including a training group, we can often notice characteristics of newness, particularly to do with anxiety and needing to find things out. This seems to apply to a considerable extent to an established group that has come together with a new objective, such as learning. Groups develop and change over time, and how rapidly and effectively they progress will have a substantial bearing upon the learning that takes place, particularly when the training requires group involvement and peer collaboration.

The trainer can make a major contribution to the development of a training group. It is, alas, equally true that the trainer can effectively destroy a group as a learning entity through indifference or incompetence in the people aspects.

The stages of group development

1 Getting together: Will I be accepted?

When the group meet, or get together for the first time in a new situation, the atmosphere is often tentative. People are cautious with each other and the trainer. Feelings range typically from mild apprehension, through worry to extreme anxiety. These feelings have a clear group dimension.

'Will I fit in?'
'Will I make a fool of myself?'
'What's in it for me?'
'What can I expect?'
'What will the trainer/others expect from me?'

The initial group members' contact with each other often involves negative behaviour (that is, behaviour that doesn't help the person or situation), such as hiding, defensiveness and cynicism. It will also include integrating and 'getting to know you' behaviour. This could be mild exchange of pleasantries and introductions; information exchange; seeking common ground; and humour. The trainer hopes for a higher proportion of the latter types of interaction! However, this is not a random factor. The trainer has substantial influence over this phase, as with the others that follow on. For example, the trainer decides the extent of opportunity for contact of this kind. Without it, the possibilities for group paranoia are considerable.

2 Getting angry: Will I have a role and influence?

If latent paranoia has not been put to rest at the start, the second stage may be more difficult. Suspicion of methods, purpose, outcomes and other people may grow. This will exacerbate the problems which will emerge to some degree, at this point, in any case.

This is the testing-out phase. It involves establishing the pecking order; who will have influence; what is the trainer's credibility; what roles will different people play? There may be internal conflict between course members. Fault may be found with anything from the plumbing to the colour of the paper. The trainer is likely to be challenged on several fronts, from administration to content and purpose of the programme.

Much of this will be valid and genuine checking and clarifying. All of it has a bearing on group development.

This phase may be overt or covert; deep or superficial; humorous or threatening; long drawn out or brief, but it will occur at some level.

If people are unable to resolve defensiveness and the questions of having an acceptable role and level of influence, and they have a competitive or combative view of the world, the group development to an effective learning team will be threatened.

3 Getting ready: Will this be my kind of group?

At some point, decisions will be being made about whether this will be a good group to belong to.

- Are there potential friends here?
- Can I expect to give and get support from some of these people?
- How are we going to work and play together?
- What are the rules we want to work to:
  - Shall we take it seriously?
  - Shall we cooperate with each other and the trainer?
  - Shall we put energy into this?
  - Shall we try to learn?
- Are we a group or a team?

If there are sufficient individuals, particularly the strong exemplars who have the respect of the group, who begin to give positives to these kind of questions, then you are moving into phase three. One or two are often left behind at this stage with their personal concerns and bad feelings. They are not now likely to hold the others back, although the stronger hostiles may attempt to do so. They will need your attention and are likely to receive the attention of the group, to encourage joining, perhaps in the social, but certainly in the learning sense. Make overtures and offers. Coercion is probably both unethical and ineffective.

The group are now ready to learn.

4 Getting going: Meeting our needs

Individuals and the group begin to produce quality work. They learn collaboratively as a team and begin to operate well independently. Initiatives are taken and problems are tackled and solved. The team take responsibility for their learning.

This is the stage for which the trainer aims and hopes. It may arrive very rapidly or may not fully arrive at all. It seems that on instructional and short courses lasting a day or less, the negativity issues are less, perhaps because the stakes are lower and the threats are not so high. The four stages are diluted, in proportion perhaps to the duration and possibly the learning potential.

The trainer may find the early stages of group development puzzling, disconcerting or even threatening. Each stage requires a trainer response which will enhance team development and learning. It is as important as content knowledge and training techniques for the trainer. If right, you will help learning. If wrong, you will cause a significant block.

ACTIVITY 28.1

▼ Reflect upon the four stages of learning group development.
Recall and visualize those you have experienced.

How should the trainer respond to each of the stages?

▽ *Trainer responses to the stages of group development*

1 Getting together: Dependence on the trainer

All people feel a degree of anxiety on joining a new group or finding themselves in an uncertain situation. This includes the trainer. If you are lucky or have prepared the ground well, others will help you in this crucial ice-breaking and scene-setting phase. However, you will have the prime task of making friendly contact, facilitating interaction between members, being helpful, reassuring, interested and human. If there are strangers to you amongst them, find out their names and spend as much time as you can with them. Generate low key humour and help people relax. The music or climate is vital at this, probably the most crucial, stage of the course.

What you have done before the group assemble will affect the climate when they first meet. Have they discussed the course in relation to their needs and development plans with you or somebody else who understands the programme? Have they had written information which helps them know what to expect? Do they know in advance who they are going to be working with?

As well as attending to the 'acceptance' needs of the group you will need to begin the process of orientation and letting them know what to expect. Help them say, do and achieve something as soon as possible, but don't push too hard too early.

2 Getting angry: Counter-dependence to the trainer

If the first stage has not been tackled effectively by the group and yourself, the second is likely to be more problematic. 'Getting angry' may involve openly aggressive behaviour, sarcasm, jokes at the expense of others, passive hostility and other forms of interpersonal negativity.

In terms of the interpersonal roles in Chapter 16 'Developing relationships', the most appropriate will be Thinker with Helper and to a lesser extent, Fun Lover as back up. The response you may most *feel* like making will probably be Judge to put down the rebels or Defendant, to protect yourself. These latter roles, however, are the ones most likely to feed the problems of 'getting angry'. You will win the respect of the 'good guys', and probably defuse the others, by the former approach.

It is important to take care of yourself by focusing on the fact that the problem is not you but a function of the new group. Rehearse and practise calmness and reduce tension in yourself and the others. Sit or stand four square.

Listen, discuss and explain. Be flexible and accept ideas and concerns as genuine and act upon them. Look for common ground and build on the positive as it emerges. This angry stage may only be fleeting. If it doesn't itch, don't scratch it!

3 Getting ready: Interdependence with the trainer

The group are in the process of forming a team. They are developing a degree of cohesion and positive relations by showing support and interest in each other's needs. Norms develop governing the way the group expect individuals to behave. If you have handled the first two stages reasonably effectively, the group will allow you to lead from the front by influencing these norms, perhaps giving guidelines and permissions. These may govern things like timekeeping, informality and whether it is OK to interject with questions.

Attempts to dominate will usually be resisted. In a sense, you join the group yet maintain a degree of separateness. The group themselves may want this anyway, and will not be free to establish their own identity if you try to get too close. Give them space. You will have to sense how much they want.

Team feeling is obviously important on a course which uses peer learning and support as part of the development process. You can help create this by collaborative group tasks at an early stage, perhaps even as a way of handling the personal introductions. Gentle subgroup competition may help to reinforce whole-group team spirit. These feelings of interdependence should be welcomed and encouraged.

It is time to press the accelerator and get going.

4 Getting going: Independence from the trainer

The final stage is when the group make the task of learning and development their own. Group and individual commitment is high. They will be a learning team no longer needing close supervision of their activities by the trainer. Too many checks and over-frequent presence may in fact be resented. The group will want to define their own priorities and needs and to negotiate these with the trainer.

This does not mean you have no role. It is simply that it is different at this stage. The trainer still gives recognition; is available as a guide; provides expert information and advice as the course requires; offers the team targets; and helps them measure performance. In other words you have become a resource for them to use. The extent to which a group becomes autonomous will depend on you, them and the nature of the programme. You will need to judge how far and when to let go. It is a remarkably similar process to both child rearing and delegation!

Remember that the objective is for them to learn, not for you to teach. The process of independence should culminate when they leave the training situation and have to apply their acquired skills and knowledge without you. Your aim is to finish so the group is independent of you and the individuals independent of the group.

Handling individuals

The previous section explored ways of leading the training group and creating a learning team. The trainer will also need to relate directly to individual members who bring their needs and personal characteristics to the training situation.

Experienced trainers will recognize both the positive and negative orientations to courses. The former need encouraging and perhaps steering, whilst the latter require attention to prevent them getting in the way of group learning and the development of the individual presenting problems.

Typical individuals on training courses

There are several types of course member that most groups seem to possess. They may present problems to you and the group. Together you need to handle them in order to meet the learning aims.

The Noble Steed: The good contributor

This is the positive type. The Noble Steed is keen, energetic and willing to take risks when the going is tough and the situation uncertain. It is bright and interested and contributes effectively. Genuinely open and wanting to learn.

When you need support, help is at hand.

The Wise Monkey: The know-it-all

Always has a clever argument and is keen to show off its knowledge. Able to quote chapter and verse. Will try to dominate the discussion and may use what it knows to intimidate. May use knowledge as an interpersonal weapon.

The Wild Dog: The aggressor

Any contribution is based upon wanting to start an argument, which it intends to win by the loudness of its bark and the display of its teeth. Finds fault with points made by others and is always negative.

The Hedgehog: The prickly hostile type

Doesn't want to be there and shows resentment. Will limit its involvement to hostile looks and comments. Rolls into a prickly ball when approached. May feel that the course is beneath its dignity but secretly is apprehensive that it may be attacked.

The Hippopotamus: The bored and impervious type

Indifferent to you and other course members. Just wants to be left alone for a quiet life. Gives 'do not approach' signals like an occasional snort. Probably experienced but only prepared to learn in its own time and on its own terms.

The Bull Frog: The talker

Will talk to others or to itself, loudly and often. Does not require invitations to speak. Rarely concise and usually rambles around a subject. Has very poor listening skills and opinions on every subject.

The Nervous Fawn: The shy retiring type

Will keep a low profile and hope not to be noticed. Very anxious about being caught out in the open and finds the situation threatening. Hopes not to be exposed thus showing its self-perceived limitations.

The Sly Fox: The inquisitor

Tricky type. Probably trying to prove how clever it is by catching out others, particularly the trainer. Asks endless questions, not to listen to the answer, but to discomfort the recipient. Feels better if others feel worse.

The Intelligent Giraffe: The intellectual highbrow

Probably both able and serious minded. Complicates rather than simplifies. Enjoys analysis and theory for its own sake. Presents difficult and abstract ideas. Can easily confuse.

ACTIVITY 28.2

Most readers will, naturally, identify with the Noble Steed, and disapprove of many of the other characters we find in a typical training group. But who then are the others?

They are, of course, ourselves on our bad days. Beneath all our Noble Steeds there lurks a Sly Fox or Bull Frog, waiting for fears and frustrations to give them their opportunity to take over and present themselves to the group.

Can you identify with one or two of the types (apart from the Noble Steed, which we all recognize as our true selves anyway!).

If you are working in a group, you would no doubt find it interesting to assess each of your colleagues in terms of your perception of their most obvious (to you) back-up group character. It could be even more interesting to receive their perceptions of yourself. I have to own to an occasional Bull Frog and Wise Monkey.

If you were your trainer/facilitator/lecturer, how would you handle yourself when you are in your negative back-up mode?

How would you approach the others?

▽ Handling individuals: Helping them and the group

The Noble Steed: The good contributor

Invite in as frequently as seems appropriate. They will not let you down. They can help influence the norms in a positive way. You both need to take care that they are not seen as the trainer's pet.

The Wise Monkey: The know-it-all

Try to build upon its ideas and get it to recognize the value of others' contributions and knowledge. Help the group not to be intimidated by asking them to evaluate the Monkey's ideas. Invite others in to provide a balance.

The Wild Dog: The aggressor

Keep calm. Don't get hooked into fighting them. It is not personal. They are like this to most people when they feel threatened. Arguing with them may alienate the group. Try agreeing with their points and listen actively to them. Tease out anything that you can make positive. Model the value of building upon rather than destroying the ideas of others. Give them your attention early on, both in and out of session.

The Hedgehog: The prickly hostile type

Acknowledge their experience and know-how and seek their contribution when you know the group will recognize its value.

Try to let them know they can help make the session successful.

Give them your time. Make a point of helping them recognize what they can and have learned, probably on a one-to-one basis out of session. Befriend them.

The Hippopotamus: The bored and impervious type

Find out what they are likely to know about the subject in quiet chats, and then make direct reference to their knowledge during session, perhaps asking them a question. Seek their advice and value their opinions. Get them involved in small group work. They are often more at home in small ponds.

The Bull Frog: The talker

Bull Frogs usually know their weakness and admit it to the group. This gives you and the others a lever to encourage them to limit their contributions from time to time. They will usually require more control than self control. When you are sure the rest recognize the problem, you can tactfully interrupt and pass the ball to somebody else. Avoiding eye contact makes it more difficult for them, but try not to put them down. Their contributions may be valuable.

The Nervous Fawn: The shy retiring type

Play it with care. Don't rush this one. When possible involve them in small group activity, where it may be easier for them to come out. Encourage and give recognition for their contributions, without over-doing it. Try to have frequent eye contact and give acknowledgement signals. Make a point of supportive contact out of session.

The Sly Fox: The inquisitor

Field some of the questions and always appear to take them at face value. Don't try to answer them all or it will become a fruitless dialogue for the rest of the group. Redirect some questions to the others and some back to the Fox itself. It will usually have a good answer and may be pleased you asked. Give the Fox some time and interest out of session. This may reduce their need for attention during the course itself.

The Intelligent Giraffe: The intellectual highbrow

They can have a lot to offer so try not to be impatient. If their heads are in abstract clouds, bring them down to earth. Don't deflate them, but help give weight to their contributions by seeking clarification about the practical implications of their ideas. Make use of their conceptual ability as collators, summarizers and scribes.

Meeting the needs of trainees

Many of the group and individual problems which beset trainers and can block learning stem from need frustration of course members. As we have seen earlier, the team leader has to facilitate the meeting of group and individual needs for the task to be accomplished effectively.

ACTIVITY 28.3

Abraham Maslow describes a set of basic human needs which can apply to all human situations, including work and training. It serves as a valuable checklist for trainers seeking by their activity and behaviour to help members meet their needs so that frustration does not block learning.

With reference to your previous experience, or perhaps by setting up an observation experiment on a course you are attending, can you identify trainer behaviour and other factors relevant to meeting individual needs and so aiding learning in a course environment? The needs are:

Physical needs
Security needs
Social needs

Reputation and self esteem needs
Self fulfilment needs

▽ Physical needs

- Comfort; lighting; ventilation and warmth.
- Seating positions appropriate for discussion and seeing visual aids.
- The time span of attention is rarely more than a few minutes without fresh stimulus, so find ways to stimulate.
- Meals will reduce receptivity for at least one hour, and alcoholic drink even longer. Organize light alcohol-free meals.

Security needs

- Let the group know what to expect and what you expect.
- Listen to their concerns and reassure as much as you can.
- Relax and reduce tension however you are able.
- Give and accept trust and support.
- Let the group know how they are doing. Exchange feedback.

Social needs

- Help individuals to feel they belong there.
- Give acceptance and friendliness.
- Show warmth and humour.
- Encourage team identity.

Reputation and self esteem needs

- Listen actively and give time to each individual.
- Give recognition and respect.
- Provide early and frequent opportunities for all to achieve and contribute.
- Acknowledge each and every contribution.
- Help individuals to maintain their self esteem.
- Avoid exposing individuals to possible humiliation.
- Confront behaviour intended to humiliate others.

Self fulfilment needs

- Create enjoyment and motivation.
- Give the group realistic challenges.
- Use a variety of training approaches.
- Encourage individuals to share responsibility for the learning.
- Provide opportunities for creativity.
- Allow scope for independence.
- Focus on the application of the course to work.
- Afford opportunity for the development of personal action plans.

In short, show genuine concern for the needs of your course members.

323

References for further reading

Argyris C. and Schon D. (1978). *Organisational Learning*. Addison-Wesley

Biddle D. and Evenden R. (1989). *Human Aspects of Management*. IPM

Clark N. (1991). *Managing Personal Learning and Change: A Trainer's Guide*. McGraw-Hill Training Series

Clutterbuck D. (1987). *Everyone Needs a Mentor*. IPM

Harrison R. (1988). *Training and Development*. IPM

Maslow A.H. (1970). *Motivation and Personality*. Harper and Row

Schein E. (1987). *Process Consultation* Vol. 2. Addison-Wesley

29

The manager as trainer: techniques and methods

A systematic approach

If you are contemplating running a course it will help if you tackle it systematically. First you need to be clear about the need and aims. This will focus you on the design and make decisions on the content, training methods and timing. Next it will pay you to consider how you will meet group, individual and task needs during the course. Finally you will need to assess how successful it was. The principles will apply equally to organizing some other method of learning, such as a self-managed package.

Need identification

What does the group need to learn?

- Is it knowledge? If so, what and for what?
- Is it skill? If so what skill and what do they have to learn to do that is new or different?

You get the answers from:

- The performance appraisals and development plans.
- Asking those involved.
- Research and observation.
- Assessing performance and pursuing an audit trail back to source.

Course design

Content
(1) What specifically do you aim to achieve so that the needs are met?
(2) What do you want to include? –
essentials: that which must be covered
desirables: that which it would be useful to cover
peripherals: that which it would be nice to cover

(3) Where can you find out all you need to know to back-up what you do know? Do not be pessimistic or over-cautious. You do not need to be a complete expert in the subject. You need some knowledge and if the group have experience to share, the capacity to help them learn not only from you, but also from each other.

'In the Country of the Blind the one-eyed man is king.'

Methods

(1) What are your preferred methods?
(2) What methods most suit the needs and content?
(3) What methods do you need to develop?
(4) What resources do you have at your disposal?
(5) Who can advise, counsel and support you?

Timing

(1) How long have you available?
(2) Can you divide it into modular units with time chunks you can manage?
(3) Is there a logical sequence?
(4) What will you need to do regarding pre-course briefing and preparation for members?

Running

Aim to meet the group, individual and task learning needs.

Validation

How will you assess how well the needs and aims were met, so that you can develop the course and assess whether it was worth doing?

- Course member's own assessment?
- Tests and measures of skills and knowledge?
- Follow-up with on-the-job assessment in relation to individual development plans?

Once you have thought systematically about the course and have decided that it needs doing, is worth doing and that you can do it, you will need to plan and prepare for the event.

Course planning and preparation: Trainer's checklist

(1) What are my training aims?
Spell out the skills, knowledge or other development aims.

(2) What do I know about the group?
  (a) Do I need to help them with information and preparation?
  (b) Who can talk to them about the course and their individual development needs and plans?
  (c) What do they know already?
  (d) What is their skill level?
  (e) What are they like as individuals?

(3) What are the key aspects to cover?

(4) Where can I get material, ideas, information or assistance?
  (a) Myself; (b) colleagues; (c) internal or external specialists; (d) course documentation; (e) manuals; (f) training guides; (g) book and journal references; (h) your own professional body; (i) other professional bodies such as the Institute of Training and Development (UK telephone 0628 890123); the Institute of Personnel Management (081 946 9100); or the British Institute of Management (0536 204222).

(5) What training methods do I plan to use?

(6) What is my course structure plan?
  (a) Opening   (i)   meeting group and individual needs;
                 (ii)   outline of aims and methods;
                 (iii) personal introductions;
                 (iv)   administration;
                 (v)   questions.
  (b) Body   (i)   content chunks and their specific aims;
                 (ii)   activities;
                 (iii) trainer input: pipe openers; where are we summaries; linking and wind up comments;
                 (iv)   key questions to ask;
                 (v)   tight or loose timetable.
  (c) Closure   (i)   final integration ideas and summary;
                 (ii)   personal action plans:
                              what I plan to do more of
                                              less of
                                              differently
                        how I will apply the knowledge
                        what I will need from others;
                 (iii) feedback review.

(7) What shall I use as my session guide and security blanket?
  How much detail? Large bold headings and key words on cards. Make light pencil notes on flip charts/blanks or write on the borders of overhead projector acetates, visible only to you.

(8) What support material will I want?
  (a) Handouts as activity brief sheets or information documents.
  (b) Visuals. Slides or overhead projector with acetates.
  (c) Closed circuit television for role plays or training videos.

(d) Flip charts, white boards and non-permanent pens.

(e) Folders, note paper and pens.

(f) Bluetack.

(g) Computers, VDUs or word processors.

(h) Realia – pictures, exhibits, models, photos.

(9) What training facilities do you require?

    (a) Rooms. How many and how large? Do you need extra for small group work?

    (b) Layout. Horseshoe? Circular? Herringbone? Tables or not?

    (c) Special needs:

        (i) Power points and extension cables?

        (ii) Television monitor and VCR?

        (iii) Refreshments?

    (d) Environment:

        (i) Noise.

        (ii) Heating.

        (iii) Ventilation.

        (iv) Lighting.

(10) Residential

    Invaluable for certain kinds of development programme.

    Base choice on visit or recommendation if possible.

Training methods

1 Open learning: guided self development

During the last decade the development and accessibility of personal computers, user friendly VCRs, camcorders and the facility to integrate the electronic and audio visual hardware has led to the rapid growth of self-directed and guided open learning on a large scale.

There are many off-the-peg packages for skill development in common core areas, such as word processing, VDU and keyboard skills, computer operation, systems programming, customer skills, telephone skills and so on.

Organizations which have a sufficiently large volume of training need have developed their own self-managed learning packages. W.H. Smith, for example, produced a sophisticated customer skills programme which linked computer to video. Trainees could explore and practise skill options, make choices, get immediate feedback and assess their own progress.

Not all organizations have the scale of need to justify that degree of investment. Nevertheless, if there is a volume of training which needs to be repeated over time, a comparatively modest investment can yield good development returns.

The self-managed learning programme development will require a little time and creativity. It does not necessarily demand professional assistance, although this is available at a price. Anybody with a thorough knowledge of a system, modest ability in logic and an understanding of training would be able to produce a manual for guided self development.

NEM Insurance, for example, requiring to train a few dozen claims staff each year, had one member of staff who produced such a manual in a few weeks, whilst fully maintaining most of her normal work load. It was a logical, step-by-step approach to learning the procedures, documentation, computer and VDU operation. It included demonstrations, examples and self-testing exercises. The trainees worked at their own pace through each phase, which was monitored by the trainee's supervisor coach. The manual could easily be converted fully to a computer based activity, but worked quite satisfactorily in simple manual form.

CASE PROJECT 29.1

The manager/trainer could produce simple packages to meet recurring training needs, which are often fudged or neglected because of the demands they place upon the time of others. How might you produce a self-managed induction training package for new recruits to Insupply if you were Bob Armstrong?

Insupply case study: Guided self development

Bob Armstrong, the Insupply Administration Manager, organized and helped produce a guided self-managed induction training package.

He produced a framework and guide for producing the package. It gave guidelines to each department on their contribution to the programme. They each produced three levels of documentation.

(1) A general simple statement of what the department does for inclusion in the Basic Induction Manual given to all new recruits.
(2) A fuller outline of the department, including broad systems and methods. The names of key personnel and their extensions were included. This would be given to all new recruits whose work would involve contact with that department.
(3) A manual which identified the key roles in a department. Each role would be illustrated with main tasks and procedures. All departmental personnel had their photos and extensions included. This would be given to all department recruits.

Bob made use of one of the staff who had developed some camcorder and video production skill. They produced a twenty-minute video which included a brief welcome from Hedi Lindstrom, the Chief Executive, and a visual visit to each department, as well as to major clients.

Each department was responsible for producing its own induction video which introduced the staff at work.

These manuals and videos varied in quality, naturally, but they were universally valued by new members of staff. On their first day they would be welcomed by their manager and supervisor and introduced to their guide and

329

mentor, usually their on-the-job coach. They were free to consult the latter as they felt the need. Each department had a VCR, monitor and headphone facility which the new recruits could use as they wished.

The trainee had the responsibility, with the support of the coach, to arrange contacts with relevant people in related departments, and time was set aside for this. The videos and manuals helped them to decide what they wanted to learn and who they could learn it from.

Each supervisor had produced a task learning programme, which in many cases used self-managed learning principles. New recruits would use them with the support of their on-the-job learning coach. It was a successful system.

Guided self development choices

There is a choice between trainer and trainee influence.

What to develop?	The development areas could be: • Self-chosen. • Part of agreed development. • Directed in relation to specific tasks.
How to develop?	There is a wide choice of media and methods:
• Books and manuals	These can include information sheets; work guide sheets; illustrations; methods of operating; examples; guided practice; and self testing, including 'Pass' and move to next phase hurdles.
• Computer aided	These range from computerized manuals to sophisticated interface with audio visuals.
• Audio visual	Videos; demonstrations; models; realia; VCR and monitors; simulation.
• Resource access	Choice of learning resources, including people who can guide, inform and encourage. Linked to job-related growth.
When and Where?	Choices of timing, duration and location.

2 Presentation: talking with a group

The lecture is probably the most used and least effective form of training. Attention span will not exceed three minutes without fresh stimulus, so there is the clue. Do not talk too long; talk with variation and enthusiasm; intersperse the 'talking to' with attention-getting devices.

'I hear and I forget,
I see and I remember,
I do and I understand.'

Trainees like talks, lectures or inputs which:

- Give clear, orderly summaries of major ideas or principles.
- Are divided into logical and linked bite-sized chunks.
- Introduce and open up a new subject.
- Simplify a difficult area.
- Put a topic into context.
- Provide a guide or map prior to independent discovery.

Trainees do not like talks, lectures or inputs which:

- Are full of digressions.
- Ramble.
- Contain too much detail.
- Are read from a text.

Getting the best from your talk with a group

Managing the talk.

(1) Prepare yourself well, but don't wind yourself up into a state of anxiety by becoming obsessive about it.

(2) Keep the numbers small, if you can.

(3) Begin by: (a) making some kind of personal contact with them;

               (b) indicating your purpose;

               (c) letting them know what to expect;

               (d) outlining what you are going to do and say;

               (e) indicating what you want from them (questions, interruptions, activities and so on).

(4) Develop your theme logically, in an orderly fashion, linking together the chunks of ideas or information.

(5) Use visual aids to support (not take over) the talk. Include objects and give demonstrations. It may help to plan the talk around these. Many presenters find these act as triggers which aid their memory and increase naturalness and fluency. It is often easier talking to and about a thing in front of you, rather than an idea in your head.

(6) Watch the group's reaction and try to respond.

(7) Build in your questions, real or rhetorical.

(8) Summarize frequently. Let the group know where they have been, where they are and where they are going.

(9) Conclude positively.

Managing yourself.

(1) Relax   (a) Have your aids and guide notes well organized.

               (b) Give yourself a few minutes to gather yourself before you start.

               (c) Focus on friendly faces; acknowledge them non-verbally.

(d) Talk to people informally one-to-one beforehand if it is possible.

(e) Consciously relax yourself, especially your jaws and shoulders. Breath very deeply and remember to do so during the talk.

(f) Don't be anxious about being nervous. It's nature's way of gearing you up.

(2) Delivery.   Vary your pace, tone and pitch. Talk clearly and tellingly to those at the back. Look at people when you are talking, as if it was one-to-one.

(3) Be you.   Let yourself 'come through'. Express your feelings and use body language actively. If you are enthusiastic, show it. If you feel something is amusing, show it. Dispense with the mental image of good talkers you feel you should imitate, but steal their methods, if you can make them your own.

(4) Gesture.   Use facial expressions, hand movements and body language. The drama of presentation is important.

(5) Eye contact.   Try to look at everybody, at least some of the time. It engages people and helps you exchange messages. This applies whatever the group size. If you are with a group sitting in a 'horseshoe', swivel your head constantly. Be aware of your left or right bias, and any obstructions, such as an overhead projector.

(6) Mannerisms.   Find out if you have any, and if so, are they distracting. If they are not, forget about them. If they are a distraction, stop doing them, probably by finding an acceptable substitute. Most mannerisms are habits which serve or used to serve you in some way. For example, 'Mmmmmm' is a device to give us time to think. There are alternatives, like holding your jaw, looking upwards or simply pausing!

(7) Posture.   Can be very distracting if it is inappropriate. Be aware how it is affecting the impact you are making, whether you are sitting or standing.

Keeping the group's attention by involvement

Effective presentation needs not only good, well-ordered content delivered with impact. Your relationship with the group is equally important, particularly in terms of members' involvement. The group needs the opportunity to be part of proceedings, so that attention and interest are engaged and the learning process enhanced.

ACTIVITY 29.1

 Reflect upon talks or presentations that you have given or received. Recall by visualizing the events in your mind's eye. Additionally, if opportunity presents, set up an observational experiment for presentations in which you will take part in the near future.

Identify:

(1) Things which switched off your involvement or that of others.
(2) Behaviour, techniques or activity which created involvement and engaged the attention.

Group active involvement methods

(1) Questions from the group.
(2) Discussion.
(3) Individual exercises or activities, however brief or simple.
(4) Group or paired activities.

For example, the activities could be reading, answering questions by making notes, making mental decisions or choices, contributing to a demonstration, acting as your assistant, responding to a questionnaire, operating equipment, handling an article, doing a calculation, taking part in a simulation exercise or engaging in a role play.

Trainer active involvement methods

These are not as effective as group activity, but they are useful supplements. If you are speaking for more than one minute, *use them.*

(1) Keep eye contact with all members, or *appear to* if the audience is large, by scanning them.
(2) Refer by name to members of the group as much as you can.
(3) Mention people and events the audience will know about,
(4) Refer to experiences you share with them.
(5) Engage them with humour as appropriate.
(6) Let your *self* get through to them.
(7) Touch on things they will have been engaged upon earlier.
(8) Demonstrate the relevance and payoff of your topic.
(9) Be enthusiastic.
(10) Keep them with you with regular summaries, linking backwards and pointing forwards.
(11) Use visuals, prepared or spontaneous.
(12) If they are going to have things to do during or after the presentation, let them know and remind them. It concentrates the mind very effectively.
(13) Use demonstrations, photos, real objects and so on.
(14) Pass things around and allow time for them to be looked at, touched, heard or smelled.
(15) Be topical.

(16) Don't speak for more than two minutes without some form of stimulus for the group. Even a pause will help.

(17) Prepare a start with some kind of impact.

(18) Give them things to do. Raise your hands if ... . Look at this ... . You will see over there... . Do you have ... ?

Visual aids

These greatly enhance a course session, but occasionally may overwhelm it and distract from the learning, when the medium is so dominant that it destroys the message.

Visual aids include flip charts, overhead projectors, slide projectors, handouts, real objects (realia), VDUs, television and camcorders, videos, films and whiteboards.

Flip chart. Almost indispensable in the training room, it can be used by the trainer or the group to steer, summarize or record discussion. It can be pre-written to give information or instructions and can have pencil written 'invisible' guide notes for trainer support.

If you are using it as a spontaneous, here and now record, use large clear letters and remember to talk to the group, not the flip chart. The standing position at the chart with the pen is a position of strength for influencing group proceedings.

Groups find it a good tool to help their discussion and are usually happy to use the 'newsprint' sheets to aid their reports. The sheets make helpful course wallpaper with Bluetack, providing a constant reference to key points.

The overhead projector. This is often a better tool than the flip chart. Certainly pre-prepared acetate slides can be colourful and have high visual impact. It is not fully exploited by most trainers, however, as a means of recording lecture or discussion points. This the trainer can do using water soluble ink, whilst remaining seated and maintaining close physical and eye contact with the group. It is also very easy to write and draw freehand upon a blank acetate sheet or roll.

When you switch on the OHP it focuses upon you and the screen. It is an attention gaining stimulus. When you have moved on, however, it is important to switch it off, as many will find it a distraction.

You can add to the drama of the talk by the seven veils method of progressive unmasking and revelation. This also works in reverse, using overlays to build up a picture or 'ideas model'.

It is usually better to point to the visual rather than the screen, but be aware that hand movements are exaggerated five times on the OHP screen. You may find it better to use a static pointer (a pencil) on the screen, moving it as you need, rather than one that is hand held and shaking.

Prepared visuals. These give impact and support to a presentation; gain attention; assist learning and recall; and are impressive. They can be prepared professionally, or increasingly easily through computer aided acetate production or photocopiers. However, neat uncrowded freehand is usually acceptable to small training groups.

Spontaneous visuals. These are good, because they involve the group and usually reflect their ideas and discussion. This can motivate the group and assist discussion leading. Aim to catch the key words and phrases rather than try to put everything down. It can help the flow and recall of what the group is creating at the time and can be invaluable for backtracking and future reference. They can be complex, because they are built up by you and the group together, so that even a tortuous diagram is meaningful.

Films and videos. These should not be used as a soft option or substitute for the trainer–group relationship. Ensure that they really fit your learning aims and approach. Don't expect them to stand alone. Good films and videos are made even better if you are able to lead into them effectively by an exercise or discussion. It is also important to lead out of a film by getting individuals and the group to reinforce the message by examining the skill or knowledge implications. Always place it in the context of the course.

Camcorders and self-produced videos. Straight reportage videos for information can easily be made by amateurs. If quality is important you will need a professional service and this is obviously more expensive. Unless unplanned humour is your aim, scripted playlets do require expert filming and usually professional actors as well. Help is quite easy to get through agencies for script writing and acting. One such in the UK is Target Casting, telephone 0524 67354.

Role play videos. Without doubt, these are powerful tools when used with playback, feedback and observation, as a means of developing self awareness and face-to-face skills. Trainees will need supportive induction and sensitive handling of feedback, but they almost always produce effective spontaneous performances with only the most basic scenario briefing. Always trust your group.

3 Learning by talking: discussion methods

Learning requires attention. Experience suggests it is very difficult for the group to go to sleep whilst they are talking. It is nearly as difficult if a person feels another may engage him or her in conversation at any moment.

Apart from these obvious advantages if you are running a training session, discussion is an activity which enhances learning. It:

- Assists memory and recall.
- Allows illustration, clarification and feedback.
- Creates 'ideas' building.
- Gives the trainee 'ownership' and motivation.
- Encourages reflection.
- Exchanges experience between members.
- Produces 'energy' in the group.

It also helps meet the individual and group needs we covered in Chapter 27.

335

Discussion leading

Preparation.	As with other training methods, decide your aims; plan your route; produce necessary visual aids and handouts.
Discuss discussion.	It is often worth considering with the group the advantages of discussion as a method:

> sharing ideas,
> all can influence content,
> helps relevance,
> creative,
> keeps attention,
> promotes learning,

and to follow this with a discussion about what helps and hinders its effectiveness. This will establish codes of conduct for the group. Factors include:

- Avoid red herrings.
- Need for clarity of purpose.
- Dominant individuals.
- Handling the quiet person.

Plan your questions.	Think of your priming and progressing questions. Open-ended questions are best. Don't over-elaborate.
Share the talking.	Observe to see who wants to speak, who is overtalked, and who is not joining in.
Manage the climate.	Keep calm, be tactful, use humour and discourage aggression.

Control and influence.

- Clarify and keep it simple.
- Summarize frequently.
- Regain attention by:
  - your tried and tested way;
  - standing up;
  - orchestrating from inside the horseshoe;
  - using a visual aid.
- Use Active Listening techniques.
- Use body language and paralanguage.

Consider different types of discussion.

- Full group.
- Syndicate.
- Buzz.
- Brainstorm.

Different types of discussion group

Four types of discussion group are:

(1) Plenary discussion   – the full training group.
(2) Syndicate discussion – small subgroup; extended discussion.
(3) Buzz group   – small subgroup; brief discussion.
(4) Brainstorm   – small group; creativity and problem solving.

Group size. A plenary group could be any size, but discussion, as opposed to commenting, decreases in inverse proportion to size. For training purposes, any number over fifteen will reduce involvement and the effectiveness of the discussion method.

Six is often regarded as ideal for small subgroup work, in terms of involvement, reduction of internal control problems and variety of contributions. However, trios and pairs can work very effectively for particular purposes, such as behaviour and skill experiments and feedback.

Syndicate and buzz group activity and discussion. These are usually popular with training groups. It helps if:

(1) The members are aware of the need for sharing the talking and the rules of feedback if that is happening.
(2) The trainer's role is clear as being 'on tap' not 'on top'.
(3) The group has organizational autonomy, deciding its own leader and/or spokesperson for the particular activity.
(4) The whole group is encouraged to share out leader roles.

Syndicate group discussion or activity. These are intended to help:

- Gain experience through a group activity.
- Reflection upon experience in the past or on the course.
- Develop ideas and guidelines, which they will 'own'.
- Test out ideas.
- Practise skills.
- Exchange feedback.

They can be used with talks, case studies, role plays, exercises, simulation games, questionnaires and so on. They are likely to last at least fifteen minutes and are best conducted in privacy in a separate room.

Buzz groups. These typically last 5–10 minutes and usually involve talking about a specific point or making a quick decision. Their use is:

- To inject energy into a flagging group.
- To raise intensity and pressure.
- To emphasize a particular point.
- To check a group's understanding.
- To get involvement in the subsequent full group session.

Brainstorming. This is a creative problem-solving technique which can be used as a training tool or a method to be learned for application at work.

The brainstorming method	Brief the group about the approach. Seek creativity. Indicate that it needs open minds, low inhibitions, fun, spontaneity and the free association of building on the ideas that others have had.
	Try to get the group in the right mood for creativity. Perhaps have a fun practice or instil light-hearted competition between the groups.
The brainstorming stages	(1) Ideas and suggestions.
	One person charts up the 'problem' and writes each suggested solution in a word or phrase on a flip chart. All are written up, no matter how outlandish or bizarre. *The cardinal rule is that nobody comments, criticizes or in any way evaluates any suggestion, either verbally or non-verbally.* Ideas should flow without inhibition.
	There is usually a time limit of 5–10 minutes.
	(2) Evaluation.
	When the list is complete the group then discuss each idea. It is important to dismiss none out of hand, but to look behind the suggestion to try to make something from it, either directly, by analogy or by association. This is another opportunity for creativity.
	If it is a real problem, owned by one of the group, that person should stand by the list and be challenged by the group before they accept that an idea should be discounted.
	Suggestions should be clarified and collated, linking related ideas. Allow 20–90 minutes.
	(3) Solution/decision.
	The group should finish up with a creative set of solutions to the problem.

4 Case studies

A case study is a way of bringing a piece of workplace reality into training. It is a description of a situation, usually with a problem related to a learning need.

A case is a good way to get active involvement in the learning process. At its simplest a case is presented to a group to read and discuss in relation to questions which focus the members on the learning areas. Each syndicate prepares a report of their conclusions for discussion by the full group. The reports are compared and contrasted and reasons behind the conclusions are explored. The trainer can help 'fix' the learning with a key-point summary.

Puzzles and problems

A puzzle has one solution. If you use a puzzle case study, with a right answer, refer to it with explanation at the end of the group discussion.

A problem has no single right answer. Perhaps there are many solutions effective to a degree, and none of them perfect. Problem cases can lead to lively interest and disagreements. The trainer should let the group know that there is no single best solution. If it is a real case, then you can tell them what actually happened.

Problem cases help the trainees focus upon what needs to be examined and done in order to avoid ineffective solutions. It stresses the process of weighing up pros and cons prior to exercising judgement and making decisions. Real life is simulated, where there are no certainties, but where success is increased by the application of relevant ideas and analysis to information which is gathered and guided by experience. A good case simulates life.

A case is an opportunity to learn how to:

- Define problems.
- Analyse problems into key components and relationships.
- Diagnose causes.
- Identify solutions and assess them.
- Make decisions and to act upon them.

Benefits of the case study

(1) A case lends itself to all the different learning styles found in groups. It is an opportunity to experience a problem; to stand back and reflect upon it; to develop ideas, concepts or guidelines; and to test out ideas and solutions.

(2) Many trainees find cases realistic, graphic, memorable and a stimulating form of learning. It is concrete and helps to anchor theory and methods. It can be enjoyable active learning.

(3) It is a very flexible method that can be tailored to the time available and can be used in many different ways:
  (a) For individual or group work.
  (b) As a challenge to seek solutions.
  (c) As a safe way of taking risks.
  (d) To examine different approaches to problems.
  (e) As illustration of complex theory and methods.

Form and construction of case studies

A case can be any length. Even very short, one paragraph cases are valuable, allowing scope for imaginative interpretation and the projection of individual ideas on to a situation.

It is not necessary to be too elaborate or to include a great deal of factual detail in cases for group discussion if your intent is to examine ideas and principles.

339

Be ready to amend your cases in the light of use. Groups will present you with good ideas for developing them or using them more effectively.

Experiment with your case questions to the group. You may ask syndicates to look at the same questions if you have time and aim to facilitate learning by discussion and comparison. Alternatively, if you want as wide a coverage as possible in limited time, different groups can examine different aspects. A stimulating approach which affords good insights is to ask different groups to view the case situation through the eyes of different individuals involved.

The case can be introduced orally, although for reflection it is useful to have it written in a little more detail. It is a 'learning from life' approach, and this can be enhanced dramatically with visual aids, photos, real documents, self-made videos and even the people involved, or role players briefed to respond to questioning.

Running the case

1 Read and discuss. The shortest and simplest approach.

2 Investigation. The trainer or others are questioned in order to gain information. Investigation is a good means of testing problem solving and prioritizing, and provides a competitive stimulus to groups investigating independently of each other. It also adds realism, because all the relevant data is not given pre-packaged to problem solvers in real life.

3 Developing case. This uses investigation, but evolves progressively from a simple start as the group makes decisions and choices. The trainer may creatively invent facts and circumstances, based upon what the group does, and to meet learning needs.

4 Live case. Course members take on the roles of characters in the case scenario in a dynamic situation. This is good as a test of solutions, and is for insight and skill development.

5 Self-generated. An excellent approach is to ask the group members to produce their own cases based on their experience, for example, cases of high and low motivation. This produces high identification, complete realism, as much detail as you want, is 'real problem' oriented and can be produced in a few minutes. These cases can be used for small or large group work and lend themselves readily for role play. They are of course very relevant for the individuals concerned.

5 Role plays

Role playing is a powerful technique for learning about the human aspects of work, especially face-to-face skills and self awareness. When handled supportively and sensitively, role plays can provide boosts not just to behaviour development or reinforcement, but also to self confidence. The impact is substantially higher when closed circuit television and video play back are used.

Learning enhancement from role playing

(1) The memory of a powerful role play can stay with the role players for a very long time and the personal lessons will be lasting. Learning points are strongly illustrated.

(2) Many find it possible to try things out without the risks that experiments may be thought to have in real life.

(3) Feedback from others, if given and received skilfully, is helpful for awareness and skill development.

(4) Observers find that their awareness of specific aspects of interaction is sharpened by observing role plays. For example, focusing on a role player's active listening can reveal subtle and deep illustrations for the observer which would not come from non-specific observation or abstract discussion.

(5) Role playing helps to develop empathy by putting yourself in other people's shoes.

Designing a role play

The trainer can provide a scenario, perhaps with a short written brief for role players. As we have seen, it is possible to bring a case study creatively to life with role playing. Groups are usually able to produce their own role plays if guided by the trainer.

Do not be too elaborate in the briefs. Too much detail and any attempt at scripting will kill the essence of role play, which is spontaneity. The best action comes from pairs or groups acting out a lightly sketched scenario in a free and dynamic fashion. This often produces interactive events of great realism and credibility.

Hints on running role plays

(1) Discuss with the group the training purpose of the role play.

(2) Be reassuring, light and matter of fact in your briefing. People can be quite nervous at the prospect, especially if it is being recorded on video.

(3) Give the players permission substantially to 'be themselves'. Let them know that you are not expecting an Oscar-winning dramatic performance, but that they should respond as they think they would if they were in that situation. This seems to take the pressure off, so that individuals feel free to project and create. I am still surprised, after very many years running role plays, how skilled and effective people are and how superbly many of the 'amateurs' perform.

(4) When deciding the players for a group role play, you may wish to select participants on the basis of your knowledge of them and the roles. If you do, there may be strong curiosity about the reasons for your choice! Once you have outlined the roles, good results are usually gained from giving syndicate groups

the responsibility for nominating the players. This is almost always done with maturity and sensitivity, with the group taking into account the needs, anxieties and potential learning benefit to the participant.

(5) Give the participants adequate time for preparation. Ten minutes usually is sufficient.

(6) Once the activity has finished, the participants will need a short time to let off steam. The emotional impact of role playing can simulate the real thing quite closely. You may need to help the players step out of the role with which they may have come to identify closely. A short pre–discussion chat between the participants aids this process, perhaps whilst the observers spend a few minutes preparing their comments and feedback.

(7) Video the role play whenever possible. This can separate the observers from the players to a degree, and the edited highlights are good for fun and learning.

(8) Plan for your feedback before the role play, allocating specific tasks to observers, who are likely to need time to prepare.

(9) Encourage self-assessment and constructive feedback. It is worth spending time beforehand talking about the value and skills of giving and receiving feedback. Players have the roles as defences if they need them. 'It wasn't really me'. It is obviously better learning if people 'own' their behaviour, but they will often do this in private, and later in public when there is trust and support in the group.

6 Training activities for involved learning

Learning requires activity and creating active ways of learning is a major part of the trainer's art. We have covered some of the main involvement methods, but there are others to consider which may fit well into some courses and sessions.

Questionnaires can be used as thinking and discussion devices, and can often be found ready-made for your needs, or developed to meet your requirements. If they are used as a means of self-assessment, it is important to offer the advice that few claim to be scientific instruments. Questionnaires have strong face validity for some people and need handling with care. If people treat them as food for reflection and information for checking out in other ways, they will serve a useful and constructive purpose.

Quiz games to test factual knowledge are usually popular, especially if they can be based upon team learning. For example, members can quiz each other on a topic which is being studied, where factual retention is important. They use this as a basis for devising a quiz to give the other syndicate on some form of competitive basis.

Group projects can be created in great variety:

For example, produce a diagram or flowchart which shows the main features of ... .

Group as trainer projects are good learning motivators. Each group is given the task of helping another group to learn about a topic. The trainers provide resources, which include themselves of course, and the group have to design a session using whatever methods they can devise to create learning. They have to learn the topic well in order to teach it, and usually do so.

Group video. 'You have to make a creative video for the Queen/Chief Executive/alien from space, to convince ... explain ... outline the main points of ...'

Group simulation exercises are fun and strongly motivating. They can be very effective learning devices.

One method is to ask the group to simulate the organizational task or activity that they are learning about. For example, if they are learning about organizational behaviour and leadership, turn them into an organization with tasks to perform and personal learning objectives to meet.

Many exercises are readily available to simulate decision making, meetings, communication, leadership, motivation and problem solving. Groups work together on a task and then examine how they tackled it, in terms of the things they are learning.

An illustration is the Cave Rescue Exercise. The group is a committee responsible for a psychological experiment of survival in confined spaces. One group is trapped underground and water is rising so that probably some will be drowned. The rescue team will arrive in 30 minutes, by which time the committee must have decided their rescue of the six trapped members in rescue order. Only one person can be rescued every half hour. The group to be rescued are a mix of gender, age, race, sexual orientation, religion, domestic responsibility, moral rectitude and societal contribution so that decision making is exciting and values emerge on the line. Post exercise analysis is potent on communication and decision making.

References for further reading

Barker D. (1980). *TA and Training*. Gower

Broadwell M.M. (1988). *The Supervisor and On-the-Job Training*. Addison-Wesley

Clark N. (1991). *Managing Personal Learning and Change: A Trainer's Guide*. McGraw-Hill Training Series

Downs S. and Perry P. (1986). Can Trainers Learn to Take a Back Seat? *Personnel Management* March

Ellis S.K. (1989). *How to Survive a Training Assignment*. Addison-Wesley

Kolb D.A. *et al.* (1974). *Organisational Psychology – an experiential approach*. Prentice-Hall

Phillips K. and Fraser A. (1982). *The Management of Interpersonal Skills Training*. Gower

Pont T. (1990). *Developing Effective Training Skills*. McGraw-Hill Training Series

Winfield I. (1988) *Learning to Teach Practical Skills*. Kogan Page

Endpiece

We suggested at the beginning of *Management Skills: Making the Most of People* that there was an 'urgent need to bridge the gap between the view of management as primarily based upon concepts and reflection, and the approach which is based entirely upon action. This gap is often more like a chasm. Those who fall in are either suffering from the 'analysis paralysis' of thinking without ever doing, or the 'action fraction' of doing without thinking. 'We hope that with the aid of this book the reader will integrate both thinking and doing, and leap the chasm with a single bound.'

We believe that the readers will find that the balance and integration of theory, research and practice in the book will provide them with useful propulsion.

The aim has been to cover comprehensively the three future key aspects of managing people and change:

The manager as recruiter:	Getting the right people
Managing people positively:	Personal growth and interpersonal relationships
The manager as developer:	Enhancing performance.

Managers will have to drive recruitment, performance-linked relationships and skill development as an integral part of their role, if they are to become the radical change agents needed for adaptation and growth. The same demands will be placed upon them whether they are in the public or private sector, or in a large or small organization.

Our hope is that the book will contribute to the enhancement of skills and knowledge both for those on the first rungs of their career ladder, and for those already at higher levels who recognize that continuous development is both their survival safety net and the way forward.

Appendix A

Insupply case study outlines

Insupply

Part One, Chapter 1

Insupply supplies office equipment and stationery and was formed three years ago by a merger of Buroquip and Gloprint.

The two parts continued to operate at their original locations a short distance apart and there was no major organizational dislocation. Insupply had 300 employees and was growing.

The Chief Executive appointed after the merger was Hedi Lindstrom. Her deputy was Colin Smith, who was also Company Secretary. He had three administrative assistants, Sally Bullen (Temps, Admin Pool, Buildings), Ekoku Inanga (Communication) and Peter Paine (Procurement).

Colin Smith needed to divest his administrative role, and after considering different options, he decided that he needed to find an administration manager. He researched the requirements and produced a job description.

Insupply: Person specification

Part One, Chapter 2

Having compared people he knew in Administration and reflected on the job description, Colin Smith compiled a person specification to assist the recruitment of the Administration Manager.

Insupply: Job advertisement

Insupply: Recruitment plan

Insupply: Application guide

Part One, Chapter 3

Colin Smith planned to work with Personnel Administration and consult his boss the Chief Executive during the recruitment of the Administration Manager, but he intended actively to manage the process.

Insupply: Modified person spec for short-listing

Insupply: applications and short-listing Part One, Chapter 4

There were 70 applications reduced to a long list of 30. Colin reduced this to six for the interview short list. He compared Bob Armstrong to Joseph Silva and preferred the former, who was short-listed and eventually recruited to the position of Administration Manager.

Insupply: Preparation for the interview Part One, Chapter 6

Colin Smith prepared systematically for the interview with Bob Armstrong and used his guide to help him during the interview, as a prompt, record and assessment sheet.

Insupply: How important are face-to-face skills? Part Two, Chapter 1

Before the short list and interviews, there had been a confrontation between an angry Ekoku Inanga and Colin Smith. Two scenarios of Colin's handling are offered.

Insupply: Colin Smith and Ekoku Inanga scenarios Part Two, Chapter 2

Awareness; self confidence; influence; behaviour skills.

Insupply: Assertion and positive influencing Part Two, Chapter 5

Illustrations of giving negative criticism; refusing a request; making a request.
   The assumption for the development of the case is that there was a positive outcome to the confrontation between Colin and Ekoku, as indicated in the Assertion and Positive Influencing section. Ekoku was mollified by the prospect of development and promotion to a marketing role in some months' time.

Insupply: Developing group behavioural skills Part Two, Chapter 7

Colin Smith held a meeting on Bob Armstrong's first day, to introduce him to his three staff. Colin also intended to outline his own new role, the changes in systems and the relocation. His hopes for the future were also on the agenda, before he planned to invite Bob and the others to chat informally about each other and the new situation.

Insupply: Developing a team Part Two, Chapter 9

Insupply moved to Midtown Complex two months previously. The Administration Department had been restructured and there had been staff changes. Bob Armstrong was aware that there were team problems so he invited a team building facilitator to help him and the team progress.

Insupply: Developing positive attitudes to change   Part Two, Chapter 13

Colin Smith's strategy for planning and implementing Insupply's move to a new location in Midtown. Problems and difficulties, and how they were handled. The lessons learned.

Insupply: Designing and implementing systems of performance appraisal   Part Three, Chapter 22

Buroquip had an appraisal scheme that was ineffective and not well supported by its management. Its limitations are outlined. Hedi Lindstrom, Insupply's Chief Executive, had experienced a good appraisal system and she asked Colin Smith to assess what would work well for the organization. Insupply's new scheme is described.

Insupply: Appraisal and target setting   Part Three, Chapter 24

Colin Smith appraised Bob Armstrong. The background and their preparation are outlined and details of the appraisal interview are given, along with the agreement of targets and the performance development plan.

Insupply: Managing the marginal performer   Part Three, Chapter 25

Bob Armstrong had recruited a young graduate trainee, Mary Jones. Performance problems developed during her trainee period. Bob Armstrong decided to tackle this outside the formal appraisal system.

Insupply: Counselling, coaching and job-related growth   Part Three, Chapter 27

Bob Armstrong decided to use different coaching styles for each of his staff. He based his choice upon their personal profiles and learning styles. Each outcome is described. He also considered counselling in some cases.

Bob decided that development could be gained for some of his staff through job-related growth. He linked this to the performance and development targets agreed at their appraisals. He used assignments, delegation, working with a model, peer learning and temporary roles.

Insupply: The manager as trainer   Part Three, Chapter 29

Bob Armstrong used guided self development through a self-managed induction training package. New staff used manuals and videos developed within Insupply, and each person had a coach and guided access to other staff whom they could use as learning resources.

Appendix B

Training modules

You may wish to develop the skills and knowledge of others by running training modules in the areas covered by this book. All chapters lend themselves to adaptation to training through the figures, cases and exercise activities and copyright will be waived when material from the book is used for *course training purposes*, provided acknowledgement is made.

The following Training Module Guides, usually broken into two hour units for internal training convenience and flexibility, have been produced for use by the manager as trainer. They illustrate module development and any part of the book could be converted into a practical training session in similar fashion.

It is always worth spending time with any new training group encouraging them to become a learning team. This process is helped, for example, by mutual introductions to break the ice, including job and career background, personal details, individual qualities and experience in the module area, and what they hope to gain from the course.

It is also beneficial to spell out the module aims and to discuss methods that you intend to use. It is important at the outset that the group are clear about their responsibility in the learning process and what you, the trainer, expect from them.

The significance of their involvement and contribution to the learning is easily demonstrated by reference to David Kolb's learning cycle, perhaps in the following terms.

(1) Experience:	We all learn from experience. Your experience of the course areas will be shared and there will be opportunity to learn from your experience of the practical work.
(2) Reflection:	We rarely have much opportunity to stand back and reflect upon our experience, but the module will provide opportunity to do that in the self-assessment and discussion activity.
(3) Guidelines:	We will produce ideas to 'fix' and harness our experience. These may be guidelines for self monitoring and development.

(4) Experiment: The guidelines and ideas will suggest skills or
                   approaches we will want to try. There may well
                   be opportunity to do this on the course, or in
                   an action plan you may subsequently make.

Module One: Leadership and motivation

Unit One   The Manager/Supervisor's role and influence
Unit Two   Leadership styles
Unit Three   Motivation: influencing the will to work well
Reference   Part Two, Chapter 18 'Developing the will to work well'

This module is appropriate for those who have or will shortly gain responsibility
for staff. It covers basic issues and builds upon experience that all members have
had. The material is easy to grasp and identify with. It helps develop self
confidence and is an ideal starter module.

Aims

- To increase knowledge of the role of managing people.
- To help members make appropriate choices.
- To explore the supervisors' and managers' influence on the will to work well.
- To enable members to identify leadership skills, assess themselves and examine
  their repertoire for development.

Unit One   *Two hours*
The manager/supervisor's role and influence

1 Syndicate discussion   20 minutes

Group A: What is management and what does a manager do?
Group B: What is the basis of a manager/supervisor's influence?

2 Full group reports and discussion   30 minutes

Hear and chart up the syndicates' reports, seeking comments and clarification from
both.

Trainer input, questions or emphasis points
A. Management   Efficient and effective use of resources to achieve results
                       and objectives.

Functions		Objectives; planning; monitoring; controlling; coordinating; deciding. (Task technical.) Communicating; leading; motivating. (People.)
B. Manager's influence	(1) Position power	Stems from the authority given to the rank or position. This is what we delegate. If the only source of influence, what effect would it have?
	(2) Expertise	If recognized as an authority. Should the boss always be more expert than subordinates?
	(3) Personal characteristics	How the manager is seen as a person. If respected, will have more influence accepted by others. Brief treatment. Lead from this direct to the third part of the unit.

3 Leadership and influence: Individual and syndicate exercise   70 minutes

Explain that one definition of leadership is 'the characteristics and skills that enable a person to influence people and decisions.' Link straight from 'Personal characteristics' above.

Individual	Think of a person who has influenced you at work. In your mind's eye visualize that person, and what they did that gained your respect and acceptance of their influence. Think of three or four things.
Syndicate	Describe to each other the influencers and the qualities or skills they showed. As a group, from your discussion of your experience make a list of the skills and qualities that you agree give a person leadership influence.
Full group	Compare and discuss the lists. There will be a great deal of common ground. Check acceptance of the differences.

Trainer input, questions or emphasis points. The syndicates will probably have identified two dozen skills and qualities from their experience of leadership. It is their list, and they will identify with it.

It will read like a syllabus for personal and management leadership development, and indeed that is how you can use it, either in relation to this module or a more ambitious development programme.

A typical list is shown in Figure B.1.

Communicates clearly	Makes time for people
Listens well	Realistic targets
Explains	Gives support and trust
Involves people	Encourages
Keeps informed	Coaches
Motivates	Sense of humour
Shows interest in people as individuals	Committed
Gives recognition	Enthusiastic
Delegates effectively	Honest and open
Sets example	Sensitive
Clear about what is expected	Fair
Gives constructive feedback	Approachable

Figure B.1   Leader influence skills and qualities: a typical list.

Individual   Think of yourself as a leader/manager/supervisor. Identify two or three of the skills/qualities that the group identified that you feel comfortable with, and two or three that are of interest to you in relation to your own training and development. The latter could be an aspect you would like to confirm or check against others' views of you; or something you are not sure about or feel you want to develop for the future. This may be a focus for the module. Your development objectives?

Self selected   Meet with two of your colleagues and share the above. Seek
trio   ideas, advice and a basis for support during the modules.

Unit Two   *Two hours*
Leadership styles

Suggest to the group that although there are the universal qualities of leadership they have identified in Unit One, there are choices we have in our approach to others at work. These are called leadership styles.

The three main style dimensions in the leader's repertoire are:

(1) Technical–people balance
(2) Decision and problem-solving style
(3) Relationships style.

Indicate that management first requires self management, which in turn demands self-assessment, which will be part of the activity. Reassure that you are not suggesting there are right or wrong styles, only appropriate choices given the circumstances.

Your aim is to help develop clarity about different style choices and their impact and appropriateness.

1 Technical–people balance: Individual and syndicate   40 minutes

Ask individuals to complete Activity 18.1 on page 193. Then in syndicate compare notes and report back on the factors affecting style balance.

In full group compare syndicate reports and offer Figure 18.1 for consideration. Conclude that there are good and not-so-good reasons that we have for our choices, and that the need is to try to achieve the former.

2 Decision-making styles   40 minutes

Option One. Ask the group to consider the four bench marks of this dimension.

          Dictates   Consults   Delegates   Abdicates

Individually think of people they know who adopt these different approaches.
What are the characteristics of these different approaches?

What are the positive and negative results of each style? (Use Figure 18.2 as your guide. Offer it to the group.)

It will pay to spend time discussing delegation as a management tool. Why are some afraid of it? How is it done badly? How should it be done effectively?

Introduce 'How groups make decisions' (Figure 18.3) and discuss its impact upon commitment to decision; satisfaction with the process; level of contribution of ideas and opinions; and motivation.

Option Two. If you wish to raise the group's energy level and feel the group could cope with the activity, the following may produce high interest and personal learning.

Place two labels 'Dictates' and 'Abdicates' in a straight line on the floor, five or six metres apart. Tell the group that 'Consults' and 'Delegates' are between these two positions. Have a chart explaining this. Ask the individuals to stand in line according to where they see their usual style of decision making. Double parking is not allowed.

If individuals are expressing feelings, perhaps unhappy or amused, ask them to talk about their feelings and thoughts. It may have something to do with their position relative to others.

Divide the members into four equal groups based on their position in the line. They will each be given the appropriate decision style label. Each group has to support its style. Give them ten minutes to agree what is good about their approach and bad about the others. They report back to the others using the style they represent. Using Figures 18.2 and 18.3 as a guide, get the group to assess the implications of the different styles.

Check if there are any bad feelings left over from the 'line'.

3. Relationships styles   40 minutes

Ask for three volunteers who will be told they will shortly have to publicly present a personal/work problem (real/imagined/mixture) to a small group of colleagues. Whilst they leave the room for ten minutes to reflect upon this, introduce the group to the relationships style dimension (Figure 18.4). Get them to fill in the factors which determine where you are on the scale.

Randomly allocate the remaining members to three groups.

A. Hostile/aloof/remote – individuals choose which they will be
B. Approachable/friendly
C. Buddy

Invite person A back to present their problem to group A for five minutes, then person B to present their problem to B, and finally C to C.

Ask persons A, B and C how they perceived their respective group relationships styles and the feelings they had about the experience. Get each group to explain the approach they were adopting to the three volunteers.

Get the group to assess the implications for relating to staff.

Alternative session
Unit Two   *Two hours*

Divide the group into equal syndicates of four to six. Present and discuss the three style dimensions with the group. Ask each member to assess where they think they are on the three dimensions most frequently, say for the last three months. Also ask them to assess where they think their syndicate colleagues would be, based on intuition or any evidence they have.

(15 minutes)

(1) Each individual has their own flip chart of the three dimensions. They take turns to mark where they see themselves on the scale and the others mark where they see the individual.
(2) Each in turn has ten minutes of the group's time, discussing why they are where they are and getting feedback about others' perceptions of them.
(3) The group compares and contrasts individual styles and notes similarities and differences.
(4) They identify from experience a list of factors that should be accounted when assessing whether a style is appropriate.
(5) Is there a best style?

(60 minutes)

The syndicates report their discussion and conclusions. Use Figures 18.1 to 18.5 to help you steer the discussion, and perhaps to offer some pointers to the group. You may prefer to take each dimension in turn for consideration.

Unit Three
Motivation: Influencing the will to work well

Two hours

1 Full group

10 minutes

Introduce the session by defining motivation as the 'will to work well', which is different from 'the will to work', perhaps. Ask the group, humorously, to divide into three groups according to how they are feeling at that moment. On the flip chart write:

Creative
Positive
Negative

Individuals write up their names against their chosen group. The groups should be of equal size, so once one is full the choice is lost to the slower responders!

2 Individual

10 minutes

Carry out Activity 18.3 on page 199. In addition, repeat the exercise with a 'switch off' situation which demotivated and produced bad feelings.

3 Full group briefing

5 minutes

The Positive Group are asked to spend 20 minutes exchanging their 'switched on' experiences in modest detail. Afterwards they should identify the factors that their experience suggests are associated with motivated high performance. These should include internal feelings and the external 'switch on' factors.

The Negative Group do the same as the above, except that they exchange and list the negative 'switch off' factors and feelings.

The Creative Group have 30 minutes to produce role plays which illustrate a positive and then a negative motivation scenario. Tell them that the other groups will attempt to interpret their role plays in the light of their respective analyses. Suggest they simply produce a story line to perform spontaneously, rather than a script.

4 Preparation in syndicate

30 minutes

5 Full group

40 minutes

The Creative Group perform their first role play which the appropriate group interprets in the light of their list. The second role play is handled the same way.

Ask the group to consider the implications for them at work of the positive and negative lists. Figure 18.7 can be used to support the positive group's findings.

They will be very similar and represent a motivation menu which is substantially in the control of the individual manager/supervisor. 'How managers and staff see worker motivation' (page 200) may also promote discussion. Figure 18.6

may help make the point that individuals need to be treated as individuals, because tastes and needs vary.

Action planning   25 minutes

At this point in the module, remind the group of the areas they have covered in the three units, and ask them individually to reflect on these, identifying things to do more of, less of or differently. Ask each to summarize briefly their plans to the group and to offer their observations on the module.

Timing is difficult to manage in these types of events. You may well find you need an additional half an hour for each unit with an energetic and committed group.

Module Two: Developing communication skills

Unit One	Leading and taking part in meetings
Unit Two	Interviewing: one-to-one skills
References	Part Two
	Chapter 15 'Developing group behavioural skills'
	Chapter 14 'Developing one-to-one behavioural skills'

This module is appropriate for all staff who use face-to-face communication as a significant part of their job. It involves sharing experience and practical activities. These may be added to by the trainer as time permits.

Aims

- To develop skills and confidence in running and taking part in meetings and interviews of any type and purpose.
- To increase awareness of the task and process aspects of face-to-face communication.

Unit One   Two hours
Leading and taking part in meetings

Video		Without video

1 Full group   15 mins   1 Syndicate/Full group   30 mins

The trainer defines a meeting as any formal communication between more than two people with a purpose, and asks the group members to recall in their minds' eyes

meetings they have recently led or have had involvement with.
Individuals note two or three help and hinder factors.

Video	*Without video*
The trainer seeks ideas in full group and records them on a flip chart. These are discussed and key points are highlighted.	The group splits into two syndicates and prepares to report to the full group for discussion. The reports are compared and key points are highlighted.

The trainer summarizes, suggesting that for groups to communicate effectively, three needs have to be met (source: Edgar Schein).

Task	Doing things that ensure that information is exchanged and processed in an efficient and effective way, so that task goals are met.
Individual	Meeting needs that individuals have, so that they are committed to participate in the task.
Group	Helping the group to work together rather than in conflict.

The trainer briefly illustrates these, if possible from the 'helps' and 'hinders' lists produced by the group.

Indicate that you are going to ask them to take part in a meeting to develop these points and to provide illustrations of the helpful skills.

2 Meeting exercise   30 minutes

If your group has eight or fewer members it is better that they all take part. More than this number and it will be better to have observers. My own preference is to have one-on-one observation.

The topic for the meeting should be chosen so that it can realistically last 30 minutes. It needs to be interesting, to produce a degree of controversy and to require a minimum of preparation.

You will need to decide if you wish to have a chairperson. As you are looking for contributions that any member can make, in the chair or not, it is not strictly necessary.

Examples are provided at the end of this unit.

3 Video   Without video

Observers discuss their feedback with the person they observed. They could usefully have been using the helps/ hinders list, and suggest things the participant could have done more, less or differently.

10 minutes

4 Full group
15 minutes

The trainer presents a framework of skills for meeting task, group and individual needs at meetings. Use a prepared chart and have handouts as support. A suggested framework is given below and full explanation will be found in Chapter 15, 'Developing group behavioural skills'.

Task	Group	Individual
Starting	Integrating	Identity
Information	Yielding	Acceptance
Developing	Encouraging	Control
Pathfinding	Progressing	Personal
Decision making	Constructing	

You may wish the group to consider behaviour which has a negative impact. For example, things done which frustrated an individual's needs; had a negative impact upon the group, such as fragmenting rather than integrating; or got in the way of the efficient pursuit of the task, such as confusing rather than pathfinding.

Video

The video of the meeting is
played back, pausing as you
or the group wish to comment.
20 minutes for highlights only.

5 Full group
Remaining time

Participants select aspects from the above framework that they felt were positive or negative contributions they had themselves made to the task, group and individual needs. These are mentioned and commented upon briefly by the trainer and group.
Conclude with individual action planning.

Examples of meetings exercises

(1) A workplace topic that all will have opinions about.
(2) Insupply case scenario. (This will take additional preparation time.)
(3) A real meeting that has a task purpose for the group.
(4) A fun 'suspension of disbelief' meeting, such as *Lost in the desert*, which follows.

Lost in the desert
Leader copy

You are the leader of a party touring from one town to another across a corner of the Sahara, on a two-week holiday organized by Sandventure Tours plc. You are following a planned itinerary. This is your first trip as leader in the desert. You have flown in from London to cover for a person taken ill, and you have no specialist training in desert survival.

Today you expected to travel 80 miles. However, after 35 miles your Land

Rover/coach engine began to overheat and the driver decided to divert to an oasis at right angles to the north of your route and approximately 25 miles from it.

After you had travelled four miles along the new route, there was a sudden sandstorm. When it was over an electrical fault caused the vehicle to burn out completely, leaving only its shell. The driver, a local upon whom you relied for desert knowledge, died of a heart attack. Your party consists of the members of your group. You must stick together. Temperatures in the Sahara at this time of year vary from 120 degrees F at midday to below freezing at night.

You have salvaged the following 15 items from the wreckage. You and your team must select ten of them and rank them in order of importance for your survival. You are allowed 30 minutes.

Lost in the desert   Tourists' copy

You are in a party touring from one town to another across a corner of the Sahara, on a two-week holiday organized by Sandventure Tours plc. You are accompanied by a tour leader from London and a local driver. You are following a planned itinerary. Today you expected to travel 80 miles. However, after 35 miles your Land Rover/coach engine began to overheat and the driver decided to divert to an oasis at right angles to the north of your route and approximately 25 miles from it.

After you had travelled four miles along the new route, there was a sudden sandstorm. When it was over an electrical fault caused the vehicle to burn out completely, leaving only its shell. The driver, a local, died of a heart attack.

Your party consists of the members of your group. You must stick together.

Temperatures in the Sahara at this time of year vary from 120 degrees F at midday to below freezing at night.

You have salvaged the following 15 items from the wreckage. Ten of them must be selected and ranked in order of importance for your survival. You are allowed 30 minutes.

Lost in the desert   Survival items

(1) A box of matches.
(2) A barrel containing four pints of water for each member.
(3) One yellow blanket per person.
(4) A machete.
(5) An orange tent – no poles.
(6) Six plastic rubbish sacks.
(7) Catering size tin of baked beans (10 lbs).
(8) Flashlight.
(9) A bottle of brandy.
(10) Book *Lawrence of Arabia*.
(11) First aid kit.
(12) Bottle of salt tablets.
(13) A compass.
(14) Ten copies of yesterday's *Times* newspaper.
(15) Book of maps of the Sahara, 1 inch to 5 miles scale.

Lost in the desert   The experts' answer

Stay with the vehicle. You have more chance of being found.

(1) Water – essential for your survival, but you will need more.
(2) Plastic bags for gathering water in the sand by condensation.
(3) Can of beans for collecting and storing the water gathered.
(4) Machete for opening can and digging holes for the bags.
(5) Tent for shelter and signal for searching aircraft.
(6) Blankets for warmth and signalling.
(7) Flashlight for signalling.
(8) Box of matches as firelighter for warmth and signal.
(9) Copies of newspaper. Sun hats and fires.
(10) First aid kit.

---

(11) *Lawrence of Arabia*. He had a camel. You do not.
(12) Book of maps. Small scale of limited value. You should not move in any case.
(13) Compass. You are not going anywhere.
(14) Brandy. Dangerous. Alcohol dehydrates.
(15) Salt tablets. Dangerous in a dehydrated state. Need to consume much larger quantities of water than you will have. They will make you more thirsty.

Unit Two   *Two hours*
Interviewing: One-to-one skills

1 Full group discussion   25 minutes

Why do we interview at work? Ask the group for the reasons why they use interviews at work. Aim to establish that it is an activity which can occupy between 10 to 60% of a person's time and has many purposes. Many will only think of the formal interviews for selection and appraisal. Remind them of the many other reasons such as briefing, coaching, counselling, problem solving, client relations, discipline and so on.

Different styles or approaches to interviewing. Suggest to the group that there are different ways of conducting interviews and give them the labels in Figure 14.1 (One-to-one styles):

            Dominant   Conversational   Counselling

Ask them questions about the differences so that the group help you build up a full definition of the approaches. For example:

- Who influences and how in the three styles?
- How is the air time shared?
- Who solves the problem?
- What is the relationship?
- What are the dominant feelings?

Suggest there are three main skill areas in an interview.

(1) Task management	Making sure the information is exchanged and processed to achieve the purpose.
(2) Rapport	Getting on the same wavelength and achieving an appropriate relationship.
(3) Active listening	Hearing, remembering and controlling the interview at the same time.

TASK MANAGEMENT

Present a chart of Figure 14.6 (Task skills and movement through the four face-to-face stages).

Discuss Figure 14.7 (Questions and one-to-one styles).

2 Individual interview preparation   Five minutes

Ask each person to identify a topic that interests them and they have strong feelings about. Tell them that they will shortly take part in a series of short five-minute interviews as both interviewer and interviewee. You could suggest that they simply be themselves, or that the interviewer will be a journalist on a house magazine which contains a short article called 'Viewpoint', giving the thoughts of a member of staff in each edition. The interviewee will be the staff member.

3 Interview Activity One   15 minutes

Use video if possible for short extracts of several interviews.

RAPPORT

Divide the group into trios. In each trio, one will interview, the second will be interviewed and the third will observe.

The interview is conducted and afterwards each trio discusses rapport and what helped or hindered it.

4 Full group discussion   20 minutes

The group recount their experience and the trainer highlights key aspects of rapport skills.

Personal impact	Behaviour which can produce positive or 'smile' reactions. Illustrate:

Smile
Handshake
Politeness
Appropriate humour
Appropriate personal interest
Choice of opening, etc.

	Also note behaviour which can lead to negative spit or swallow reactions.
Relaxation	Consider how one person's tension can communicate itself to the other, and consider self-relaxing techniques, like deep breathing and sitting four square.
Non-verbal	Explore the impact of tone, posture, eye contact, facial expression and so on.

ACTIVE LISTENING

5 Full group discussion   10 minutes

Explore the concept of active listening skills with the group, using Figure 10.5 as your framework. Suggest the headings and ask the group to fill in the details.

6 Interview Activity Two   15 minutes

The trios change roles and the second interview takes place, with the interviewers aiming to apply as many active listening skills as they are able. The observer keeps score and the trios discuss the results when the interview is complete.

7 Interview Activity Three   15 minutes

The trios rotate roles again, and the final interview takes place. This time the interviewer displays poor listening skills, preferably without too much exaggeration. The trios explore the results and the effects on the feelings and attitude of the interviewee.

8 Full group discussion   Remaining time

Explore the trios' experience, review the unit's main points and get individuals to self assess and action plan.

Index